Compassionate

Words From Hell

and other Reflections

in the

Eternal Mirror

Earl C Davis

Rocky Comfort Press

Copyright © 2010

Earl C Davis

Cover:

Detail from the parable windows of

St. Mary's Church

Banbury, Oxfordshire, England

ISBN 145375251X

EAN-13 9781453752517

Rocky Comfort Press

For

Pegeen

on the occasion of our 50th wedding anniversary

In the words of a long-time friend

who jokingly said,

"She's listened over and over to the same

twenty sermons for the last fifty years!"

Other Devotional Writings by Earl Davis

Christ at the Door

Forever, Amen

Somebody Cares

Life in the Spirit

Why the Angel Sat Down

When the Sparrow Falls

38 Years is a Long Time
Reflections on Biblical Characters

The Promise God Made to Thieves
Reflections on Biblical Promises

How Moses Got to the Promised Land
and other Studies in the Life of Moses

The Tragedy of Remembering Jesus
and other Meditations for Special Occasions

I Can't Forgive Myself
and other Reflections on Emotions

What Should I Do?
Meditations on moral issues

The Conversions of Simon Peter
and other reflections on Spiritual Growth

How A Good Jewish Boy Gets Himself Crucified
and other reflections on the Heart of the Gospel

The Unpardonable Sin
and other Studies in Probing Texts

The Stories Jesus Told
Studies in the Parables for Pastors and Laymen

Table of Contents

Because: The Face of Motivation	9
If: The Larger Half of Life	16
Never: The Word that Locks Doors	24
Nevertheless: The Word that Leaps Hurdles	32
P'like: The Power of Imagination	40
Just Too Busy	48
Compassionate Words From Hell	54
Facing Change	60
Dealing With Regrets	67
Did Jesus Praise a Scoundrel?	72
A Focused Vision	78
The Eyes of God	85
The Changing Form of the Eternal Gospel	92
A Plea for Ignorance	98
The Harvest that Didn't Happen	104
The Haunted House	110
The Five Most Crucial Minutes	115
The Last Temptation of Jesus	121
Getting to Know Jesus as Messiah	127
Jesus as the Man of Prayer	132
The Gift of Kindness	138
The Law of the Echo	145
A Lion on a Leash	151
The Naming of a Mystery	157
The Lord's Supper as a Symbol	162
Love Beyond	168
Neither Sand Nor Beast	174

Never Before . . . Never Again . . .	180
Full Armor for Fierce Battle	186
The Power of Positive Giving	193
The Priority of Evangelism	198
Listening to the Wrong Voice	204
The Sin of Overwork	211
Retire From Church? Never!	218
Stones	225
The Career of the Soul	232
The Gospel Truth	239
The Present	246
What Jesus Thought of Money	252
What Really Is Faith	258
When Satan is Most Active	264
Christmas and Common Things	269
Christmas and the Cradle	275
Christmas and the Crown	281
Christmas and the Curse	287
Can Santa Come to the Manger?	293
God's Will and Christmas	298
Going Home Another Way	305
Hidden Truths of Christmas	312
The Joy That Belongs to Christmas	317
Packaging Christmas	322
The Peace of Christmas	328
Which Jesus in the Manger?	335
Christmas Expectations	340
The Great Reunion	345

Foreword

This volume of sermons is collected from the pastorates at First Baptist Church of Memphis, Trinity Baptist Church of Memphis, and even one or two from interim pastorates since I have "retired." It will no doubt be noticed that the sermons have been left in their *sitz im leben*, their life setting. It did not seem helpful to send these thoughts on their way shorn of the circumstances of their preparation and delivery, for sermons that are most helpful come from the daily life of the pastor and congregation. And leaving them thus gives a window into the life of the church, the city of Memphis, and the nation.

It is my hope that these volumes might find a place in the devotional life of some Christians, and might encourage pastors in their task of bringing fresh "bread from the oven" Sunday by Sunday.

If you find a idea or a devotional germ here that might fly, have at it. None of us are original, and I here render my acknowledgement of debt to many in both the pulpit and the pew.

August 2010

Earl C Davis

Because: the Face of Motivation

Deuteronomy 7:7-8; Mark 6:5-6; Luke 10:20;

John 14:19; I John 4:19

We begin a series of messages built on words; little words, common words, Biblical words, powerful words. I feel a bit like Fred Craddock's description of the time when he went to speak at a conference, and decided to take only two words. His wife, a good minister's wife, urged him to take more words. His answer: "They said they just wanted a few words from me, so two will do." As she packed, his wife kept on trying to be helpful: "Fred, there's plenty of room in your suitcase for a good many more words; take as many as you wish." "No, no, two is enough." As I recall, he "took" the words church and faith to that conference, and spoke on those two topics all week!

Today I have brought to the pulpit only one word, the word *Because*. Now, this word may look very common to you, and we all do use it every day, but it is a very religious—or perhaps I should say, Biblical—word, with over 1000 references (all of which I have checked!).

The Face of Motivation

The Oxford Dictionary says because comes from the old English phrase, *by cause*, after which the cause was stated. Remember the stock answer George Leigh Mallory always gave when asked why he was so driven to climb Mt. Everest: "because it's there!" Remember that T-shirt that made a hit with all parents? On the front of the shirt were these profound words which every child loathes to hear: "Because I'm the Daddy, that's why!" The little word because is the face of motivation! The becauses of our life reveal the motivations which guide our decisions and determine our destinies.

Look with me at some of the becauses of the Bible; it will help us to realize the nature and power of the becauses in our lives. The because of guilt (Gen 3:10); the because of giving (Gen 33:11); the because of favoritism (Gen 37:3); the because of stability (Psm 16:8); the because of Divine refusal (1 Sam 16:7); the because of love (Deut 7:7-8); the because of Divine anger (Mt 11:20-21); the because that led to glory (Isa 53:12); the because that crippled Christ (Mk 6:5); the because that prompts rejoicing (Lk 10:19-20); the because that put a man up a tree (Lk 19:3-4); the because that leads to greater trust (Lk 19:16-17); the because that calls us to commitment (Lk 19:31); the because that explains why men love darkness (Jn 3:19); the because that prompts our witness (Jn 11:42); the because of the thief (Jn 12:6); the because that gives hope (Jn 14:19); the urgent because (Eph 5:15-16); the because of imitation (1Jn 4:17); and the most beautiful because (1 Jn 4:19).

The Problem of Wrong Becauses

We see both divine and human, worthy and unworthy becauses in the Bible, and when we look at the becauses of our own lives we see the motivations behind our words and our deeds. Consider your life; what are the most powerful becauses, most powerful motivations in your life? What are the motivations that make you think like you think, act like you act, live like you live? Are they the right ones? Good ones? Pure ones? Do they spring from your relationship to the Father? For many years I used, as an illustration of the power of our tendency to rebel against God, the desire of our children when babies to feed themselves! You name it, oatmeal, chocolate pudding, squash, whatever, it went on the parent, the baby, the ceiling, and everywhere else as the child insisted on trying to feed itself! I'm getting feelings of *deja vu* as I watch our daughter Dawn trying to feed our grandson Alexander! His one and only because , his primary motivation is simply, me first! I fear that is still the motivation, the because that dominates too many of our lives as adults. Me first, I want, I'm angry, I'm ashamed, I'm proud I'm hurt, I'm jealous, I'm insecure, I'm scared, I'm greedy. Some of these are natural and understandable feelings, yet they too often motivate us in a destructive way; these are our becauses and too often they lead us to grief and empty dreams.

Biblical Becauses

Let's examine a few of the Biblical becauses, because they help us choose more solid becauses, more solid motivations for doing what we do, both as individuals and as a church; both in church and during the week.

Consider first *the because of guilt* (Gen 3:10). ". . . and I was afraid, because I was naked." Here is the conclusion to the familiar story of the sin of Adam and Eve in the garden. Adam says he hid because he was afraid to be found naked. That because was only the fascade, the front door to the real motivation for his hiding. Guilt was the real motivator, even as it is today in so many cases in our lives. See how God cuts to the heart of the problem as He responds, "Who said you were naked?" What's being naked got to do with it? I made you that way! Have you been eating of the forbidden tree? Adam tried to blame his hiding on Godyou made me naked! Do you ever lash out at others when the problem is a guilty spirit within you? But it is not God's craftsmanship that is at fault, but our guilty hearts when we disobey Him and twist His law, made for our good. Peace comes when we replace a guilty spirit with a spirit of obedience and trust.

Or consider *the because, the motivation for giving,* found in Genesis 33:11. ". . . because God hath dealt graciously with me, and because I have enough." What a marvelous ending to the miserable story of Jacob's treachery to Esau! Jacob urges Esau to take his gifts for two becauses: (1) God has been good to me What a because upon which to base your tithing upon! The realization that God has been good to us is foundational; but we find it so easy to count our misfortunes, our misblessings, rather to count our fortunes and our blessings! What blessings would flow if we took to heart the old hymn, "Count your many blessings." And is it not true that most of us do have enough of this world's goods to live on a level most of the world only dreams of? Are we grateful? You will never give the tithe joyfully and cheerfully to God until you give from a grateful heart that knows it has been blessed of God. And the second because:: " I have enough." Let me tell you a simple, profound truth: "enough" doesn't have anything to do with amount! It has to do with a realization that we are blessed to the extent that it doesn't matter what we have; whatever we have is enough to share with others and give a tithe back to God! Ask yourself this question: what is the because behind my amount of giving to this church? Complete this sentence: I do (or do not) tithe because . . .

Now turn with me to two *passages which link a Divine and human because,* Deuteronomy 7:7-8 and 1 John 4:19. "The Lord . . . set His love upon you . . . because the Lord loved you" And the human side of that love: "We love Him, because He first loved us." I suppose there is no because in the Bible with more power to change our everyday life than this one in Deuteronomy! It tells every one of us, the good and the bad and the ugly, that God loves us; "that God don't make no junk." God believes I'm okay and you're okay in Christ. God's because in choosing us in Christ is not because we're smart, or rich, or famous, or anything like that. God's motivation in blessing us, in sending Jesus to die for our sins, in forgiving our sins and mistakes every day—the motivation is divine love. You remember the answer the great theologian Karl Barth is said to have given when asked his deepest theological truth: "Jesus loves me, this I know; for the Bible tells me so." The fact that God loves us in Christ to the depth and reach of the cross is the most profound truth in human experience. One of my favorite theologians, James Denny of Aberdeen, had the habit of holding a crucifix up high before his class (no, he was not a Roman Catholic) and saying, "Men, go into every church in the land, hold this high, and say, 'God loves like that!'" And such divine love surely constrains all those who have experienced it to give our best devotion in return: We love Him, because He first loved us. Perhaps it cannot be put better than in the 3 questions the four-year-old put to me: "Does God love us? Why does God love us? Do we love God?"

In the face of such love, *the because that crippled Christ* is especially poignant, as we read it in Mark 6:5-6. "He could there do no mighty work . . . because of their unbelief."

Brethren, negativism is one of the most powerful forces in our lives! Doubt, disbelief, negativism—these actually crippled the work of Jesus; prevented Him from blessing His home village as He desired. While negativism will cripple us in our businesses and our homes, and that is terrible, it is sad to realize that negativism in the house of God, whether Nazareth or our church, has tremendous power, too. Unfortunately, there are those in every church who feel called to pour cold water on fires of enthusiasm wherever they find them! And, even without such spreaders of gloom, many of us find negativism welling up in our own heartsI say to myself, and I say to you, let us remember the awful power of negativism in Nazareth, and resolve to keep our hearts open and turned toward Jesus.

To help defeat negativism, consider *the because that prompts rejoicing* (Lk 10:19-20). You know, we Christians overlook one of the greatest motivations for rejoicing—the fact that our names are written in heaven! This is one of three great passages of scripture which speak of our names in God's book: in Malachi we read of a Book of Remembrance (Mal 3:16-17) of God's people, those whom God calls His special possession. And again, in the Book of Revelation we read of the opening of the Books, and of the Book of Life (20:12) out of which a person is judged. But the Christian need have no fear of judgment, for his name is written in heaven! That's so much better than his name cut in stone on magnificent monuments on the earth, so much better than his name on the sweepstakes winner's notice, so much better than having your name up in lights. Rejoice, for your name is written in heaven!

Turn to Luke 19:16-17 and *observe the because that leads to greater responsibility.* Remember the parable of the king who gave his servants money to trade with in his absence? Hear his words to the faithful servant: "Well, thou good servant: because thou hast been faithful in a very little . . .have authority over ten cities." Faithfulness to their master motivated these men, and he rewarded their faithfulness. It teaches us that God rewards faithfulness in little things with greater opportunities and responsibilities. If a steward is not found faithful in the small things of life, how can God trust him with larger blessings and opportunities? It is a piercing question as we fill out our offering envelopes. It tells us a lot about how God operates, motivated by the faithfulness of His servants.

In John 11:42 we see *the because that prompts our witness.* "Because of the people which stand by . . ." When He said this prayer Jesus was standing at the tomb of Lazarus. He knew the Father was always with Him, and that all the power of heaven was standing by at that moment, but He was keenly aware of the people standing there, and their need to see Jesus acting in the love and the power of the Father. And that need, that because, was the motivating power. So He witnessed to that relationship by this prayer. It speaks to the motivations of our witnessing for the Lord. Too often church members feel a motivation to witness only when the preacher "steps on their toes," or out of guilt, or habit, or to get ready for revival. But here we see three powerful motivations for our witnessing: (1) the conviction that He was sent as a witness to the Father; (2) the desire to see others believe; and (3) the awareness that others were standing by watching His actions. Let that because be present in your life!

And finally, let us note *the because that gives us hope*. In John 14:19 we read: ". . . because I live, ye shall live also." What a wonderful promise for the hereafter, and a wonderful motivation to make these days a testimony of faith, to live for Jesus. We have no innate claim on immortality; the idea that we live forever is Greek, not Biblical. Jesus promises that those who believe in Him shall never die, but live forever with Him. Remember the beautiful hymn, "Because He Lives":

> *Because he lives I can face tomorrow;*
> *Because he lives all fear is gone;*
> *Because I know he holds the future,*
> *And life is worth the living just because he lives.*

That's the most wonderful because of all! But can you claim that because? Because He lives . . . I shall live.

If: The Larger Half of Life

Matthew 4:3; 6:30; Luke 23:39; Revelation 3:20

Rudyard Kipling gave fatherly advice in a poem that was widely quoted a couple of generations ago:

If you can keep your head when all about you
Are losing theirs and blaming it on you;
If you can trust yourself when all men doubt you,
But make allowance for their doubting too;
If you can wait and not be tired by waiting,
Or, being lied about, don't deal in lies,
Or, being hated, don't give way to hating,
And yet don't look too good, nor talk too wise;

If you can dream—and not make dreams your master;
If you can think—and not make thoughts your aim;
If you can meet with triumph and disaster

If: The Larger Half of Life

And treat those two impostors just the same;
If you can bear to hear the truth you've spoken
Twisted by knaves to make a trap for fools,
Or watch the things you gave your life to broken,
And stoop and build 'em up with wornout tools;

If you can talk with crowds and keep your virtue,
Or walk with kings—nor lose the common touch;
If neither foes nor loving friends can hurt you;
If all men count with you, but none too much;
If you can fill the unforgiving minute
With sixty seconds' worth of distance run—
Yours is the Earth and everything that's in it,
And—which is more—you'll be a Man, my son!

Wonderful advice, I am sure—if you can do it! A preacher was waxing eloquent before a captive audience of hungry and homeless street people, and ended his sermon by quoting with great pomposity the challenging lines, *If you can fill the unforgiving minute with sixty seconds' worth of distance run—Yours is the Earth!* There was a long silence, then came a tired voice from the back of the room: *"And if you can't?"* Many of us can't! "If you can fill . . ." Consider with me the word if and let God speak to you about it this morning. If is a very large word in terms of its influence upon us, and yet it is one of the smallest words we know. That may be why it is so easy for us to pick on it and misuse it. Remember how we used to pour scorn on this tiny word in rhymes like:

If ifs and ands
Were pots and pans,
We'd all be tinkers.

And there's a blue million others like that. This little word often travels in the company of "white collar" bullies: "If you do this or that, I'll do so and so . . . or I'll not do something I promised." It travels in the company of manipulators: "If you love me, you will give me, or let me . . . It travels most often in the caravan of the losers: If only I had done thus and so, or not done such and such . . . But if so and so had happened, or not happened.

You may remember, if you are of the older generation or have an old-fashioned English literature teacher, Alexandre Dumas' novel, The Count of Monte Cristo. The novel's hero, Edmond Dantes, was imprisoned for 14 years in the dungeon of an old castle on the island of If. That island does exist, in the Mediterranean Sea, just outside the harbor of Marseilles. What an appropriate name, If, for an island and its dungeon—for so many people go through life confined in the prison, the dungeon of if, a prison from which we spend our years trying to escape.

Sometimes we say of an uncertain situation or opportunity: it's real iffy. Listen! Life itself consists in half measure of If! It is vitally important how we relate to this word; how we use it.

If: In The Rearview Mirror

Sadly, most of us see if only in the rearview mirror; we see this word if as a hand waving good-by to what might have been. And if that is the primary use of if in our vocabulary, it is about the biggest, heaviest word we have.

That delightful and insightful author, Authur Gordon, has in his book **A Touch of Wonder** a story about if. He had a psychiatrist friend with whom he often had coffee, and one day when all was going wrong, he asked his friend to meet for coffee. He shared his gloomy feelings for perhaps 15 minutes, then the doctor invited him back to his office to listen to a tape recording. The tape had on it three case studies; three people—unnamed—who had come to the psychiatrist for help. He played it and asked Gordon to spot the two-word phrase which controlled the three people. The first was a businessman who was berating himself for not having worked harder and looked farther ahead. The second was a woman who never married because of a

If: The Larger Half of Life

sense of obligation to her widowed mother, and she bitterly recalled all the marriage chances she let pass by. The third voice was that of a mother whose teen-age son was in some trouble with the law, and she blamed herself. "Six times in this tape," said the psychiatrist, "they used a phrase full of poison: *If Only*. The doctor went on to say these are the two saddest words in any language, and that "the trouble with if only is that it doesn't change anything. It keeps the person facing the wrong way— backward instead of forward."

Biblical Uses of If

He's right, you know; we can go through life looking in the rear view mirror and saying if only . . . or we can let this little word If open all kinds of windows on the future. There is a sad, perverse streak in us that leads us feed upon ourselves, to relish the rehashing of old mistakes and decisions that cannot be altered. The Bible is full of such thinking, for it is a mirror of all walks of life, all states of mind and heart, all mixtures of spirituality and carnality. A survey of various popular translations of the Bible finds if often on the lips of the characters of the Bible: early on we hear the Children of Israel muttering at Moses and Aaron as they trekked through the desert: "if only we had died in Egypt!"

Apparently Moses got a bellyful of their if attitude, for in one of his farewell speeches he says, "If you disobey, God will punish you, and in your despair, in the morning you will say, if only it were evening, and in the evening, if only it were the morning!" And faithful as he was, in a time of hardship Joshua wailed, "if only we had been content to dwell on the other side of Jordan!" Absalom set up his rebellion by commenting to oppressed citizens, "if only I were the judge in Israel!" And who can forget David's sad cry at the news of the death of his son Absalom: "O Absalom, if only I had died in your place! Daniel comes before King Nebuchadnezzar with a black interpretation of the king's dream and says: "if only the dream were to those who hate the king!" In the New Testament we find a rebuke to Jesus in the if of Mary and Martha when their brother Lazarus died: "If you had been here, he would not have died!" And we see how lightly Peter takes the if of his rash vow to Jesus: "If I should die with thee, I will never deny thee!"

If: Pointing to the Rock

Among the many uses of if in the Bible, positive and negative, I want us to focus on the use of if in a positive sense, for there is more to this word than what we see in the rearview mirror! The first emphasis I call to your attention is the use of if in the New Testament to point to a wonderful work of God, an accomplished fact on which our faith can rest. Instead of looking back at what we have not done, or have done wrong, use if to emphasize what God has done!

". . . If God so clothe the flowers of the field . . . will He not clothe you, O ye of little faith?" If God so painted the flowers with the colors of spring, and He did, then we as His children need have no fear. God will take care of you. Let us focus not on our ifs, but on His! " . . . If with the finger of God I cast out devils . . .then the kingdom of God is in your midst." And Jesus did indeed cast out demons, giving proof that a new and more powerful force than satan was at work in this world. Let us rejoice in that affirmation!

And Paul uses if in this fashion to point to the rock of our salvation, to underline the power and work of God in our lives in the process of salvation and sanctification. "If when we were enemies, we were reconciled by his death . . .we shall be saved by his life." What a grounds for rejoicing when we realize that if the death of Christ brought us reconciliation with God—why, the continuing life of the Risen Christ in us will bring us salvation here and now in the struggles of this world, and will bring us salvation when we stand before God in the Judgment.

In I Corinthians 15 Paul rings the changes again on this little word If, for he says, "If there be no resurrection of the dead . . .but now is Christ risen from the dead!" If Jesus did not rise from the tomb; if the Easter story is just a futile, beautiful but empty hope, then we Christians are of all people the most deceived and hopeless! But we know Jesus was raised; the if only serves as a backdrop to the heart of Christianity—the sure and certain resurrection of Jesus. In these words of Jesus and Paul we see them using if as a backboard of uncertainty off which to bounce a certainty of the faith—God cares, God is at work, Jesus is alive!

If: The Stepping Stone to Higher Faith

In the New Testament this little word if is often used in another positive way to encourage the person who realizes he or she is weak in faith. Listen to these words: "If I can but touch the hem of his robe, I shall be made whole . . ." so spake the woman with the flow of blood. She could have said, "if I could get to him, I might find healing, but of course there's no way!" Or hear the leper pleading to Jesus: "If you wish, you can make me whole." Here if is robbed of its defeatist attitude, for the man is persuaded that Jesus certainly will heal him—and his faith is rewarded! And remember the father with the convulsive son who could not be healed by the disciples? When Jesus came down from the Mount of Transfiguration, the father begs him to do something, if he can. Jesus replies, "If you can believe, all things are possible." In all these cases the if is not a put-down, not a looking backward at what could not or did not happen; rather it is a stepping stone, a leg up, to higher faith.

I would mention one other use of the word if in connection with the Christian walk. We see it used as a reminder of how even the Christian can fall back in his Christian walk and disappoint God. We see it used as a reminder of our responsibility to each other as Christians, and we see it used as a word of reminder to keep on keeping on. Hear Jesus' warning about falling back and growing cold: "But if the salt has lost its flavor, how shall it be salted?" The grim reality is that some Christians talk the talk, but fail to walk the walk! Every Christian and every church stands under the possibility of this if—that we will fail to be the flavor and preservative of this wicked world.

And a second if, from Paul, reminding us of our responsibility within the household of faith. "But if meat causes my brother to stumble,

I will eat no meat so long as the world stands." What a gallant if! Would to God we all had that kind of attitude toward our Christian brothers and sisters. Of course it is not easy; who ever said it was? It means just what Paul says it means: the giving up of our rights and privileges for the brother or sister who is weaker and may stumble because of us. And the third instance of the encouraging if is a reminder of reward: "In due season we shall reap," says Paul, "if we faint not." Over against the work is the harvest, over against the struggle the victory, over against the past is the future—all divided by a tiny word, if.

If: The Arrow of Doubt

I quickly point out to you the dark side of if. This little word is so powerful the devil makes use of it whenever possible as an arrow of doubt, and was not afraid to use it even on Jesus. At the beginning of Jesus' ministry, the devil used all the power of this word: "If you are the Son of God, then turn these stones into bread; then jump from the steeple; then worship me and receive all the kingdoms of the world!" And not long afterward, we hear Jesus' brothers saying, "If you really can do miracles . . . go down to Jerusalem for the feast." And just a bit later, at the dinner where the woman of ill reputation anointed Jesus' feet, we hear a pharisee saying, "If he were a prophet, he would have known what sort of woman she was." And so it goes, under the hand of the devil, right on up to the cross, as the by-standers jeered and taunted, "If you are the Son of God, come down from the cross!" That is the most vicious use of the tiny but powerful word, if. The devil wanted to plant the seeds of doubt in the mind and heart of even Jesus himself. So never think for a moment that the devil does not want to plant a million doubtful ifs in your heart; doubts about yourself, your salvation, your Saviour. Let not that use of if find lodging in your heart.

If: The Gospel Hinge Word

One final use of if, and that is as a hinge word in the Good News of salvation through Christ. From the Book of Revelation we hear the

If: The Larger Half of Life

appeal of Jesus: "Behold, I stand at the door and knock; if any man hear my voice and open the door, I will come in." The choice of hearing the knock of Jesus upon your heart is up to you. Nobody else can open the door of your life, your future, your hope, but you. From Paul's letter to the Romans we read, "If thou wilt believe in thine heart and confess with thy mouth that God raised Jesus from the dead, thou shalt be saved." Only you can take that step of belief and public confession, but you can do it today. And a last if from the Book of Acts, as Philip preaches to the Ethiopian. The man believed in his heart and was ready to go all the way with Christ. "What doth hinder me to be baptized," he asked Philip. "If you believe with all your heart, you may," said Philip.

Never: The Word that Locks Doors

II Samuel 12:10; Psalm 10:11; Matthew 7:23; John 8:51

Norman Schwarzkopf must have a mother just like mine. I read in the newspaper yesterday that when asked recently if he had any political ambitions, General Schwarzkopf replied, "I have never considered any political aspirations, but you know somebody once said, 'Never say never . . .'" I guess both our mothers used to say that same phrase! *Never say never!* Because you just may have to eat your words! "Never," my mother used to say, "is a mighty long time."

And it is usually true that when a man says never, his love or his anger, his hatred or his sorrow, has the best of him. We usually live to rue the day we swore never to do a certain thing, or go to a certain place, or perhaps even marry a certain person!

But when God says never, it carries the eternal ring of authority. Sometimes God's never is a command, sometimes a judgment, and sometimes a blessed promise. Look with me this morning at the word of blessing and curse, the little word never.

The Never of the Fire

There is not a long list of things God commands His people never to do; but here in Leviticus 6:13, in the middle of those unending lists of laws for every occasion under the sun, given to the Israelites in the middle of the wilderness, we find a striking instance of something God commanded His people to never do: never let the fire on the holy altar in the tabernacle of God go out. Why was it so important that God attached a never to this commandment? Why not just light the fire on the altar whenever they needed it, or every morning?

The context verses speak of how each morning the priest, dressed in his priestly robes, should reverently take from the altar the ashes of the burnt offerings of the day before, and add wood to the fire which was to burn continually on the altar. He was to never let the fire go out because the fire was a symbol of God. The fire, just as the tabernacle, represented the constant presence of God among His people. Fire throughout the Bible is a symbol of God, of His presence, His holiness, His righteousness. From the burning bush of Exodus to the burning eyes of the Eternal Christ in Revelation we see fire as a symbol of the presence and work of God. So it appears in this scene. As they journeyed, God's people needed to know God was always present, in the middle of the night, in the midst of the storm, in the midst of great sin, in the midst of great sorrow. God is always with His people—therefore never let the fire, the symbol, go out.

The fire also reminded the people of the sacrificial nature of their relationship to God. The fire needed tending, the fire required sacrifices. It reminded them that their God was like a consuming fire, as the Scripture says. Jeremiah says God's Word is a fire in his bones, and even Jesus speaks of "being eaten up by the zeal for God's house," and Paul reminds us that our lives are to be a living sacrifice on the altar of God. How can these things be if the fire goes out? Now First Baptist Church doesn't have a fire burning on the offering table, but we certainly have the necessity to do what the flame on the altar reminded the Israelites to do. We must be faithful in bringing our best offering and our tithe to God's house, we must be sure that we reverence this place as being filled in a special way with the presence of God, and we must offer ourselves to Him every time we come to worship.

The Sinner's Never

Let us turn from the never of this commandment of holiness to what I call the sinner's never. It is found in 2 Samuel 12:10. You know the background story here. You remember that David, caught in lust, desired the wife of Uriah his general. He tried various and desperate means to put a respectable face on his sin when Bathsheba, Uriah's wife, became pregnant. Finally David had Uriah killed and married Bathsheba. Perhaps he had fooled the world, but not God, for here comes the prophet Nathan. He first snares David in a parable about a man who, though possessing many sheep, stole a poor neighbor's only lamb. When the angry king demanded to know who would do such a thing, the prophet declared the king himself guilty! Here is the curse pronounced on David: "Now therefore the sword shall never depart from thine house . . . " We know the outcome of the story. Absalom, David's son and proper heir to the throne, led a rebellion to overthrow David and very nearly succeeded before being killed in the battle.

Now hear the bitter truth of this sinner's never. Some sins carry a never in their heart like a bitter seed, and we find that when, like David, we commit these sins, even deep remorse and repentance cannot remove the temporal fruit of our sin. A sin with a never in its heart means when all is over, there is yet a grief that never leaves; remember Longfellow's poem about the judge who presided over the terrible witchcraft trials in Salem in the 1700's—he stood each year in church and confessed his sin *"with a lifelong sorrow that never slept."* Some sins carry a never in their heart that results in a crippled life, spiritually and physically, even when God has forgiven. We can pull the nail out of the tree, but we cannot pull the nail hole out, nor the scars that remain. This sinner's never reminds us of a bitter truth that many of us have experienced, and warns us again of the devastating power of sin.

The Wicked Man's Never

In Psalm 10:11 we see what I have called the wicked man's never. The wicked man says, "God will never see my sin." Such a statement conjures up images of John Dillinger, or the Godfather, or Jesse James, or in these days thoughts of Adolph Eichmann, or the man whose daughter recently remembered how he killed her little friend 30 years ago and now he is finally being brought to justice, or the man in Chattanooga, who is being sent back to Mississippi to stand trial for an alleged civil rights days murder he committed decades ago. But the wicked man of this verse may be very respected in the community and in the church. Most of the wicked men I know don't think about God enough to consciously say, "God will never see my sin." What he does say in his heart are things like this: God isn't important; God doesn't matter in this world. Deacon Howard Lee expressed this inward mindset very well when he said to me a few days ago: "Preacher, I know why many people don't tithe, yet they pay to Caesar what is his—Caesar sends out the tax forms and the bills. God isn't visible and He doesn't send out bills!" That's right—out of sight, out of mind!

You see, if you truly believe in God; if you are aware of His all-knowing, all-powerful, all-loving, all-holy presence in your daily life—why, it is impossible to say God won't know, won't care, won't see our sin! The truly wicked man is the one who denies the reality of God in his daily life. So this statement, the never of the wicked man, is most likely in our time and city to be the word of the busy man or woman, who has no time for God, no time for worship, no time to practice Christian ethics, whose life is immoral, unethical, uncaring because they live as if there is no God! "God will never see my sin." But He will! In due season God will confront the man or woman who says or lives as if God will never know of their sin. And that leads me to the next never.

The Never of Judgment Day

In Matthew 7:23 we find the never that ought to be seen as a companion never to Psalms 10:11. The wicked man, the man too busy to acknowledge God in his life, the man who may even have his name on a church roll as an a "left-over" from childhood even though he never darkens a church door except for funerals and weddings—that man ought to be aware that there is a coming Judgment Day.

Look at the background of this verse in Matthew 7. Jesus is speaking of the need for the walk to match the talk, the life to match the lips. Then Jesus speaks of the Day of Judgment, and what He will say of such folks: "I never knew you; depart from me, you that work iniquity." Now, all of us can preach more Gospel than we can live out; but here is the end of the story of those who block God out of their conscious life and its decisions—as they have forgotten God in this world; so God will forget them in the next. Who is the person Christ will know in the Judgment Day? The person who does God's will (v. 21) and the person whose inner life is right before God (vv 22-23).

The Never of the Unpardonable Sin

The dread of hearing Christ say on Judgment Day, "I never knew you," is often paired with the fear of committing the "Unpardonable Sin" by many devout Christians. A man asked me just this past week: "Will everybody be saved? Is there anything you can't get forgiveness for?" Look at Mark 3:27 for the answer I gave him.

I have heard all kinds of sins proposed for the honor, or the disgrace, of being the unpardonable sin. Most people have no clear idea what this terrible sin is, but I will tell you today. Notice when and why Jesus spoke of the unpardonable sin. Scribes had come from Jerusalem to trap Jesus, and when they saw the miracles and how Jesus was casting demons out of folks, they said, "He has Beelzebul, and by the power of the ruler of demons he casts demons out." So Jesus responded with the comment about the unpardonable sin.

Only blasphemy against the Holy Spirit is unforgiveable! And the greek word for blasphemy refers to those who by "contemptuous speech intentionally come short of the reverence due to God." This they surely did, when they said Jesus was being controlled by Beelzebul, the god of the dung heap! They made two fatal mistakes: they looked at what God was doing and said the devil did it; and they blinded themselves to the realization that God was at work in this world. So how could God break through to them, seeing they could look at the deeds of Jesus and credit them to the devil? He couldn't. And those who will not hear and see God at work finally reach the point at which they cannot hear and respond to God. They are in a hopeless condition, refusing to acknowledge God's hand. They cannot be forgiven because they have closed their eyes to the light. So the only unforgiveable sin is unrepentance, refusal to acknowledge God's saving work through the Holy Spirit.

Judas' Never

Another *never* fits right in here. It is Judas' *never*. In Mark 14:21 we hear Jesus saying of the one who betrays Him: "The Son of Man goes as it has been written of Him: but woe to that man by whom He is betrayed! It were better for him if he had never been born." What a terrible thing to say! But it nails to billboards some great spiritual truths. First, it tells us that God intended Jesus to go to the cross. God foreknew that when He came to us. Mind you, in His humanity, Jesus had to be willing to go to the cross, trusting the Father to do all things well. But in this dark verse we see the plan of God for salvation through the cross of Christ. And second, we see here an emphasis on the free will of every man. Just as no one has to be in the group of which Jesus says, "I never knew you;" just as no one has to commit the unpardonable sin, so in this matter Judas did not have to be the one to betray Jesus. He, like all of us, had free will in his decision to betray Jesus. To say that Judas was predestined, that he had no choice but to betray Jesus, is to say that God has done a monstrous injustice to Judas.

This passage merely says that Jesus goes to the cross as planned; that it is a terrible thing to be the one to betray Him; and that it were better for him never to have been born than to do this foul deed. Judas' deed of betrayal boils down to this: he refused to trust, to follow, to believe in Jesus. He thought he knew best for them both. He ruined his life both here and hereafter. And what is true of Judas—that it were better if he had never been born—is equally true of every person who turns his back on Jesus and goes to hell, isn't it? It could be said of some "good" people, some rich, some kind people, some people sitting here in church this morning—better never to have been born than to reject the Gospel of Jesus.

The Blessed Never

Now turn to three nevers which richly bless the Christian. The first is found in John 8:51 "Verily I say unto you, if a man keep my saying, he shall never see death." What a blessed hope! But most folks today react to that promise as did the people who heard Jesus say it—"you've got a devil! Abraham is dead; the prophets are dead—and you say, keep my saying and you will never die!" Jesus isn't speaking of physical death here; He speaks of something much worse; eternal spiritual separation from God. If a man keep my saying means: if he accepts who Jesus is, and what Jesus teaches about Himself and the Kingdom of God, that man will find physical death to be but a shadow, the entrance hall into the presence of God He shall never see death.—what a blessed hope when we stand by the graveside of a loved one in Christ.

The second never of a precious promise is found in John 10:28. This is a famous verse with us Baptists; it takes John 8:51 a step further. Speaking of His followers, Jesus said "They shall never perish, neither shall any man pluck them out of my hand." The Bible breathes with the assurance of God that He who truly believes in Jesus will never wish to fall away from such fellowship and salvation—an assurance set in the frame of the cherished doctrine of free will. Here we see the believer's security is certain not just from the believer's side, but from God's side; no one, not even the devil, can tear God's child away from Him. The One within us is stronger than the one who rules this evil age. So long as you desire to live at the foot of the cross, God is able to surround you with a band of angels, and keep you safe.

And in closing, the third blessed never, found in Hebrews 13:5 "For He hath said, I will never leave thee, nor forsake thee." This verse has been an anchor in the storm for Christians through the centuries. Immortalized in song, whispered in prayer, it is power and strength and comfort and protection. Never leave you, no matter what you do, for if we only repent, no sin is unforgiveable. Never leave you, no matter how bad things seem. Never leave you, no matter how long the night, how deep the river. When the One who went to the cross because of your sins and mine tells us repentant sinners that he loves us, forgives us, never leaves us—believe it; that's the Gospel!

Nevertheless: The Word that Leaps Hurdles

Luke 5:1-11

There are, I am told, around 600,000 words in the English language. Yet 359 words make up 81% of our speech! The chances are that the word I want to focus upon is not an everyday part of your vocabulary, even though it ought to be. It is the small Biblical word *nevertheless*. This word wears several faces; it is the word of the winner and the whiner. It is the word of the sinner and the saint. Examine with me some of the Biblical uses of this word and ask yourself what role this word plays in your vocabulary and life.

The Word of Conflict

Let us begin by pointing out that this is one of those words that frame the paradoxes of life; a word that reminds us of the now and not yet aspect of life, the tug-of-war between that which is and that which ought to be, that which is good and that which is evil. Perhaps a perfect illustration is seen in Philippians 1:24. The writer of this letter, Paul,

Nevertheless: The Word that Leaps Hurdles

is in prison and expects to be executed. Even with his head "on the block" he says he is in a dilemma: It is better to go and be with Christ, nevertheless, to stay in this world is best for the church. he would like to face death, get it over with, and go on to be with Christ. Says he, "I do not know what to choose." Throughout the Bible we see the tug-of-war of life described by the word nevertheless.

The very word nevertheless is itself a combination of three words which in recent centuries have come to travel through life together: never the less. The word implies that some thinking has been done and it indicates that there are two considerations, two sides. A dictionary definition of nevertheless includes phrases like "in spite of that . . . however . . . in light of the foregoing . . ." Two concerns, two views, two values are balanced. And it is not an easy task.

Turn to Numbers 13:28 for a classic use of the word nevertheless to express the conflict in each life between what is right and wrong, between obedience and disobedience, cowardice and bravery. This passage relates the sending of the 12 spies into the Promised Land by Moses, and their report. It is easy to imagine the scene as these men arrive back in camp with their prizes and proofs of the bounty of the land God has promised them. Pomegranates, figs, and the most marvelous cluster of grapes they—or you or I—have ever seen!

Two of the spies come puffing down the path under the burden of the grapes slung on a pole between them! The camp is thrown into an uproar, a frenzy of excitement and hope that the long trek is over. But listen to the report as it begins in verse 27: "We came unto the land whither thou sentest us, and surely it floweth with milk and honey; and this is the fruit of it. Nevertheless the people be strong . . . and the cities are walled . . . and we saw the children of Anak there . . ." And Caleb said, "Let's go up and take it!" But the men who went with him said, "They are stronger than we . . . and they brought up an evil report of the land . . ." Their evil report spoke of men who made the spies feel like grasshoppers!

Is not this the story of life? For every positive there is a negative voice. For every man who says it can be done there is a voice saying it cannot. And so the first value of this word is that it helps remind us that life is made up of decisions and choices. Today each of us is faced with decisions for the coming weeks and months in our business, our family, our church. And there is a nevertheless in the midst of each choice. And because this word is a word of conflict, it leads some people to make of it

The Word of Compromise

We have the advantage of hindsight; we can look back on the decision of 10 of the 12 spies Moses sent out and say they really blew it! They made of the word nevertheless a word of compromise and cowardice. The children of Israel would come to realize that no matter how compelling the call, no matter how spirit-led the vision, there would always be those who flee from opportunity on a donkey called nevertheless, folks who cannot focus on the one prize before them. James calls them the double-minded and Jesus contrasts them with the pure in heart, those who have the ability to will one thing.

This word, nevertheless, is an old companion of those who would be friend to God and the World and mumble nevertheless as they count the cost. Turn with me to Matthew's Gospel, chapter 14. Here in verse nine we see another instance of the word nevertheless. King Herod is throwing a birthday party, and all his political and military cronies are there. Part of the entertainment of the evening is the dancing of Herod's niece, Herodias. Deep into his cups and appreciative of her dance, Herod offers the girl whatever she desires, up to half the kingdom! Goaded by her mother, the girl lays a strange request on the drunken king: she desires that the head of the preacher down in the dungeon, John called the Baptist, be brought to her upon a platter! Herod is not so drunk that he cannot realize his mistake. He really does like the preacher, and in fact has protected him, thus far, from the queen. But tonight, in light of his promise to give her whatever she wants, and in front of all these guests—how can he deny the girl her wish? How can he summon up the courage to say, No way, Hose! Matthew tells it like this: "And the king was sorry: nevertheless for the oath's sake, and them that sat with him at supper, he commanded it be given her." Sometimes it takes courage, and plenty of it, to recognize the dilemma and say, nevertheless I will not take the coward's way out! How easy it is to look at the cost and find it too much to afford integrity and courage. But I hasten to say that the Bible is not merely the story of spies and Herods. There are those who by their use of this word made it

The Word of Confirmation

The man who took his pen under the guidance of the Spirit to record the deeds of the kings of Israel made the word nevertheless a confirmation of the mercy of God, and so it remains until this very day. I Kings 15:4 paints in a few strokes a picture of God's mercy. "Nevertheless for David's sake did the Lord his God give him a lamp in Jerusalem, to set up his son after him." This verse follows the description of the reign of King Abijam over Judah. He was a wicked king, walking in all the sins of his father, yet God had mercy on him for David's sake. I read that verse and I thought, "I wonder how many times God has had mercy on me because of the godly life of someone who has been praying for me?" How many times do you suppose God has been merciful to you because of the righteous life of another person?

And Paul, sharing his thoughts with the Corinthian church, shows us how in a time of trouble nevertheless can become a sentinel to the soul, confirming the comfort of God. In 2 Corinthians 7 he says that when he came to Macedonia his heart had no peace: "We were troubled on every side: without were fightings, within were fears. Nevertheless God, who comforteth those that are cast down comforted us . . ." So life gets hard; sometimes we feel we haven't the strength to contend with the battles within our selves, let alone the battles on the outside. But over against all that is the comfort of God. The tragedy is that so often we turn to anything and everything before God.

But this word nevertheless is a word of confirmation not only of God's mercy, but also of God's judgment. In Exodus 32:34 we read of God's reply to the bold request of Moses following the sin of the people in making the golden calf. You remember that Moses asked God to forgive the people but blot him out of the Book of God's remembrance. God's reply is worth pondering, as He affirms the individual's responsibility before Him, and tells Moses to return to the people and say, "Behold, mine angel shall go before thee: nevertheless in the day when I visit I will visit their sin upon them." Let the word nevertheless be in our vocabulary as a reminder that our God is both merciful and righteous, and that there is a judgment day coming.

But I have been inspired as I see how nevertheless has been used by God's people in a way that rises above the conflict, that puts away the compromise and cowardice, for this can be

The Word of Commitment

This word nevertheless is a winner's word. It ought not be a whiner's word, a loser's word. Surely by birthright this word belongs to the winner, the fighter, the bold dreamer, the visionary, the one willing to dare, the person who, in the midst of adversity, does not fold up but rather looks up and keeps on going. Fanny Crosby was physically blind throughout her life, yet she had marvelous spiritual sight; she could see forever, and she penned some of our most beloved hymns including, Redeemed, Redeemed, How I Love to Proclaim It! Blessed Assurance, Jesus is Mine; Pass Me Not O Gentle Saviour, and many others. She simply said nevertheless to all her handicaps. She once expressed her nevertheless this way:

> *O what a happy soul am I!*
> *Although I cannot see,*
> *I am resolved that in this world*
> *Contented I will be;*
> *How many blessings I enjoy*
> *That other people don't!*
> *To weep and sigh because I'm blind, I cannot, and I won't.*

Nevertheless: The Word that Leaps Hurdles

That's how a little girl of 8 years said Nevertheless! It is a word of resolution, of determination, of unswerving commitment to a goal higher than ourselves. Or take Martin Luther.

The Cardinal thundered, "The Pope's little finger is stronger than all Germany. Do you expect your princes to take up arms to defend you—a wretched worm like you? I tell you, No! And where will you be then?" "Then, as now," cried Luther, "I shall be in the hands of God!" And so he stood, against all odds, realizing the powers arrayed against him; nevertheless "Here I stand," said he, "So help me God!" What a way to express a nevertheless! Remember the poem Ulysses by Tennyson, in which Ulysses urges his companions, now old and weary, to turn, nevertheless, to the goal:

'Tis not too late to seek a newer world.
Push off, and sitting well in order smite
The sounding furrows; for my purpose holds
To sail beyond the sunset, and the western stars until I die.
Tho' much is taken, much abides; and tho'
We are not now that strength which in old days
Moved earth and heaven, that which we are, we are—
One equal temper of heroic hearts,
Made weak by time and fate, but strong in will
To strive, to seek, to find, and not to yield.

And those closing words are inscribed on the lonely cross in the vast and icy plains of the South Pole, marking the resting place of Robert Scott and his brave comrades who perished saying, nevertheless, we will press on!

Still, the highest glory of the word nevertheless is found when it is used as a marker in the spiritual dimension of life; when it affirms that the spiritual, the unseen, the challenging vision is more real and true and worthwhile than the familiar world of sight and sound. Thus we say, "Hither by thy help I'm come; grace has led me safe thus far and grace will lead me home." Look with me at several examples of the way nevertheless should fit into our spiritual vocabulary.

In Luke 13 we see a strange situation. We are told that some of the Pharisees, usually the antagonists of Jesus, came to Him to warn Him of Herod's murderous hatred. Jesus' response was for them to go tell "that old fox" that Jesus wouldn't be a thorn in his side very long, for today and tomorrow are given to casting out devils and healing, and on the third day it is completed. "Nevertheless I must walk today, and tomorrow, and the day following: for it cannot be that a prophet perish out of Jerusalem." Here is our Lord using nevertheless in regard to God's plan. It matters not that Herod is angry; God's plan must be carried out. And He "set His face like a flint" to go to Jerusalem. I wonder how many of us can use nevertheless in that manner?

In Luke 5 is our text passage. Here Peter puts all his common sense in the balances over against obedience to Jesus. He has fished all night and done no good; "nevertheless, at thy word I will let down the net." Again, I wonder in my own life, and you may wonder in your life, if we are willing to say to conventional wisdom, to your common sense and my common sense, to the pressure of the society around us—nevertheless I will obey God.

And a last example of the commitment stance of nevertheless as seen in Matthew 26. Here we go to the Garden of Gethsemane, and see our Lord kneeling beneath the old olive trees. And here nevertheless reaches its highest use on the lips of men, as Jesus prays concerning the will of God: "O my Father, if it be possible, let this cup pass from me: nevertheless not as I will, but as thou wilt."

None of us can use nevertheless with the depth of Jesus. But how glorious it would be if all of us went out of this place with nevertheless written in our hearts with the passion of the garden, with the obedience of the fisherman Peter.

The world is always with us, calling and clamoring; our own heart is pulled between our will and God's will; our sins weigh us down and cripple us; our problems rise up taller than our resources; what shall we say?

Let us say nevertheless I will seek God's will.

Let us say nevertheless I turn away from my sins.

Let us say nevertheless I ask Jesus to be my Lord and Saviour.

P'like: The Power of Imagination

I Chronicles 29:11-18; Hebrews 11:13,27

Remember the book, **All I Really Need to Know I Learned In Kindergarten?** Robert Fulghum in that book put his finger on a truth we need to keep in mind—Children and childhood have a lot they can teach grown-ups.

Take p'like, for instance. We all played p'like as children; "P'like I'm the cowboy and you're the Indian . . . p'like I'm the marines and you're Tojo . . . p'like I'm Eisenhower and you're Hitler." At least that's the way we boys played in the closing days of World War II. P'like turned the piece of cardboard we fastened to our bicycle wheel with a clothespin into a motor, and the little grapevine next to the house into a jungle. P'like: the power of imagination. I remember how our son, as a preschooler, had an imaginary friend he would hand over to his mother to put in her pocket or purse during church! But most of us lose the tremendous power of imagination as we grow up.

P'like: The Power of Imagination

Let's talk about this powerful tool called imagination. Listen carefully or you will imagine me saying things I do not say! Begin with some facts about imagination. *(1) Imagination is very real and powerful. (2) Imagination is a Biblical concept. (3) Imagination is neutral and can be used for either good or evil. (4) Imagination is essential for our maximum usefulness to God.*

The Power of Imagination

I venture to say that imagination is more powerful than either the pen or the sword! Every doctor can attest to the power of imagination as he tries to deal with the imaginary aches and pains of the hypocondriac. And maybe some of you remember the panic of Halloween night, 1937, as Orson Welles' radio program, *War of the Worlds*, led to folks seeing alien spacecraft all over the country! About 250 years ago the power of imagination led to the condemnation and execution of nearly two dozen persons as witches in Salem, Massachusetts. The power of imagination turned the cold wood floor of my childhood home into a magic carpet as I read the adventures of Richard Halliburton in his **Book of Marvels**. I traveled to the pyramids, I saw the Taj Mahal by moonlight, I visited the forbidden Muslim city in disguise—I traveled the world in my imagination. The dictionary says imagination is "imaging," or seeing something in your mind which does not have concrete reality—yet.

The Dark Side of P'like In The Bible

When I turn to the Bible with the idea of "P'liking" I immediately think of the folks Jesus called hypocrites. One of the sharpest chapters in the Bible is Matthew 23, in which Jesus condemns the pharisees and scribes as hypocrites, as folks who imagine themselves to be righteous. This chapter, like a double-edged sword, will cut the modern reader as well as the ancients! The very word hypocrite literally means to "speak from under," and comes from the Greek theatre in which one actor would play several roles by putting first one mask over his face and speaking, and then another mask and another role. The hypocrite speaks from behind a mask, thinking—imagining—himself to be what he is not. Much of what the Bible has to say about imagination and its power speaks of its dark use.

The first reference to imagination is in Genesis 6:5 as God sees the wickedness of mankind, evaluates it and arrives at a conclusion—to send the flood. "And God saw that the wickedness of man was great in the earth, and that every imagination of the thoughts of his heart was only evil continually." It didn't have to be, but it was. And that is the general tenor of the explicit references to imagination. The Bible says that the imagination of man's heart is evil from his youth (Genesis 8:21); the reason for scattering the people from building the tower of Babel is that "nothing will be restrained from them, which they have imagined to do" (Genesis 11:6). A favorite description of evil in the Old Testament is that one "walks in the imaginations of his heart."

The Value of Imagination in the Bible

But look at the positive uses of the imagination. In I Chronicles 29 David, who wished to build the temple but was restrained by the Lord and only gathered the materials for the building of it, leads in prayer blessing the project. The people have brought worthy offerings and David himself has given of his wealth; now he prays in this manner: "O Lord god of Abraham, Isaac, and of Israel, our fathers, keep this [the temple and the building of it] for ever in the imagination of the thoughts of the heart of thy people, and prepare their heart unto thee" (29:18). The temple was not yet built, and for the reality to come to pass, the imagination, the vision, of it must be kept in the heart of the people. Why? Because the imagination, the vision, is the motivating force. Their imagination was their motivation.

In the roll-call of faith in Hebrews 11 it is said of Abraham, Isaac and Jacob: "These all died in faith, not having received the promises, but having seen them afar off," and of Moses we read: "By faith he forsook Egypt, not fearing the wrath of the king: for he endured, as seeing him who is invisible." What is meant by seeing the invisible but

P'like: The Power of Imagination

seeing it in the mind, imagining it? When Isaiah, in the year that king Uzziah died, went to the temple and saw the Lord, high and lifted up, with his robe filling the temple—he saw in his mind, in his imagination what a man beside him may not have seen at all. And John, on the island of Patmos, looks right into heaven through a door, as it were, cut into the sky. Did other prisoners looking up at the blue sky see the same? Or was it painted on the screen of his imagination?

In II Kings 6 when Elisha the prophet is being hunted by the king of Syria, his servant rises early one morning and looks out to the surrounding mountains to see the Syrian army encamped around about. He asks Elisha what they should do, and Elisha replies that "they which be with us are more than they that be with them." The look of disbelief on the face of the servant must have been something to behold, for Elisha begins to pray that God will open this man's eyes. And God did, and the servant looked out again and saw the mountains full of horses and chariots of fire, the horsemen of God. What was this on Elisha's part but having faith to see the invisible, to imagine what the fearful could not see—the very present help of God.

The Corruption of Imagination

We can put this neutral power of imagination to either good or evil use, and once pointed in a particular direction it is like a big dog on a leash dragging a little boy along. The bad influence of imagination is easily illustrated. Take pornography—it appeals to the imagination and turns all the vast power of that faculty to degrading and unworthy thoughts. And once corrupted the imagination leads the way to evil action. Or consider gambling. Common sense says the casino owners will make money, the gambler will lose money. I pass a billboard several times each day that plugs gambling. The image on the sign is that of a nice, friendly dog with a mouthful of money. The two statements on the billboard are these: Nice Doggy. (Agreed; but this billboard is about gambling, not about a nice doggy). And the other phrase is: Everyday is Payday. (But for whom? Only the owners of the gambling establishments have payday everyday!) There's no common sense on that billboard, but common sense isn't the driving force in gambling; imagination is—the gambler imagines himself winning a pile of money; money that should have stayed home and provided for the needs of a family. Imagination is not harnessed to either morality or truth.

Imagination's power is so great that it is essential we keep a tight rein on it. We ought not do all we can imagine; we should not, must not let our imagination lead us into evil. Imagination was given to us to use for God's glory. And Paul expresses our individual responsibility in the matter of imagination in Romans 1:21 when, speaking of natural man, he says: "When they knew God, they glorified him not as God, neither were thankful; but became vain [lit., empty] in their imaginations, and their foolish heart was darkened." They didn't have to have vain, empty, corrupting imaginations; they—we—choose it to be so.

The Right Use of Imagination

So the question is, How can we use our imaginations rightly, in the service of God? We can remind ourselves that "seeing is believing." Seeing in the mind, imagining, visualizing brings us closer to the reality. Recently when a new section of Disney World opened and a group of executives were touring it, one of them, a friend of the late Walt Disney, said, "I just wish Walt could have seen this!" To which the other replied, "Oh, he did; he did!"

When a person says "I can't even imagine that!" they certainly won't do whatever it is they cannot imagine; they won't even try, for they do not believe in its reality. "Seeing is believing" means that we only believe that which we can at least see in our mind and envision and dream about, that which lives in our heart and is fed on imagination. That's why many dieting programs urge you to visualize yourself skinny! William Carey was a great missionary because he could see the multitudes without Christ around the world. A cobbler, he worked on shoes during the day, and at night read about missionaries and lost millions around the world, marking places of need on a rough leather globe made of shoe scraps. He could see the need; he could see the

P'like: The Power of Imagination

power of the gospel—in his imagination. "Attempt great things for God; expect great things from God," he said.

Proverbs 23:7 says that as a man thinks in his heart, so is he. As he imagines himself to be, so he becomes. Paul, in Philippians 4:8 tells us to think upon, meditate upon—imagine?—things that are lovely, pure, honest, just. Which leads me to point out that Norman Vincent Peale's emphasis on positive thinking is Biblical; it is a way of imaging, of seeing the good. Do you know how he came to see the importance of positive thinking? He says that a group of men including Lowell Thomas, Eddie Rickenbacker and himself decided to begin publishing a magazine they would call Guideposts. They slowly built a subscription list of 25,000 while operating on a shoestring out of a grocery store attic in Pawling, New York. But one night a fire broke out and destroyed the publishing house and the list of subscribers. Lowell Thomas plugged it on the radio, and soon they had a list of 40,000 subscribers—and a big financial problem. They called a meeting which dripped with pessimism. At the meeting was a wealthy woman who had helped before. In the midst of the pessimism she spoke up: "I suppose you would like me to make another financial contribution. I might as well put you out of your misery. I will not give you another cent." Says Peale, "That did not put us out of our misery; it merely deepened it!" "But," the woman continued, "I will give you something more valuable than money. You are all sitting around talking about what you lack. When you think about lacking, you will focus on lacking and you will, indeed, lack. To correct that situation—reverse the mental process and begin to think positively.

Now," she went on, "how many subscribers do you need at the moment to keep going?" Peale and the others thought quickly and said, "100,000." "All right," she said, "that's not hard. Visualize 100,000 people being helped by this magazine and you will have them. In fact, the minute you can see them in your mind, you already have them." She turned to Peale and asked if he could see the 100,00. "Well, maybe so, but they seem pretty dim" he said. "Can't you imagine 100,000?" All Peale could see was 40,000. She turned to the man next to Peale and asked him if he could see the 100,000. Peale remembers thinking it unlikely that this man, a rubber manufacturer, would do much imagining, but the man stared straight ahead for a moment and then cried out with eagerness—"Yes, I do see them!" Peale was jolted; "Where? Point them out to me!" And he too began to see the multitude. They bowed their heads right there and thanked God for giving them the 100,000.

Peale goes on to say that the approach of "seeing is believing" is Biblical and must be used in a Biblical way. You cannot simply visualize yourself being rich and suddenly have it. That is the old prosperity religion, which is a lie and a heresy. But releasing the power of imagination in a Biblical fashion is something different, and is the key to some troublesome verses like: "If you have faith as a mustard seed, you can say to this mountain, be lifted up and planted in the midst of the sea and it shall be done . . " "If you abide in me, and my word abide in you, you shall ask what you will, and it shall be done to you." "If we ask according to his will, he hears us, and if we know that he hears, whatever we ask, we know that we have the petition we desired."

Don't these verses tell us to ask for God's will, and then according to our faith, our vision, our desire, our imagining of this matter in His will, it will be done? Do you dream big enough in the circle of God's will? Do you—does our church—imagine big enough? To imagine small, to have a small vision, a small dream is lack of faith and sin. After all, Peter described the new Christian community on Pentecost in these words from the prophet Joel: "Your old men shall dream dreams, your young men shall see visions."

A Sanctified Imagination

"Where there is no vision, the people perish." What are the elements of a worthy vision, dream, imagination for a church? There are at least four aspects to keep in mind: (1) We must have a common imagination about what God would have us do. If every member has a different vision, imagines a different goal for the church, it cripples rather than gives wings. We can say all we wish about the priesthood of the believer, but the church is a body, says Paul, in which all the parts must work together for a common imagination and vision. (2) The imagination must be a converted imagination. Our dream, our vision, that which we imagine must be God's plan for us, not just our human desires and wishes. (3) We must have a consecrated imagination; that is, we must be willing to sacrifice for the dream we can visualize. A worthy vision calls for our best in support, as David pointed out in the building of the temple. And (4) we must have a challenging imagination. By that I mean a converted imagination never thinks small. God is not in the "little" business. Jesus' parables told of the small mustard seed growing into the giant tree.

I have a vision for our church for this decade; I can see it. Do you have a vision for our church? Can you imagine it, see it? Is it a common vision, a converted vision, a consecrated vision, a challenging vision?

And a closing word: Have you ever imagined what God could do in your life if you would let Him have control? Close your eyes and imagine the kind of person God could make of you, and the influence for good you could have.

Just Too Busy

I Kings 20:40; Luke 10:38-42

I believe I speak for every person in this room when I say that we have a spiritual problem. The problem revolves around the pace of our lives—the incessant, relentless, endless demands of job and school and family and church. It seems that in every segment of our society there is an insatiable hunger to stay busy, to do more, get more done, do it faster and faster. And, unfortunately, for most of us, the faster we go, the behinder we get! I often think of a cartoon in which a frightened young priest —it could just have easily been a Baptist minister!—comes rushing into the office of the bishop in the rear of the cathedral, with a worried look and a wringing of the hands: "Your Reverence, there is a man outside in the congregation who says he is Jesus Christ! What shall I do?" As he came to his feet and began to straighten his desk, the bishop replied, "Look busy, man; look busy!"

This mindset of busyness and work means all too often that our sense of self-worth and the worth of others is tied up with our work, with what we do, rather than who we really are. Have you noticed how, when we meet new people, almost the first question we ask is what kind of work this person is in. We know the question is merely a way to get acquainted and a hook to hang a face and facts upon. But it also true that all too often a person's worth is measured against what they do for a living. I remember a tombstone in England on which is carved this epitaph: Born a man; died a Grocer! Far more important than what we do for a living is who we are spiritually.

That Animal Called Work Ethic

As I say these things, I realize that there is a segment of our society who do not work; not because they cannot, but because they will not! They are parasites upon the rest of us, and it is proper to remind such of the words of Paul: If they will not work; they shall not eat. But for most of us it is the Protestant work ethic that has so shaped us. The idea is ingrained that everyone should be working, and that work at its truest form is physical. I can remember thinking as a teenager—and have not yet fully overcome the idea—that I was not really working unless I was cropping tobacco or pulling corn tassels for hybrid corn (back when that was still in the experimental stages). To me that was work; the artist, the philosopher—these who worked with their heads instead of their hands—they were not really working! The official hymn of the Protestant work ethic is *"Work, For the Night is Coming!"* And we generally assume that a man cannot go wrong if he is busy! Most of us find it difficult not to portray ourselves as always busy! So most of us find ourselves in a furious pace of life which we allow to rob us of a deeper spiritual life—or at least we lay the blame on the pace of our lives.

While I Was Busy Here and There

Our problem is well illustrated in an Old Testament story. It follows directly on the heels of our text last week in which Elijah fled from

Jezebel. In the following chapter, 1 Kings 20, Ben Hadad, the king of Aram, goes to war against Ahab, king of Israel, not once but twice. On the second occasion Ahab won the battle by the grace of God. But having won, he let the enemy king, Ben Hadad, go free.

Now a prophet of God, hearing about this, had a friend knock him around a bit and, bandaged up, the prophet sat by the roadside until the king came by. Then the prophet cried out to the king, the chariot halted, and the bandaged "soldier" made his plea to the king. It seems that this man, in the heat of the battle, had been given charge of a captured enemy soldier and told to guard him. "If he escapes, either your life is forfeit, or you must pay a ransom!" Well, as the miserable man tells the story in 1 Kings 20:40, "While your servant was busy here and there, he was gone!" The king had no sympathy and declared the punishment just. Then the prophet ripped off his disguise and the king recognized a prophet who then chastised him for letting the enemy go free. Our point is the excuse the man in the story made: "While I was busy here and there, he was gone." Yes, that's our problem: While we are busy here and there, our spiritual life is gone.

While we are busy here and there: making a living, helping at the school, working with the civic club, coaching little league, doing church work, our spiritual life is being ignored or made a stepchild. Now we feel guilty about this; we know the water in the well of our spiritual life is deeper than our rope can reach; we want to experience more—but we find the spiritual compartment of our life reduced to Sunday mornings; no devotional life to speak of. But, we say to ourselves, there is just no time!

Mary Has Chosen the Best Part

There is a New Testament example of the same problem in Luke 10. Here we see Jesus as a dinner guest in the house of Martha in Bethany. It is pointed out that Martha owns the home; she is the sensible one with a head for the good old work ethic. In verse 39 we read that she had a sister named Mary, who also—mark that word; it is translated moreover in some versions—sat at Jesus' feet and listened to his teaching.

Now verse 40 says that Martha was cumbered, distracted with much serving. Literally, the word pictures one who is actually drawn, pulled around, a twisted expression of seriousness and duty. So poor Martha is taking care of the necessary arrangements and a whole lot of other arrangements that don't matter a bit. But finally she grows irritated at Mary's abdication of duties, and bursts in where Jesus and Mary sit talking, and demands, "Lord, is it nothing to you that my sister has left me to do the serving? Tell her to carry her end of the load!" Now notice the reply of Jesus. He tells Martha that she is distracted with many things—many dishes of food for the meal—but really only one thing is necessary. And then he adds, "Mary has chosen the best part, which shall not be taken from her."

An Anchor In A Material World

There is a message here for us. Consider a couple of points with me: *(1) Jesus himself practiced and taught that the spiritual world must be our anchor in this material world.* We will all become imitators of the Rich Fool if we ignore that truth. Jesus spent much time in prayer and meditation; in communion with the Father. Sometimes he prayed all night. If Jesus needed that kind of spiritual life to keep an anchor in the unseen world, surely we need, as the poet says, to lean our arms awhile upon the window sill of heaven and gaze upon his face, and then turn strong to meet the day. Halford Luccock of Yale tells how it was the custom of the early Puritans in New England to leave the view of the ocean clear, so that people could see out across the sea into the mists, and remember another land. But as time went by, buildings began to block the view of the sea, and the people stopped looking to an unseen land.

That is what has happened to many of us spiritually; like Martha, we have let the cares of this world blind us to a greater reality. Our inner, spiritual life is "the still point of a turning world" as T. S. Eliot put it, and if we do not pay attention to the quiet, still point, we will grow dizzy. Jesus rebuked Martha not because the quiet life was superior to the active life—there are, indeed, meals to prepare and jobs to be done—but because she was becoming a slave of the things she had to do.

The Bible shows us that man was made for fellowship with God, and we have a spiritual hunger for God. I found it passing strange that just this week, in a conversation with a Muslim friend, he commented on the obvious fraud among some TV religious programs, and his word was, "They go to these guys because there is a spiritual hunger." The catechisms say that man's chief end is to glorify God. But is that uppermost in folks' mind, even in the minds of evangelical Christians on a daily basis?

The Spiritual Life Is A Choice

(2) In this scene Jesus is saying that our relationship to him, the deepening of our spiritual life, is a choice we make. Mary chose that good part. We will not automatically become more spiritual; we must seek it. Notice that the text says speaks of "Mary, who also sat at Jesus' feet." Mary found a place for both contemplation and work. So must we. But how can we make Mary's choice and find room for it at our frenzied pace?

First, we must seriously desire the Kingdom of God first in our lives. I think it is not by accident that the passage of scripture immediately following this story is the account of the Lord's Prayer. Notice what that prayer says about the still point in our lives: hallowed be thy name; thy kingdom come; thy will be done; then, and only then, does the child of God come to material things: our daily bread, and then our forgiveness and protection from evil. If you seek first the kingdom, you will glorify God in your job, your school, your home.

Second, we must develop a plan that provides time alone with God. We have no trouble getting up early to go fishing or hunting or golfing. Perhaps we will need to get up earlier to have a regular devotional time.

Third, we must build upon this devotional time a conscious awareness of the spiritual and eternal dimension of life throughout the week. I remember the comment of the chairman of a pastor search committee some years ago. The committee had come to hear me and talk with me, and Pegeen and I had visited their church. The chairman took me on one of those visits to his office, and there he showed me the open Bible on his desk. He said that in one of my sermons that he heard I had pointed out the necessity of not being ashamed of our faith; of bringing the spiritual world into the work world. And so he had begun to read the Bible for a few minutes at work each morning, and leave it open on his desk as a reminder to himself and all who came to his office that there is an unseen world. In what ways do you let people know of your faith at work?

Fourth, we must join our life and our faith with that of others by finding our place in the house of God on the Lord's Day. You know, the church steeple used to be the tallest object on the city skyline. How that has changed in our modern world! Pegeen and I have enjoyed travelling the "Romantic Road" in Germany several times; on a couple of occasions we stayed the night in Nördlingen, and I walked the more than 300 steps to the top of the church tower. And from the tower you could look over all the town; every road came to the church! It was the center of the life of the village in the centuries past. Let it be the same today in your family's life.

Now let us take stock. Some folks have their priorities backward:

> *They worship their work;*
> *They work at their play;*
> *They play at their worship.*

But if you are among those who are weary of being empty spiritually, hear the words of Jesus: Come unto me, all ye that labor and are heavy laden, and I will give you rest. And so he will.

Compassionate Words from Hell

Luke 16:19-31

Recently I saw an interesting list; a list of the 40 richest Americans of all time. Fascinating list, and their wealth was given in today's dollars. Who do you think topped the list? Bill Gates? Wrong! The top five were John D. Rockefeller at $190 billion (oil), Andrew Carnegie with $100 billion (steel), Cornelius Vanderbilt with $96 billion (rails, shipping), John Jacob Astor with $78 billion (fur trading and real estate), and William H. Gates III with a lowly $62 billion (software). I've rounded off all these figures to the nearest billion, give or take a few hundred million!

When I see a list like that, with all the needs of our land and the whole world, I am brought to the parable we have before us. Perhaps this parable is the most relevant parable to our world today. We Americans, with our affluence and our sins, ought to find it most disturbing and challenging. It is the only parable in which Jesus gives a character a name—a fact which has led scholars through the centuries to wonder if this really is a parable, or a description of an event which was taking place as Jesus told it. Some scholars feel there is a relationship to Lazarus of the Fourth Gospel. I think so. It is the only account of compassionate words from hell in all of Scripture. Let's walk through this scripture this morning and let it speak to us.

The Rich Man

First we have the rich man (v. 19). He is clothed in purple and linen, the garments of wealth and royalty. He lived sumptuously, that is, like you and I live. He has plenty to eat; he always conjures up in my mind an image of King Henry VIII with grease all over his chin and a turkey leg or chunk of roast beef in his hand. In our story, the idea is that he lived merrily in splendor and without fear of lacking.

Since we all know the end of this story, let us notice what the text does say about the Rich Man and what it doesn't say. The text does say he lived just like you and me. We are rich. The text does not say he was a miser, for he freely spent his money and lived well. He wasn't stingy. The text does not say he was cruel and mean to Lazarus every time he saw him; for Lazarus sat at his gate regularly. Those paintings which show the rich man whipping Lazarus are wrong. The text does not say that the Rich Man was not compassionate—he simply never saw Lazarus.

The text does not say that the Rich Man's wealth sent him to hell. It is saying that wealth is a dangerous thing, or else Jesus would not have described this man as wealthy. What we have here is not a picture of what sends a person to hell, but a picture of the life-style the saved person won't live. This rich man ignored the basic teaching of the Bible on wealth, which is this: we are given wealth for three reasons: (1) to care for our family, (2) to have money to give to the needy, and (3) to have money to give to God. That which sends a man to hell, and sent this rich man to hell, is self-love and self-trust above God.

Lazarus

So much for the first character. Now to the second character in our story, a beggar named Lazarus (vv. 20-21). We do not know why he is named Lazarus, or why this is the only character in any of Jesus' parables who is named. Lazarus was daily brought by friends or relatives to the huge ornamental gates at the entrance to the estate of the rich man. And had you been a guest of the rich man and glimpsed the beggar out of the corner of your eye as the limo turned through the gates, and asked about the beggar, the rich man would have been surprised—for he had never even noticed the man! Now to get the impact of this parable we need to know the customs of the time. They didn't have napkins by their plates at meals like we do; you simply wiped your hands on a piece of bread and flung it under the table for the dogs. Well, it seems that some of the servants in the "big house" would gather up some of these scraps and give them to the beggar, Lazarus, who sat outside at the gate at the end of the long drive.

Sometimes when I read this passage I feel the guilt of being in a country where we throw away enough food to feed the world's hungry folks and yet ignoring the children of Lazarus who are starving every day. Somehow I seem to rationalize most of that guilt away. But sometimes as I read this passage I feel the greater guilt of not seeing those at the gate who have greater needs even than food; those who die from lack of spiritual bread. And sometimes I think that all churches have reached a point where we ought to cease and desist our work overseas until we can see the spiritual needs around us, at our very doorstep. While this parable sent Albert Schweitzer to Africa, it ought to send all of us to our neighborhoods.

Both Men Died

Now consider verse 22. What depth of truth and economy of words! It happened that Lazarus died. The rich man didn't read of Lazarus' death in the newspapers or hear of it on the television; he didn't know Lazarus had died because he didn't know Lazarus had ever existed! So Lazarus just disappears from the gate. Perhaps some of the servants, or the chauffeur said, Thank God the beggar's finally died. Get him out of the way and we don't have to feel guilty. Nobody even heard the rustle of the angels' wings carrying Lazarus home to the bosom of Abraham. Lazarus may not even have had the dignity of a burial, for none is mentioned. His body may just have been flung into the bushes or burned on the trash dump.

I knew Lazarus, I think. He went under the name of Lee Brown, in my seminary pastorate at Ekron, Kentucky. Lee lived three doors down from me in the little village of 200. Lee had leathery hands from working in the soil. He was always at church; I never knew anything about a family. My wife knew when I had stopped by and visited with Lee Brown, because I would have dusty knees on my trousers. Lee would always ask for prayer, then kneel down on the floor, and I would join him. Well, Lee got sick. And one night at the hospital, with Pegeen on one side of the bed holding his hand and I on the other, we had prayer with him. When we finished the prayer we realized Lee was not breathing. Seven people turned up at Lee's funeral. He just faded away without anybody really noticing it, although most of the village passed by his house every day going to the post office to get their mail.

But in this same verse we read that the rich man also died. Fancy that! We somehow expect the poor and lowly to die; but nobody seems to expect the rich and powerful to die. The rich man died, and was buried. Odd, isn't it, that no mention is made of a funeral for Lazarus, but there was a big lamentation and huge funeral for the rich man. And note the contrast—Lazarus is carried to heaven, while the rich man goes to hell.

Helmut Thieliche, German preacher of the last generation, says in a sermon on this parable that surely the rich man had contemplated, as we all do, the matter of his death. No doubt he thought of the crowds of elite folks, the leaders of the city, the movers and the shakers, all standing around with long faces. And as the coffin is lowered into the ground one of the friends would say, He lived a full life! And the rich man would cry from hell, I never lived at all! And as the shovels of dirt began to fall, some crony would say, He was so kind; why, he even let beggars eat the crusts from under the table. And the rich man would scream in the torment of hell. And perhaps even the preacher at the rich man's funeral would mumble, He was so religious. Well, we can fool folks here, but we cannot fool God. Perhaps you have heard the little joke at the expense of pastors: It seems that St. Peter was showing a new resident of heaven around, and as they walked the golden streets a nun came by in a Cadillac. The new resident inquired and was told that transportation in heaven was commensurate with faith and deeds below. Later they saw a well-known politician—in the world below—riding a bicycle, and it was explained that a bicycle was all he deserved. And just then a late prominent pastor came whizzing by on roller skates! I'm not sure about the system of rewards, but I know we cannot fool God.

The Rich Man In Hell

Now consider the rich man in hell, in verses 23-24. He sees Abraham and Lazarus. "Abraham's bosom" is another term for heaven; for eternal bliss. He is in torment. He pleads for mercy. There are three points we ought to notice in these verses. First, he appeals to a religious relationship: "Father Abraham." Yet he never had a true relationship to God. He asks Abraham to send Lazarus to cool his tongue with water. Now he knows Lazarus' name! And what a difference between that name, if he ever noticed it, and its meaning for the rich man now—Lazarus means God my help. Second, note that this man who is used to extravagance doesn't ask for much mercy—just the tip of a finger dipped in water, touched to the tip of a tongue. Third, notice that he doesn't complain that his punishment is unjust.

We see that beyond the grave, personality and consciousness continue. Death doesn't change the rules, just the places involved.

Abraham's Reply

In verses 25-26 we hear Abraham's reply. First, you received your good things in life—and you used them wrongly! He stored no treasure above, and he thought he had no responsibility to help others. Lazarus, on the other hand, received bad things, but he let them draw him to God. Mark that it is a sick interpretation that says the future automatically brings a reversal of fortunes! Not all rich people deserve hell, and not all poor people deserve heaven. But conditions beyond the grave are a direct result of the life we live on earth. Which means that faith must issue in a changed life.

Second, Abraham points out that besides all this (the righteousness of God) there is a great gulf fixed. There always was a great chasm, a gulf, a dividing canyon between the rich man and Lazarus. Think of the Grand Canyon. The nature of the afterlife is irreversible and unchangeable.

Compassionate Words From Hell

And then we have the compassionate words from hell in verses 27 and 28. It seems so odd to hear unselfish and caring words from hell. Do most of us have to be in hell before we care about others? If we wait til then, there will be nothing we can do. To the rich man's request to send Lazarus to his brothers, he is told they have Moses and the prophets. The despair is evident in the voice of the rich man—no, no, if one came back from the grave they would repent! Notice that here the rich man acknowledges his brothers' sin and need to repent, and it is also an acknowledgement that his sins and lack of repentance have sent him to hell, too.

If they will not listen to Moses and the prophets . . . How true! They had seen Lazarus raised from the dead and they had not believe. You have seen sorry, wicked, weak men and women raised to be God-fearing, righteous followers of Jesus. Yet so often you wait . . . What is Moses and the prophets saying to us? That all of us have sinned and deserve to go to hell. That God so loved the world that he sent his only son to die for our sins, to bring us forgiveness and new life and eternity in his presence.

Facing Change

Acts 6:9-15; Mark 2:21-22; II Corinthians 3:18
A Graduation Sermon

Everything must change,
Nothing stays the same.
Everyone must change,
No one stays the same.
The young become the old,
And mysteries do unfold,
Cause that's the way of time;
Nothing and No one goes unchanged!

Even Barbra Streisand knows everything changes. Today we congratulate our graduates, a group of folks moving—changing—from one stage in their life to another. And while you think you know something about change, what you have already experienced is only a drop in the bucket compared to what you will see in the next 50 years. In your lifetime you will experience more change than the society has seen since the garden of Eden.

Facing Change

In that light I want to give some pastoral advice. And what I say this morning applies not only to those graduating from high school and college, but to us all. All of us plan to live a few more years, and in that light none of us can escape change.

The Reality of Change

Let me speak first of the reality of change. The first observation I would make is that change is inevitable. We have no choice concerning change. Change indicates life. A living thing is distinguished from a dead thing by the changes going on within it. Consider a rock and a tree. Change is inevitable. Our own bodies are constantly changing; cells are dying and new ones are born. Moving through life is like stepping into a stream. We can never step in the same place twice. The second observation is that change is neutral in itself. It's odd that so often the very word "change" produces negative reaction. Change is inevitable, and in itself change is neutral. The third observation is that the outcome of change can be either good or bad depending on our reaction and use of change. A fourth observation is that we tend to resist change. All of us tend to want to leave things the way they are—or were! If you graduates think different, why do you want your room to be left just as it is when you go off to college? We all resist change. Here's a list of 51 reasons not to change.

We'll Not Change!

1. We've never done it before. 2. Nobody else has ever done it before. 3. It has never been tried before. 4. We tried it before. 5. Another company/person tried it before. 6. We've been doing it this way for 25 years. 7. It won't work in a small company. 8. It won't work in a large company. 9. It won't work in our company. 10. Why change—it's working OK. 11. The boss will never buy it. 12. It need further investigation. 13. It's too much trouble to change. 14. Our competitors are not doing it. 15. Our competitors are doing it. 16. Our company is different. 17. The ad department says it can't be done. 18. The sales department says it can't be sold. 19. The service department won't like

it. 20. The janitor says it can't be done. 21. It can't be done. 22. We don't have the money. 23. We don't have the personnel. 24. We don't have the equipment. 25. The union will scream. 26. It's too visionary. 27. You can't teach an old dog new tricks. 28. It's too radical a change. 29. It beyond my responsibility. 30. It's not my job. 31. We don't have the time. 32. It will make other procedures obsolete. 33. Customers won't buy it. 34. It's contrary to policy. 35. It will increase overhead. 36. The employees will never buy it. 37. It's not our problem. 38. I don't like it. 39. You're right, but. . . 40. We're not ready for it. 41. It needs more thought. 42. Management won't accept it. 43. We can't take the chance. 44. We'd lose money on it. 45. It takes too long to pay out. 46. We're doing all right as it is. 47. It needs committee study. 48. The competition won't like it. 49. It needs sleeping on. 50. It won't work in this department. 51. It's impossible.

It reminds me of the story of the young man who was traveling and came upon a tiny village where he stopped to get a coke. Seeing an old codger sitting on a bench, he said, "I bet you've seen a lot of changes in your life." "Yep," the old fellow replied, "and I've been agin ever one of 'em." Once when the German rocket scientist Werner Von Braun was giving a lecture about space travel and putting a man on the moon, he followed the lecture by inviting questions. One little old lady raised her hand and said, "Why can't you forget about putting people on the moon, and stay home and watch television like God intended? A lot of folks—and a lot of churches—are like that. But it doesn't have to be that way if we can learn how to deal with the changes that inevitably face us.

Steps To Successfully Face Change

The first step in successfully dealing with change is to be clear about your goals in the midst of a changing world. I remember the story of the buggy whip company that went out of business because they did not know their goal; they did not know they were in the transportation business, not the buggy whip business. And there is a lesson here for churches: we are not in the business of protecting traditions, or keeping the past, or even in the business of keeping the present church strong. We are in the business of proclaiming the Gospel of Jesus Christ and demonstrating in our personal and corporate lives the difference Jesus makes. Graduates, if you know what your goal in life is, then you are already forearmed to deal with change. If you know what your purpose and goal is, then you can shape the future by means of the changes you face.

Which leads me to say, embrace the changes that carry you toward your goal; shape the changes that hinder your progress toward your goal. I saw the story of how Pizza Hut came to be. Two college boys—during the years I was in college—began to make pizzas to sell other students. They were so popular the guys decided to franchise the business. Today everybody knows Pizza Hut because two guys needed to work to put themselves through college. By the way, the name Pizza Hut was chosen because it was the only name they could think of that would fit on the sign they already had. James Mitchner, the author, said, "What we must do, I believe, is to accept change, even embrace it, but at the same time to control it, to mold it to our ends, so that it contributes to the quality of life rather than subtracts from it."

Missionary Elizabeth Richards likes to relate a story which shows how the bedouins of the Arabian desert have embraced and used some of the changes in their life-style. You know that bedouins are the folks who move with their herds and flocks across the desert. They live in tents made of goat's hair, etc. Well, nowadays you are quite likely to see a TV antennae sticking up from the tent! One of the missionaries noticed a bedouin driving his tractor (yes, some of them have accepted that change) back and forth in front of his tent. When asked what this was all about, the man said he was charging up the tractor battery so he could power his TV with it!

Change And The Christian Life

Change affects all of us, even Christians and even churches. We are all aware of the changes in church music and in the style of worship in many churches, especially in those churches reaching unchurched people. It is interesting that even Billy Graham is changing the way he presents the Gospel. At a festival —not a revival or crusade—in New Mexico earlier this month, both Billy Graham and his son, Franklin, showed up in denim and leather coats and blue jeans, with Franklin wearing a baseball cap. Billy Graham said the word "Crusade" has negative baggage that "festival" doesn't have. And even the standard invitation hymn Graham has used for decades was changed from "Just As I Am" to "Come Just As You Are."

And I am pondering news reports of many churches changing the invitation ritual most Baptists grew up on. Many churches are inviting people who wish to make a commitment to Christ or join the church to either come forward at the close of a service, or to speak with the pastor in a get acquainted time in another area following the service such as we have, or simply to fill out the card and bring it by the church office. In other words, there is a trend toward de-emphasizing the "walking the aisle" in a good many Baptist churches. I admit I was a bit dismayed about that until I began to think it through, and listened to one of our theologians who pointed out that we have made "coming down the aisle" the public profession of our faith. That is not biblical, nor was it the tradition of the church for 1800 years. "Walking the aisle" began in the 1820's and gained momentum with the revivalism of the last century. But the public profession of faith, in the Bible and in the church for 18 centuries, is baptism. And by putting our emphasis on the public coming forward, we have taken away from the meaning of baptism. I have usually said that coming forward is a small thing to do if you really are committed to Jesus. And that is true, but I think I'd rather have a person who is shy about coming forward in front of folks, but is willing to serve Jesus by teaching children or just living a committed life-styles—than to demand you "walk the aisle" to be a card-carrying Baptist even if you never darken the door again. So I will be trying various ways of receiving members in our Saturday evening service in the fall.

Facing Change

One of the disturbing realities is that churches are often the slowest segment of society to make changes. Why is this? Are we so foolish as to think "the way we've always done it" is the only way or even the best way in a changing world? Is the slowness to make changes a sign of the insecurity of churches? An effort to hang on to the familiar, the old, the known? Probably. But I think the main reason churches have trouble with change is that we know we deal with eternal things, things that do not change. I think churches are afraid that if we make changes in the way we do things, we may change that which is eternal and ought not be changed.

The problem with this approach is that we have confused the wine with the wineskin; the clothes the Gospel wears with the Gospel itself. Look at the charge made against Stephen in Acts 6:9-15: Stephen is accused of having said that Jesus said he would change the customs of the Jews. If we turn to Mark's Gospel, we see Jesus accused of turning all the religious rules on their head—and again and again he separates the peeling from the fruit, the shell from the nut, the wineskin from the wine. Folks, so much of the way we do church is not the Gospel; it is the hull, the peeling, the clothes that the Gospel wears. And the Gospel can—and does—change its clothes as it goes from situation to situation. It is rather humorous when we realize that the Lord of the church, Jesus Christ, was seen as, and accused of, being a change agent in his day. If we want to look and sound and act like Jesus rather than the pharisees, we as a church must separate the Gospel from tradition, the Gospel from the clothes it wears, and speak to our times. The Bible clearly states that change is a natural thing for the Christian. We move from glory to glory, as we move through this life on our pilgrimage, becoming more and more like Christ, until that perfect day when we shall know as we are known.

But Some Things Never Change

Now I have spoken of change. Of the *necessity for change* and the *inevitability of change*. Of our *resistance to change*. In closing let me look with you at the flipside. Some things never change. And if we assume they can or do, we make a serious mistake.

Man's sinful nature will always be true. Every person who comes into this world, comes into it as a selfish, proud rebel against God. When society, and especially the church, forgets this and thinks that by education or evolution, by medicine or psychiatry, we can alter that nature, we are wrong. There is only one way to deal with the unchanging natural nature of mankind, and that is through the second unchanging factor, the Gospel of Jesus Christ.

The Gospel of Jesus Christ does not change. It will always be the plain and simple story of how God the Father put on human flesh and came to this world as Jesus of Nazareth, died for your sins and mine, and rose from the grave to give us a spiritual power to change our lives. How we tell that story, with what music it is accompanied, what apparel we wear—those things can and do change. But the old, old story of Jesus and his love for us will never change.

But for the Gospel of Jesus Christ to be effective, we must tell people of a third unchanging, eternal reality in this sinful world: the mercy of God. A man, woman, boy or girl is saved not by singing the hymns I love, nor by wearing a coat and tie, nor by worshipping in slacks and pantsuits, nor by walking down the aisle, nor by coming to church on Sunday. . .but by realizing the eternal mercy of God revealed in the cross of Jesus Christ. Every one of us needs to hear the unchanging mercy of God. It was there for Abraham, it was there for David, it was there for the thief on the cross, it was there for Paul, and it will be there for you and me. Hear the words of Psalm 103:10-17.

Dealing with Regrets

Philippians 3:13-21

A New Year Sermon

Someone has said we come to year's end like so many cows looking over a gate, chewing the bitter cud of hindsight! In many ways 1985 has been a year of joy, blessing, and happiness—yet we have also blotted, smeared, wrinkled and torn those 365 fresh white pages we received a year ago. Isn't it a shame we cannot have the year over again to do it right! I'm sure every person here has some regrets about the year we're closing out. Something we did, or didn't do which made all the difference to our life or someone else's life; things we said, or didn't say which built a wall. Regrets about things that happened, or did not happen in our relationship with our husbands, wives, children, neighbors, fellow Christians, or even in our relationship to God. Regrets that keep us saying in our hearts: *"If only...if I had just... if I could do it over..."*

I want you to pick out one regret from this past year—or further back if it still haunts you, call it up and let it stand before you during this sermon. It may be as sharp and painful as a divorce or a bitter quarrel; perhaps you stole something and would give anything to have that day back to do over; maybe your regret is a lie that broke a special person's heart; perhaps it is the day you began to drink or first tried drugs; maybe it is the day you had the abortion. But call it up and let it stand again in front of you. I do not generally recommend that folks delve into the past, although I know a man who for years would play a fantasy game of calling up the 10 worst mistakes he had ever made and "writing" new scripts for those days! To continue to live in the past serves no good purpose; but we can use the experiences of the past, in proper perspective, to change our future. Leslie Weatherhead tells of seeing in an old orchard a plum tree that had come down in ruin. It was in the Fall, and the tree was full of ripe Victoria plums as it lay on the ground. It seemed at first that the weight of the fruit and the winds of storm had worked together to bring down the fine tree. But the farmer said that the tree had been ravaged by insects which had attacked the tree over a long period of time. What storms could not do alone, the insects had accomplished. When asked what he would do now, the farmer replied immediately: "Gather the fruit and burn the tree."[1]

Take Paul, for instance. Look at our text. It's one of those favorite passages in which we ring the changes on how Paul forgot the past and turned to the future. How true, but see how he gathered the fruit before burning the tree of the past. He reflected on his boasting, his trust in the flesh, his zeal for Judaism—the Book of Acts tells of his holding the coats while Stephen was stoned. Paul wasn't proud of those days, and they made him an outcast for awhile after his conversion, but he does glory in the mercy and the plan and the wisdom of God who could and would touch someone like him with salvation and make him a minister. He did not live in the past; he gathered the fruit and then burnt the dead tree!

So look at your regret. Part of its fruit is that God will use that sad fact, as He would use everything that happens to us, to teach us and draw us closer. God wastes nothing! The Holy Spirit works in all that

Dealing with Regrets

touches us for our blessing. So ask yourself, How and why did this happen, and how can it be avoided next time. What does God want me to learn from this?

Another fruit of your regret is that God will use it to help you understand yourself. We are the result of what we do (as well as what we eat!) What is this regrettable thing saying about who I am? Is this the kind of person I want to be?

There is a sad story about the great team of Gilbert and Sullivan, playwriter and composer, which seems almost impossible in light of their music. But once upon a time they purchased a theatre and Sullivan bought a carpet for it which Gilbert thought cost too much. The quarrel over it brought forth many harsh words, and they even went to court about it at one point. After buying that carpet they never spoke to each other again! Gilbert wrote his words and mailed them to Sullivan, who wrote the music and mailed it to Gilbert. On many occasions when they had to appear together and take a bow, they stood on opposite ends of the stage and bowed outwards, so as not to have to face each other. In like manner our regrets, if not tended to, can do the same for us.

One especially precious fruit of our regret is that it allows us experience God's forgiveness, and to offer our forgiveness to others. That's what shines through so many of David's psalms written after his sin with Bathsheba, and Paul walked the rest of his life in this same realization after the Damascus Road. "I will put your sins, and mistakes, and regrets as far from you as the East is from the West," says God, and Isaiah even says God will put our sins behind His back. So often our experience of God's grace is made all the more bright and beautiful in our hearts when we show mercy and forgiveness to others. As a part of that regrettable incident—do you need to pluck the rich fruit of forgiveness both for yourself and someone else?

The glory of the fruit of regret is that it can be a motivation for change. Our regrets can either cripple, smother, drain us, or provide the motivation for the future—be the stepping-stone, the building blocks, the hard soil out of which the beautiful flower can bloom. Our regrets can be a powerful springboard, for while one end of the board is firmly fixed in the past—the other is free to launch us, a better person, into the future.

Arthur Gordon, that delightful story-teller, tells of being depressed and lonely one winter afternoon in New York, an important project in his life having fallen through. He arranged to meet an old friend, a psychiatrist, at a cafe. Gordon describes him as an energetic gnome, muffled in his overcoat, and with his shapeless felt hat pulled down over his bald head. After they had talked for fifteen minutes, the Old Man asked him to walk back to his office so he might show him something.

In the office the Old Man took out a tape and played it for Gordon. On the tape were comments from three unidentified folks who had come for help that day. "Listen for the two-word phrase that is full of poison. All three of these people use it. —You used it three times in fifteen minutes in the cafe."[2]

The two words which he said are the most sad in any language are "If only..." The trouble with our constant "If only..." is that it doesn't change anything. It doesn't render any fruit, and it doesn't provide a launching pad for the future. It only keeps us facing the wrong way—backwards. There is a perverse streak in all of us that makes us like to hash over old mistakes and regrets. I guess it's because in doing that we are at least still on center stage.

The answer is to change the key words from "IF ONLY" to "NEXT TIME". Gordon summed up the little story as he and the psychiatrist left the office. They hailed a cab, but another pedestrian beat them to it. The Old Man slyly commented, "If only we had come down ten seconds sooner, we would have caught that cab, wouldn't we?" To which Gordon laughed, "Next time I'll run faster!" That's it!

If we can remember to pick the fruit and burn the bush, and look forward to "next time," we are on the right track, and 1986 will be different in many ways.

Dealing with Regrets

How can we put this sermon into practice? You've been thinking about a certain regret—what are you going to do in order to pick the fruit from it? Do you need to write a letter forgiving or asking for forgiveness? Or pick up the phone and make that call? Do you need to face up to the truth of being a shallow, critical Christian? Of being a thief towards God? What will you do to make "next time" a reality? Will you seek a closer walk with God by a daily time of devotion? Will you begin reading the Bible and allow the Holy Spirit to guide you? Will you open your life to Jesus here at the end of the year?

That's the essence of the sermon today —gather the fruit and burn the tree! Take the fruit and burn the incident forever! Learn from the past, from your regrets, and then let them go. Now, don't burn the bush before you gather the fruit! Every regret has its lessons to teach, and the wise person will find that fruit before burning the bush.

[1] Leslie Weatherhead, **That Immortal Sea**, pages 138f.

[2] Arthur Gordon, **A Touch Of Wonder**, pages 68f.

Did Jesus Praise a Scoundrel?

Luke 16:1-13

We Seldom Hear a sermon on the unjust steward. Why? Because we find this parable embarrassing and confusing; it certainly appears that Jesus commends a scoundrel, and so we go through all sorts of mental and theological gymnastics to extricate Jesus from this mess. We really ought to let Jesus be Jesus, and tell his parables as he wishes!

Praising a Wicked Man

Listen to a story which, although but a pale shadow of this parable, may help you get the point of Jesus' story. A few years ago a man dropped by church on a Sunday morning. He was a stranger, and said, very apologetically, that he had just been released from prison, where he had been saved and had begun to study the Bible and earn all kinds of study course awards. He dropped all sorts of names in Biblical scholarship—he was even familiar with sets of commentaries, etc. As he told his story, he just needed a boost to get started on the right path; he had a job at a Memphis business beginning the next day.

Did Jesus Praise a Scoundrel?

Well, I talked with him a bit, bought his story, told him I would see what we could do after church, and turned him over to some laymen with my blessing. During the Bible Study hour he managed to wander into several Sunday School classes and, on the strength of my positive comments to our folks, began to take up an offering for himself. After church he was nowhere to be seen, and I have not seen him again to this day.

I have sometimes told his story and commented that he was one smart cookie! He had apparently been in so many pastor's offices that he had taken note of the names and titles of commentaries so he could drop those names in his story. I do think that, of the hundreds of folks who have tried to sell me their hard-luck story through the years, his story was the best and most believable! I would have to commend him for his craftiness and shrewdness in planning ahead.

Jesus' Story of a Wicked Steward

Jesus told a parable in which just that sort of man is praised. Not praised, mind you, for his wickedness but for his prudence and zeal and foresight. Let's look at Jesus' story. Now the main characters are the boss, the manager or steward, and the debtors. But before we even tell the story, let us understand that this story is a parable, not an allegory. The boss does not represent God, nor does the steward stand for Jesus or Paul or the church or the devil as some folks have said. This story is simply a parable about money, and how it ought to be used.

Now this story is tied to the three stories of chapter 15, which we looked at last Sunday. Perhaps the wasting, squandering of the prodigal son's resources prompted Jesus to tell this story, for the same word is used of the wasting, squandering of the master's resources by the unjust steward. Notice also that this parable is told to the disciples (verse 1); that is, to those who would gladly hear Jesus, to the prodigals who would return home (see 15:1) as well as to the twelve.

The story itself perhaps reflects a common situation in those days. The boss, the master, the landowner is probably an orthodox Jew who is prohibited by his religion to charge interest on loans, so he has hired a Gentile as his overseer, his steward or trustee. The system worked much like the tax collection system in Biblical times—the tax collector and the steward were required to collect a certain percentage or amount for the boss, and then all beyond that which could be squeezed out of folks belonged to the collector or the steward. But one day word came to the boss that his steward was wasting his master's money. The steward is called in, told to prepare an audit, and get ready to turn in his boss's checkbook.

The steward goes to his office, locks the door and begins to pace and think. What can I do? It was a foregone conclusion that his job was gone. "I cannot dig," he says. His life-style has left him unfit and probably unable to do manual labor. "I am ashamed to beg." That appeared to be the other option open to him and while he was ashamed to beg, he was not ashamed to steal and cheat! Suddenly the light comes on in his head; he snaps his fingers—"I've got it!" (The KJV takes six English words to say what one Greek word says here). He picks up the phone and begins to set up appointments with those who owe his boss. We are given two examples of what happened when they turned up in the steward's office. He tells the man who owes 100 measures of oil (100 *batos*, or about 1200 gallons) to change his account sheet to show only 50 measures due. The man who owes 100 measures of wheat is told to write 80. Now, obviously these folks are scoundrels too, and most likely aren't told and don't care why the steward has this sudden fit of generosity with his master's resources. But they are glad to take part in this clear deception of the steward's boss.

The steward's reason for reducing the bills is obvious to the listeners of this parable; he will put these people in his own debt; they will "owe him one." When he loses his job, he'll have made some friends in this 12th hour strategy who will rescue him from being shut out in the cold. This steward, this scoundrel, is so clever that even his boss has to grudgingly admire the way he has taken care of his future (verse 8a). But just when the disciples and the whole crowd are chuckling over the smoothness of this scoundrel, Jesus drives home his concerns

Did Jesus Praise a Scoundrel?

about money and how we use it. Let me point out four truths this story emphasizes in the area of stewardship.

Realism and Foresight of the World

First, we note that while Jesus is not praising the thievery of this steward, he does put words of praise in the boss's mouth for the cool-headed realism and foresight of this wicked steward (verse 8a). "He who chose his path like a fool, walks along it like a wise man." This man is a realist. He didn't kid himself about the gravity of the situation. His options appeared to be either manual labor or begging. No rose colored glasses here. But he does not waste time crying over what might have been, or looking back. He sees it as it is and acts decisively. He has the courage to be consistent. He will act in the future as he has acted in the past in looking out for himself. He is a man of foresight who will try to shape his future. Apparently he has been a clever manager, keeping one eye on where the market is going and the other on his master's portfolio. So now he has his eyes on the future. He does not make the mistake of the snobbish young man at the turn of the century who boasted he would never have to worry, because his father owned the biggest buggy whip factory in the country!

Sons of this World and the Sons of Light

Second, note that Jesus broadens the lesson as he uses this fellow to represent the "sons of this world"—the "sons of this world" are more prudent, that is, they exercise more realism, more wisdom and more foresight concerning the affairs of this world than do the "sons of light" in regard to the next world! (Verse 8b). Now that's where this parable begins to smart! John Wesley comments on this verse that the sons of the world are really fools; but they are more consistent with themselves, truer to their principles, more steadily pursue their goals than the sons of the light. Jesus is saying this rascal is a better example of zeal and foresight than we Christians! Now isn't that really so? Consider a young man of the world in this city who has no regard for spiritual things, yet is an up-and-coming young executive. He works long and hard, and at the end of the day he "gives himself with the fervor of a saint to the study of the psychology of salesmanship." The sons of this world are zealous in the pursuit of money.

They are zealous in the pursuit of pleasure—is it golf? Then the man of the world will study as if it were the Bible books on the proper golf stance, grip, swing and follow through. If he fails to hit the ball right, he tries another 100 times. But the zeal of the sons of light often flags in the face of a worship that runs five minutes beyond the hour; we cannot bear the burden of the Biblical call to witness or minister or tithe. Jesus is saying that the sons of this world, those whose vision and hope are bounded by this world, are more consistent and zealous than the sons of light who, even on a cloudy day, can see forever! Folks committed to this world which is passing away show more dedication than those of us who say we are spiritual! Let me suggest a little exercise: when you get home, take a pen and paper and examine your life. Ask yourself, Am I living, acting, thinking, feeling as one who marches toward a goal, a reality beyond this world? Make a list of the great spiritual beliefs you as a Christian hold—perhaps something like the following—and ask yourself if you really believe these statements and if they shape your daily life as they should: (1) Jesus is Lord in my life; (2) material things are not as important as spiritual things; (3) unsaved people go to hell; (4) the Christian is saved to serve God; (5) the tithe is the Lord's.

How Money Opens Doors

Third, Jesus urges his followers to use money in such a fashion that when it fails (when death comes) you will be welcomed into heaven by friends made through your money (verse 9). Now the term "mammon" is simply a Greek translation of an Aramaic term for money. Note that Jesus does not say to beware of money, but to use it rightly. Money itself is neutral, although it is often used for unrighteous purposes. What a tale a dollar bill could tell if it could talk! But Jesus is here saying that just as this man used money to secure a place for himself among friends in this world, even so should we use our money in the cause of friendship. Not to buy friends but to win souls. As Christians we are to use our money to heal those broken of heart and limb, to put the Bible into the hands of every human being. So that when "it"—our money—fails us, and that is in the hour of death, we shall be welcomed into "eternal tents," into heaven, by those you have blessed by a kind deed and a compassionate word, by those who have come to know Jesus through you—through your life, your word, your witness, your money. Jesus said in John 14 that in the Father's house are many mansions, and that he was going to prepare for us a place—will there be anyone to welcome you as a fruit of your Christian witness?

In the fourth place, Jesus reminds us that money is of small consequence, and the Christian walk of great consequence (verse 10). And if we are not faithful in little things like money, we obviously cannot be good stewards in more important things (verses 11-13). This much about this story is a comparison; this wicked man was a steward and so are we. Stewardship implies that we are dependent upon using what belongs to another. Stewardship implies that we are expected to use it in keeping with the owner's wishes. Stewardship implies that we must someday give an accounting of our stewardship.

This story brings together both God and money in verse 13, and points out that they cannot be equals. The wicked steward put money first, and did it so cleverly that his cheated employer had to admire him. Jesus says we must put God first. And if we do so, we can move from the Old Testament law of the tithe to the higher joy of being a true steward, of using all we have as God leads. If we put God first, we can change the money we have been given into something we can take with us.

It is significant, I think, that the parable of the Rich Man and Lazarus follows this story, for that parable is the best commentary on this story. The Rich Man there did not use his money to gain friends either here or in the world beyond. Let's don't make his mistake.

A Focused Vision

Mark 8:22-25

The physical eye is an amazing creation of God. We could spend hours marveling at the intricacies of the human eye. But equally fascinating to the student of the Word of God is the use of the eye as a symbol in the Bible.

The Importance of Seeing

The Bible is full of comments about sensory perceptions, especially about the eye, from the 7 references to God seeing what He had created in the first chapter of the Bible to the comment in the last chapter of the Bible that the redeemed "shall see His face."

Sprinkled throughout the Bible are inspiring and curious comments about how we see and what we see and what we do not see. There is Balaam, whose donkey could see what he could not see—the angel standing in his path with drawn sword! The man in our text story needed two touches of Jesus for healing, for after the first touch he

A Focused Vision

saw "men as trees walking." The angel in Jesus' tomb tells the women early on Easter morning to "Come, see where he lay." When the early church went about replacing Judas, the criteria was that the person selected must have been an eyewitness to Jesus' ministry.

The Eye: Symbol of the Heart

So often, when the Bible speaks of our eyes, it really means our hearts. For the eye is often a symbol in the Bible for our hearts. For instance, when we read that Sarah was despised in Hagar's eyes, it says more about Hagar's heart than about her eyes (Gen 16:4). When Potiphar's wife casts her eyes on Joseph, it is her heart that is at work (Gen 39:7). When the Bible says that "every man did that which was right in his own eyes" it means that he followed the dictates of his own heart and mind rather than the laws of God (Judge 17:6;21:25). When Job says the eye of the adulterer waits for the night, saying no eye shall see him, it is the wicked heart that is speaking (24:15). When Job says "mine enemy sharpeneth his eyes upon me" (16:9) he means his enemy's heart is full of hatred. When the Psalmist says he is weary of weeping, "mine throat is dried, mine eyes fail . . ." it is not his eyes but his heart that is broken and discouraged (69:3).

When old Simeon says in the temple, holding the baby Jesus, "Mine eyes have seen thy salvation . . ." it is not only his eyes that have seen the baby, but more importantly, his heart bears witness to the reality of God's work. This use of the eye as a symbol of what is really in the heart is seen most clearly in the Sermon on the Mount where Jesus says, "The light of the body is the eye: if therefore thine eye be single, thy whole body shall be full of light. But if thine eye be evil, thy whole body shall be full of darkness. If therefore the light that is in thee be darkness, how great is that darkness!" (Matt 6:22-23). And again in John 9:39-41 Jesus says of the pharisees that their problem is that they say they can see; therefore their sins remain, whereas if they were really spiritually blind, they would be guiltless.

Problems of Spiritual Vision

There are those folks, perhaps you among them, who are blessed with near perfect—20/20—physical vision. But that cannot be said of our spiritual vision, which reflects our hearts. Let me point out to you some common spiritual eye problems.

3-D Disease

There is, first of all, the 3-D glasses that didn't work. Do you remember, way back in the late '40s and early '50s, when there was a rash of three-dimensional movies designed to be seen through special spectacles? Those spectacles could make you think that horse and wagon was running right over you; those screaming Indians were galloping right up the aisle at you! But not really—it was a clever deception. Just like the clever deception used on Adam and Eve by the devil. The devil said that choosing—in the form of eating the forbidden fruit—to disobey God and live independent of Him would open their eyes, and Adam and Eve would be gods, too. They believed the snake, and entered into a new world in which their eyes were indeed opened—they found themselves possessed of the knowledge of guilt and shame and sin and of their broken relationship to God through disobedience. The devil promised them they would be a god; what happened is that they hid from God. Each of us has made the same decision as Eve; disobedience to, and independence from, God has put the "apple" of guilt and shame in every eye, and we wear the devil's 3-D glasses which make this world seem to be more and different than it really is. This is the basic eye problem shared by every human being.

Proud Eye Disease

There is the eye problem demonstrated by the pharisee who went up to the temple to pray to God, or so the Good Book says (Luke 18:10-14). He really went up to talk to himself. And everything he said smacked of spiritual pride. He was proud of keeping the rules and regulations; he was proud that he wasn't like the poor sinner he saw off to the side also praying. This parable bothers me; it makes me wonder if, in the

A Focused Vision

sight of God, I am often like the pharisee . . . it makes me wonder if some of you are not also in that category. Spiritual pride will blind you as surely as the gold that blinded the rich man from seeing Lazarus at his gate every day for years.

Speck and Beam Disease

There is the eye problem Jesus called "speck and beam" disease (Matt 7:3-5). He told of a man who was terribly anxious to get the speck—one of those little floating bits of dust you see in a stream of sunlight—out of his brother's eye, while ignoring the fact that there was a six foot long 2x4 sticking out of his own eye! Jesus called him a hypocrite, and said we need to work on our own life before criticizing others. And folks, he is talking to the church here with the term "brother." Let us take Jesus' admonition seriously.

Menpleaser Disease

Paul, in Ephesians 6:6, diagnoses another common eye problem among church members—that of giving "eyeservice," being "menpleasers" in this world. As you look at the way you live, the things you say and the things you do, how much of it is "eyeservice?" We are so concerned about what other people will think and say of us! All of us ought to reread that old classic, Charles Sheldon's **In His Steps**, or his grandson's updating that work as **What Would Jesus Do?** Both books center on asking ourselves the basic question about every area of our lives: What would Jesus do in my place? Asking that question would rid us of Menpleasers disease.

But the worse form of spiritual eye disease is self-blindness. It is seen in the unpardonable sin, discussed in Mark 3:22-30, in which Jesus condemns the pharisees for observing the work of God and attributing it to the devil! That attitude, and only that attitude, is unpardonable. And that attitude is spiritual self-blindness; closing our eyes deliberately to what God is doing in our midst. Jesus is often called the light, and if you keep running from the light, hiding in dark places, you lose your ability to see, just as the fish deep in underground lakes in caves have lived in the dark so long that they have lost their sight. Folks, let us mark this. If we resist God's will over and over, it is possible to lose the ability to tell what is His will.

Simon Peter tells us that for the Christian, spiritual eye disease is the result of his not cultivating Christian character —faith, virtue, knowledge, temperance, patience, godliness, brotherly kindness and love (2 Pet 1:5-9). And he tells us that the lack of these Christian traits blinds us spiritually; he "cannot see afar off," and leads to poor memory "he hath forgotten that he was purged from his old sins."

The Great Physician and Our Blindness

What does the gospel do for our spiritual eye problems? First, it opens spiritually blind eyes. In the prophecies and in his first sermon in Nazareth, Jesus said he came "to open the blind eyes" (Luke 4:18). To open the eyes of our heart to more than the guilt and shame we have known ever since Adam and Eve; to open our eyes to the grace of God in Jesus Christ. Charles Spurgeon was saved while listening to a Methodist layman, struggling to preach and repeating over and over Isaiah 45:22 "Look unto me, and be ye saved, all the ends of the earth." 'Ere since by faith I saw the stream Thy flowing wounds supply Redeeming love has been my theme And shall be 'til I die. Jesus came to open our eyes and our hearts to see the cross, and through it God's grace.

A Focused Vision

After our eyes are opened to the love and grace of God, God focuses and trains our vision so we who belong to Jesus can see more than and further than the man of the world. It is a sad reality that most Christians need a second touch for our spiritual vision to be what God intends, and that may be why we have the unusual miracle of this man whose blindness required a second touch of healing from Jesus.

Let me just point out some of the powers of a focused spiritual vision. It is a tremendous and beautiful study to examine the scripture in this theme. In all the changing scenes of life, the person committed to

A Focused Vision

Christ, the person with a focused spiritual vision, can see more and see further than others. A beautiful example is found in the story of Elisha, as he prays that his servant may see more in the hills around them than the enemy army. And as a result of that prayer, the servant stepped to the door and saw chariots and horses of fire, sent by God. Elisha could already see them (2 Kg 6:17)! We also see this truth in Joel's prophecy—applied to the church by Peter on Pentecost—that in the last days "your old men will dream dreams, and your young men will see visions." Folks, a major difference between the church and a similar group of pagans is that the church can dream dreams and see visions!

In adversity, the Christian can see heaven opened, as Stephen did (Acts 7:56) and as John did on the island of Patmos. The spiritual person endures, as seeing him who is invisible (Heb 10:27).

The Bible makes some promises to the one who has a focused spiritual eye: the pure in heart shall see God (Matt 5:8); he who has the spiritually focused vision will never see death (John 8:51); he will see Jesus as he is when he comes again (1 John 3:2); and in heaven they shall see His face (Rev 22:4).

A Spiritual Eye Test

When Jesus controls the heart, the spiritual eye is focused, purified and clarified. How can you tell if your spiritual eyes are focused? Test your vision this way: Are you an open witness, having publicly professed faith in Christ? Does your life give evidence of Christian character? Are you a forgiving, loving person? Can you see things the world cannot see? Is Jesus in control of your pocketbook? Gold has a greater power to blind us than almost any thing else.

Three Great Eye Truths

Let me close by pointing out 3 great truths about our eyes. First, *conversion is essential* if we are to ever see heaven. As Jesus told Nicodemus: "Verily, I say unto thee, Except a man be born again, he cannot see the kingdom of God" (John 3:3). A new birth is required, not riches, education, social standing or any other substitute, if we intend to see heaven. Let us be mindful as individuals and as a church that there is a world needing to see Jesus in us. Second, *sometimes churches get eye diseases.* The church at Laodicea was diagnosed by the eternal Physician as having a spirit of pride, thinking they were rich, stuffed with goods, needing nothing—not realizing that they were blind! He urged them to anoint their eyes and see clearly again (Rev 3:14-18). And third, *sometimes it takes a second touch for a person to see clearly as Jesus intends* (Mark 8:22-25). Let us never get too proud to ask for a second touch of grace and forgiveness and vision in our own life.

The Eyes of God

II Chronicles 16:9

Have You Ever thought about the eyes of God? Job did. "Hast thou eyes of flesh? Or seest thou as man seeth?" Have you ever wondered what color God's eyes are, or if his eyes have the laser beams of Superman's eyes? The eyes of God are directly described only twice in Scripture, in Revelation 1:14 and 2:18.

What does the Bible mean when it speaks of the eyes of God? When it says the eyes of God run to and fro over the earth, what is the idea behind the imagery? It is this: When the Bible speaks of the eyes of the Lord, of God seeing, we realize that seeing is the same as knowing and judging.

God Knows Everything

The Bible says God sees and knows everything. That may be an uncomfortable thought, but we all affirm this idea, even the biggest "atheist" in the land affirms that God sees and knows everything. We do it by the money in our pockets—pull out a dollar bill. On the back side we have both the obverse and the reverse of the Great Seal of the United States. On the reverse, the back side of the seal, we see an unfinished 13-step pyramid, topped with the eye of God within a triangle. Above the triangle is the Latin for "He has favored our undertakings." God knows all about Danny Owens and Jessie Misskelly and Tanya Harding and you and me. The book of Psalms tells us the wicked man "hath said in his heart, God hath forgotten; he hideth his face; he will never see it" (Psm 10:11). But he is wrong! This is a hard lesson for us all to learn: God knows everything. Even Moses, down in Egypt land, having killed the Egyptian slavedriver, looked this way and that—but he didn't look up, where God was watching from. And Moses was one of God's chosen. It is interesting, and shows the influence of the world upon us, that we are so secretive about our giving in the church. Some are secretive, no doubt, because they know the pull of pride if others knew how much they gave, but others are ashamed to have fellow Christians know how little they give. But God knows. God knows everything.

God sees and knows the toil and trouble of the least of his people. Remember the beautiful gospel song, *His Eye Is On The Sparrow*, "his eye is on the sparrow, and I know he watches me." Jesus said two sparrows are sold for a penny, five for two pennies, and your heavenly father knows when that spare sparrow falls. We see this illustrated in the widow and her mite. The Bible tells us God looked down upon the sorrow of the people in Egypt and brought them out. When they came to the Promised land, we read that God told them it was a land of milk and honey, and that "the eyes of the Lord are always upon it, from the beginning of the year even unto the end of the year." When the Israelites insisted on having a king, we are told that God looked upon the people and selected Saul. In the New Testament we remember how Nathanael was surprised that Jesus saw him under the fig tree when he was not even in the area. Folks, the drama of our lives is played out under the watching eye of God. This realization that God knows all about us ought to help us lay aside our phoniness, our masks, our

The Eyes of God

deceit and live righteous lives before him. Saint Teresa of Avila testifies to this; she said that as a nun she actually stopped praying to God because she felt so sinful. And then God gave her a "vision," actually the realization that he already knew all about her and still loved her, and it freed her to become one of the great saints of the church.

God Judges Everything

The Bible says that not only does God know and see everything we do and think, but God also judges us with his eyes. At the time of the flood "God looked upon the earth and behold, it was corrupt; for all flesh had corrupted his way upon the earth" (Gen 6:6). Isaiah said Israel was the vineyard of God, and "he looked for judgment, but behold oppression; for righteousness, but behold a cry" (Isa 5:7). Amos speaks of the wicked people of his time, saying that God will set his eye upon them for evil, not good—"Behold, the eyes of the Lord God are upon the sinful kingdom, and I will destroy it from off the face of the earth" (Amos 9:8). God's eyes are a symbol of his judgement, his righteous judgement on the world. That is why in Revelation 2:18, in the message of the Eternal Christ to Thyatira, one of the seven churches, Christ is especially described as having "his eyes like unto a flame of fire, and his feet like fine brass," for he tells this church he knows all about them; about both their good and their bad deeds.

And that leads me to say that today we begin our annual emphasis on stewardship. We understand that we are stewards of our time, our abilities, our lives as well as our financial resources, but in these days we emphasize our stewardship of money. Our theme is A Focused Vision, and this sermon lays a foundation as we look at God's eyes, what God sees, how good God's vision is. We need to begin by trying to see ourselves as God sees us. Let us mark it down, that God knows, God sees how much money we have, as surely as he knows the thoughts of our hearts. You know, sometimes when someone walks in front of us when we're watching TV or at the ball game, we say, "Hey, you've been drinking muddy water; I can't see through you." But God can see right down to the pocketbook no matter what fasçade we put on our religious life.

The Eyes of Jesus

In the New Testament one can make a striking and disturbing study of the looks of Jesus. For instance, when Jesus was about to heal a man with a withered hand and the pharisees muttered, we read that Jesus looked "round about on them with anger, grieved for the hardness of their heart" (Mark 3:5). When the Rich Young Ruler walked away rejecting the gospel, Jesus "looked round about and said to his disciples, How hard it is for the rich to enter the Kingdom of God" (Mark 10:23). In the last week of his ministry Jesus came to Jerusalem to die, and we read that he came into the city, went straight to the temple, "and when he had looked round about upon all things" he went back to Bethany to spend the night before cleaning out the temple. In the last book of the Bible we have a description of the Eternal Christ who is illuminated for a darkened world by the torchlight of the churches: he has eyes like a flame of fire (Rev 1:14). Just because all the accounts are not balanced in this life does not mean that God does not see, or judge, wickedness in the world and in the church.

God Looks to Strengthen

But one of the most unusual verses about the eyes of God, and one that is foundational to understanding how God feels about us, is 2 Chronicles 16:9: "For the eyes of the Lord run to and fro throughout the whole earth, to show himself strong in the behalf of those whose heart is perfect before him." Here again we read about the eyes of God. It is a vivid image; God's eyes running across the earth. The meaning is that God knows everything that happens across the earth, and knows it in a flash. And the reason for the eyes of God running across the earth is this: The greatest desire of God is to show himself strong in behalf of those who love him. God's eyes search us, try our very hearts, so that he might strengthen, encourage, protect, guide and bless those who love him. And as long as we try to hide from him he

The Eyes of God

cannot fully bless us. From the garden of Eden to the garden which held the body of the crucified to the garden at the end of time, God's eyes are on his people for good. Our part as Christians is to live a life open to the searching, guiding eyes of God. As the old hymn puts it:

Trials dark on ev'ry hand, and we cannot understand
All the ways that God would lead us to that blessed
   promised land;
But He'll guide us with His eye, and we'll follow til
   we die . . .

Surely, "in the shadows standeth God, keeping watch o'er his own."

Some Folks' god Can't See

Some folks think God can't see; can't see their wickedness and deceit. And some folks' god really can't see, because their god is no god—a figment of their imagination, a pale reflection of their own desires. But the God of the Bible, the God of Abraham, Isaac and Jacob and the father of our Lord Jesus, can see and know and the Bible makes plain that in God's sight all men are sinners, all men are equal, all men are precious.

A Haunting Look

Yet after we have studied these references to the eyes of God, there is a verse that haunts all sincere folks. It is Luke 22:61. The scene is the trial of Jesus, and outside in the courtyard Peter stands warming himself at the fires of this world, denying that he ever knew Jesus. And just as Peter denied knowing Jesus for the 3rd time and the rooster crowed, just at that moment they led Jesus down a walkway which opened to the courtyard, "And the Lord turned and looked upon Peter . . .And Peter went out and wept bitterly." None of us can stand the look of God, for we are all sinners. And yet that look recreated Simon Peter, and made him into a choice servant of Jesus.

Sir James Barrie, the creator of Peter Pan, illustrates the look as he tells the story of Joey McQumpha. At least Barrie tells the story of

Joey's mother, poor Jess, and she tells us about Joey. He was only a child, but he already had a text, and it was the dream of his brief life to be a minister and go into the pulpit and preach on his special text. He was a special child, as we will see. Once, long years ago, Jess was taken ill, and the family and the doctor abandoned hope. She called little Joey and told him she was going on a long, long journey and that he must be a good boy after she was gone. He was puzzled, because he knew she was very sick, and could not even get up without her stick. So that night after everyone was asleep, Joey rose in the darkness, took her cane out into the garden, and there, with his little body shaking and his teeth chattering, he buried his mother's staff among the cabbages. For, thought he, how could she go on a long journey without the cane? Happily for the family, mother Jess did not go on that long journey after all. It was Joey who took it.

One day the little boy ran merrily down the road to play. A cart rumbled around the corner, the driver asleep at the reins; there was a thump, a cry, a mother's scream, and a handful of men brought Joey's body home. That was the tragedy of Jess's life. She could not go to church, but on Sunday mornings, she seemed to feel the presence of the little lad who used to run home from church to tell his invalid mother about the service and to wave his hands in a reverent way just like the minister. Joey never wavered in his resolve to be a minister. And his first text, he said, would be from Genesis 16:13, "Thou God seest me." "We'll get a carriage for ye, mother," he would tell say, "so 'at ye can come and hear me preach on Thou God seest me. It doesna do, mother, for the minister in the pulpit to nod to ony o' the folk; but I'll gie ye a look an' ye'll ken it's me. Ye'll be proud o' me, will ye no, mother, when ye see me comin' sailin' alang to the pulpit in my gown? The other folk will be sittin' in their seats wonderin' what my text's to be; but you'll ken, mother, an' you'll turn up to Thou God seest me afore I gie out the chapter." Said his mother twenty years later, on her deathbed, "Ye'll wonder at me, but I've sat here in the lang nights dreamin' 'at Joey was a grown man noo, an' 'at I was puttin' on my bonnet to come to the kirk to hear him preach on Thou God seest me."

And when I read the Book, when I come to Thou God seest me, I let the Book lie in my lap, for aince a body's sure o' that they're sure o' all."

"Aince a body's sure o' that they're sure o' all." Once we're sure, convinced that God sees us all the time, and still loves us, we can be sure of all the other big questions—like What's the point to life? What will happen to me after this life?

Thou seest me, O God, and plain beneath Thy sight appear

The tale of years that vanish, and all secrets deep as night;

Thine eyes are searching through me, yet I will not

    shrink nor fear:

Thy heart is full of tenderness, Thine arm of help is near,

And Thou, O God, art Love as well as Light![1]

---

[1] Lines by Frederick Mann.

I am indebted to that special Australian preacher of the first decades of this century, F. W. Boreham, for the story of Joey in his book, **A Casket of Cameos.**

The Changing Form of the Eternal Gospel

II Corinthians 4:3-7; II Timothy 2:8; Revelation 14:6

Mark starts his Gospel with the words: "The beginning of the gospel of Jesus Christ." We all know what he means by the "gospel;" he is speaking of objective facts—"the facts, ma'am, just the facts," as Sgt. Friday used to say on Dragnet. Mark is going to tell us the facts: a certain man lived in a certain time at a certain place and certain things happened as part of God's plan to redeem the world. Luke also has a special interest in nailing down these objective, time-bound facts: they had their beginning in the days of Caesar Augustus, in the time of the taxing, when Cyrenius was governor of Syria.

Mark's basic facts are that this man Jesus went about doing good—healing, comforting, preaching, raising the dead and in general giving the devil a hard time. He fell out of favor with the religious authorities and was nailed up by the Romans on charges of sedition. He died on the cross, was buried and rose again on the third day by the power of God Almighty. Those are simple facts clear to anyone.

The Eternal Gospel

Jesus' works and words; what he did and what was done to him, is what we call the Gospel, the Good News of God to mankind. These facts, this revelation of God's plan to redeem mankind through Jesus, is the everlasting gospel which that angel in Revelation has in hand as he flies across the heaven in the end of time, warning of the coming judgment of God. The everlasting, eternal Gospel is the objective facts of Jesus Christ: the same yesterday, today, and forever. It is this factual body of information that Paul refers to in Romans 1 when he says he is not ashamed of the Gospel of Christ (1:16).

My Gospel

But then we hear Paul speaking in Romans 2 of my gospel, and 2 Corinthians 4 of our gospel being hidden, and again in 2 Timothy he mentions my gospel, and in 2 Thessalonians 2 he speaks of God calling you through our gospel. When we read these statements alongside the gospel of Jesus Christ, we realize there is the objective, unchanging, eternal gospel of what God did in and through Jesus—and there is my gospel, your gospel, that portion of the eternal gospel that we have embraced, which has become real in our lives, which has shaped and molded our character and ethics and actions; that part of the eternal gospel which has laid claim on us. And it is always smaller than the eternal gospel.

This same truth is seen with respect to the Bible. There is, on the one hand, the Bible; sixty-six books of varying size and written across 2000 years by men guided by the one and same Spirit. A divine book filled with everything from admonitions not to eat pork to instructions about how and when women are to speak in church; from sexually explicit stories to the glorious resurrection accounts; from Habbakuk to Jude, from Nahum to Revelation.

Now if I look at your Bible or you were to examine mine, each of us would have certain parts heavily marked and underlined, some tear-stained and smudged and torn from frequent reading. Other parts of our Bible may never have seen the light of day. So your Bible, my Bible, is always smaller than the Bible. We disapprove of Thomas Jefferson making his own Bible by cutting out all the sections with which he disagreed; yet we all perform surgery on our Bible by our use of it! My Bible consists of those portions of the Bible which have come alive to me, reached out and seized me because of my experiences, my investment of myself in studying the Bible, my surrender to its claims.

In the same way the eternal gospel is always more than my gospel or your gospel. As the gospel flows into the contours of our lives, nobody is ever able to fully embrace, to embody and live out, to contain the fullness of the eternal gospel. That's why Paul, under attack by a faction of the Corinthian church, says we have this treasure in earthen vessels. And since the eternal gospel is bigger and greater than the gospel of any one of us, it is so sad to see someone measure a church, or measure the power and effectiveness of the eternal gospel by that gospel they see reflected in the life of one Christian or in one group. The eternal gospel is not to be judged by any individual reflection of it—my gospel or yours—and, thank God, none of us is going to be judged by any other human being's gospel, either!

Changed Lives And Changed Gospel

Along with the reality of the eternal gospel and the gospel each of us presents, consider with me a second truth, that whenever the eternal gospel flows into a life, both the gospel and that life is changed. As we embrace the gospel, as we grow in its grace, the gospel blooms in our life and because of the uniqueness of each life the eternal gospel, even in its "condensed" form, can be more glorious and wonderful than ever. We think of folks like John Newton, the slave trader who came under the power of the eternal gospel and was converted, and gave us the beautiful hymn Amazing Grace. Less than the eternal gospel, but what a beautiful expression of it!

We think of Francis of Assisi and marvel at the power of the eternal gospel to flow into the contours of each surrendered life and be ever richer and more powerful. A few years ago I stood before a glass case in the crypt of the church where Francis is buried and beheld his worn, patched robe and reflected on the soft touches of the gospel in his life. Not long ago at the tomb of Martin Luther I reflected on the way the eternal gospel had flowed into his life in a dynamic way. Two very different—and marvelous expressions of the eternal gospel. I am challenged to ask myself and you—what shape has the eternal gospel taken in your life and mine? What shape have we allowed it to take?

Here is a word both to those of us who fall into the error of binding the eternal gospel to tradition and those who chafe under the old ways— the gospel is alive, it is the new, fermenting wine being poured into the wineskins. If the skins are brittle, they will not survive; if the skins are fresh and supple, they will stretch and change even while the wine flows into the contour of the skin. No two wineskins are exactly alike; no two leaves, no two flowers, no two snowflakes are exactly alike. And just so, no two gospels are just alike because no two people are just alike. Remember when, after the resurrection, Peter said to Jesus, speaking of the Beloved disciple, "Lord, what shall this man do?" and Jesus said to Peter, "If I want him to remain alive until I come back, what is that to you? You follow me." Each life is different, each life is a plan of God, each life has potential to portray in a beautiful way the eternal gospel.

A Gospel You Cannot Hand Down

Add to the twin truths of the two gospels and the change both in the eternal gospel and our lives a third truth: this gospel each Christian possesses for himself cannot be inherited or handed down. There are many things in life that we can know about only in general terms until we experience them for ourselves. For instance, we can talk of marriage all day but it is not something you can inherit or hand down; each person must experience it for himself or herself to know what marriage is really about. The same is true with death; for young people death is simply a word, a concept, a fact that happens to other people; it is only when we grow older that the reality sinks in. Or take being deacon chairman in a Baptist church—now there's something you can only dimly understand until you have served in the post!

So it is with the eternal gospel of Jesus Christ. You can talk about it all day, the media can write articles and do their feature reports on it, but until you stand as one under the lordship of Jesus Christ, you can never really understand what Christianity is or have a gospel of your own. Christianity is not simply copying what your parents did concerning church or morality. Miss Whittie Dickinson used to work diligently with me in the first grade, earnestly trying to teach this southpaw to copy the gracious, flowing strokes of the alphabet penmanship on the top of the blackboard, but you can't copy Christianity like that.

Dangers Of Our Personal Gospel

A fourth truth follows hard onto these three. There are weaknesses in the personal gospel of each of us. Consider that we are helped and strengthened only by our gospel, not by that portion of the broader eternal gospel we have not yet embraced. As you know, Satan is attacking the family in these days with remarkable success. Part of the problem is that the teaching in the eternal gospel about God's intention for marriage, God's plan of permanence is not a part of the personal gospel of many church members. Another example; many people, during a difficult time in their life, feel defeated, unforgiven and rejected because the acceptance and forgiveness of sinners by Jesus has not really been a part of their personal gospel, or the personal gospel of the folks in their church. Another example; many people, black and white, are filled with prejudice because the love of God for all people is not a part of their personal gospel. Or again; many church members are lukewarm or downright disinterested in reaching the unchurched and lost because the reality of hell has never been part of their personal gospel.

How true it is that my gospel or your gospel may be a narrowing, a constriction of the eternal gospel. I spoke of Saint Francis a moment ago. We are told that Saint Francis met the great Muslim general

The Changing Form of the Eternal Gospel

Saladin in the 1200s. At the end of their encounter, Saladin is reported as saying, "If ever I meet a second Christian like you, I would be willing to be baptized. But that will never happen." Some three hundred years later, a king in Peru said something similar and devastatingly different to a Franciscan priest who had come to Peru with the Spanish conquistadors. The priest offered to the defeated Incas the choice of conversion or death. When the king objected, his hands were cut off. Then he was again asked, "Be baptized and you will go to heaven." The king replied, "No, because if I went to heaven I might meet a second Christian like you." What a sad misshaping of the eternal gospel in our lives. Thank God that many of the difficult experiences in life drive us back to the eternal gospel, and our own gospel can grow and change.

I close by challenging those of us who are already Christians to remember that there will always be a difference between the gospel and our gospel, and let our smaller gospel be lovely and winsome. As the poet said,

> *You are writing a Gospel, A chapter each day,*
> *By deeds that you do, By words that you say.*
> *Men read what you write, Whether faithless or true;*
> *So what is the Gospel According to you?*

I close by asking those of you who are not professing Christians to consider the joy and the power of the eternal gospel. I ask you to remember that the eternal gospel is the story of one particular person, Jesus Christ, who lived and died and rose again to set us free from sin and death. I ask you to allow the eternal gospel to flow into your life, expressing the good news of Jesus in a way that no other life can do.

I am indebted to Harry Emerson Fosdick's sermon *"Every Man's Religion His Own,"* in **The Power To See It Through**, pp. 142ff.

A Plea for Ignorance

Genesis 2:15-17; 3:1-8

A Graduation Sermon

May is the graduation season across our land, and millions of young people and not-so-young people are proudly celebrating milestones in their acquisition of knowledge—or at least the acquisition of a diploma—whether from kindergarten, grade school, high school, college or graduate studies. I come, then, swimming against the stream this morning with a plea for ignorance. That may be a shocking statement to many of you—for all these years you have been, by parents and teachers, encouraged, cajoled, commanded, bribed and threatened to get you to drink from the fountains of knowledge. Why then would I carry the banner for ignorance?

Well, perhaps I should defend myself. Paul once invited his people to just consider him crazy and indulge him while he bragged on himself, so I would hide behind his example. I appreciate the value of education. I suppose I possess one of the finest private libraries in town; at least in theology. I endured—no, I enjoyed—11 years of college

A Plea for Ignorance

and post-graduate study leading to an earned Ph.D. Surely, then, you know that I am not an anti-intellectual; I am not opposed to gathering all the knowledge you can— of the right kind, in the right way, for the right purposes.

We Worship Knowledge

There is, however, no denying that our world worships at the altar of knowledge. We so often express the idea that knowledge is the cure for everything. We buy into the statement of Emerson that "There is no knowledge that is not power." We agree with Keats that "knowledge enormous makes a god of me." We rush to the fountain of knowledge—all kinds of knowledge—as if we can never quench our thirst. I'm told that by the time we are adults, we have accumulated 100 million bits of everyday wisdom. The store of our knowledge, or at least of our information, keeps mounting up at an astonishing rate. Many fields of study find their information doubles in 3 to 5 years, and what was considered a good education 10 years ago is hopelessly obsolete today. NASA plans to orbit by the end of this decade a series of remote sensing platforms which will send back to earth 1 trillion bytes of data each day for 15 years! Talk about trying to drink from a fire hose!

Is Knowledge the Answer?

But is knowledge in itself the answer to all mankind's problems? Is even "Know Yourself," as was inscribed as the great motto on the temple of Apollo in Delphi by the Greeks sufficient? Our society seems at times to echo the old Greek idea of gnosticism—that salvation comes by possession of secret knowledge. The Bible doesn't hold that view; in fact, it is interesting to remember that beautiful passage in Daniel 12:3-4 where the writer speaks of the world to come in which those who have been teachers of righteousness shall "shine as the stars," and also says in pessimistic vein that in the end of time "many shall run to and fro and knowledge shall be increased." The writer of Ecclesiastes says, "He that increases knowledge increases sorrow" (1:18). Humorist Josh Billings put it well a century ago: "The trouble with people is not that they don't know, but that they know so much that ain't so."

Knowledge has many faces. Paul, in 1 Corinthians 13, includes knowledge among those things that are worthless without love, and in 1 Corinthians 8:1 he says knowledge "puffs up." My biblical word to you this morning is to see knowledge for what it is and seek the right kind of knowledge. Not all knowledge is good. The Bible says there is a blessed kind of knowledge, a knowledge that God wants us to embrace; you should gain all the right kind of knowledge you can. But the Bible also says there is an evil knowledge, a useless knowledge, a dangerous knowledge, a perverted knowledge, a knowledge the devil is anxious for you to gain, a knowledge that binds and enslaves us, that destroys relationships and produces alienation and corruption—and of that knowledge God would have you ignorant.

Adam and Eve and Knowledge

The authority for what I am saying is found in the story of the fall of Adam and Eve in Genesis 2 and 3. Like modern man, Adam and Eve thought knowledge was the highest prize in life. They bought into that saying that "He who binds his soul to knowledge, steals the key to heaven" (N. P. Willis). They were already given all that mankind needs for perfect peace and fulfillment: all their needs were met, they enjoyed fellowship with God, and they had a meaningful task to do in the keeping of the garden. God placed only one restriction upon them—they were not to eat of one certain tree in the midst of the garden: the tree of the knowledge of good and evil. All other fruits were available; but to eat of this tree, said God, would mean death (Genesis 2:15-17).

Then came the devil in the form of the serpent. He's peddling dissension and alienation and disobedience. "Did God really say you couldn't have that particular fruit?" The implication is that God is, at best, being arbitrary or childish, and, at worse, does not have the welfare of Adam and Eve in mind. Eve explains that God has warned

A Plea for Ignorance

them that to eat, to disobey, will mean death. Now it is clear that she hasn't the faintest idea what death is all about; she has never seen anyone or anything die. She is ignorant of death. She is as ignorant of death as my little less-than-two-years-old grandson; he has no notion—yet—of the reality or power of death. The snake scornfully calls God a liar: "Ha! You will not die if you eat that fruit; on the contrary—He knows that the moment you eat that forbidden fruit you will be as smart as God! He knows that you'll know all that He knows if you eat that forbidden fruit. He just doesn't want that!"

Now notice that suddenly the hitherto undistinguished fruit of the tree of the knowledge of good and evil suddenly takes on new appeal. Eve saw that it certainly was food like the apples and oranges and pears . . . it certainly looked good—she wondered how they could have overlooked this fine fruit all this time! . . . and after all, it would make one wise. You'll notice that the benefit of wisdom is listed last behind nourishment and beauty, but it is clear what was uppermost in Eve's mind. So she ate, and gave some to Adam to eat, while the snake ambled away whistling to himself, "I never promised you a rose garden."

A Knowledge—But of Death

Now hear me—the Bible says the result of the new knowledge gained by Adam and Eve was not a heightened experience of life, but of death! Even the reprobate poet Lord Byron can see that: "The tree of knowledge is not [the tree] of life . . ." Adam and Eve disobeyed, ate the fruit, and indeed gained new knowledge; now they could see the difference between good and evil; now for the first time they saw evil over against good—and now for the first time they experienced shame and guilt and alienation from God. Look at verses 7 and 8. Folks, God wanted them to be ignorant of what it means to be ashamed, to feel guilt, to feel alienated from each other and from God.

What God Wants You Ignorant Of

I say again—God wants you to be ignorant of some things. God wants you to be ignorant of what it feels like and what it means to have alcohol or drugs control your life and make you curse the ones you love and deprive your family of love and hope; God wants you to be ignorant of the guilt that rides on the back of the adulterer, ignorant of the self-hatred of the person who has thrown away morals and integrity and has walked on those who trust him . . . God wants you to be ignorant of destructive experiential knowledge; the knowledge that comes from experiencing the power of the devil. The devil wanted Adam and Eve to have knowledge, all right; but it was a damning knowledge, a knowledge of sorrow and pain and lost hopes.

There is a right kind of knowledge and a wrong kind of knowledge. I would urge you as young people to go out into this world carrying a precious ignorance of some things. For instance, I am ignorant of the destructive power of alcohol on my own life, although I have certainly seen what it can do in the lives of others. I have never drunk anything stronger than wine, and that only at communion services. I came to marriage ignorant of the guilt of pre-marital sex. And I'm glad I did. I don't know personally what it means to run around on your wife, although God knows I have agonized with scores of folks through the years who do know of the guilt and shame of it. But listen—I haven't missed a good thing in the world by being ignorant of things God wants us to be ignorant about. The Ten Commandments are there to keep us ignorant of the painful and destructive knowledge that comes with breaking God's laws. I make a plea for you to keep a certain kind of ignorance all the way through life; keep that ignorance gladly and proudly—nothing else will enrage the devil so!

A Right Kind of Knowledge

Now let me change gears and speak of a kind of knowledge God wants all of us to have. While there is a knowledge of evil and its power in your life that God doesn't want you to ever have, there is also a knowledge that builds up and blesses. Jesus said to his followers: "You shall know the truth, and the truth shall make you free [John 8:32]." What kind of knowledge is this truth? Is it different from what Adam and Eve gained when they disobeyed God? Is it different from the bitter

A Plea for Ignorance

truths we become aware of when we disobey God? Jesus is speaking of a spiritual knowledge; it is not about atoms or galaxies or biology or computers.

No matter how much education you may have this morning; no matter how much knowledge you may have about any particular field—whether it is medicine, law, politics, real estate, computers or whatever—if you don't have the knowledge God wants you to have, there is something wonderful missing in your life. If ever a man was educated, it was Paul. He was steeped in Jewish rabbinic training, knowledgeable in Roman culture as a Roman citizen, and could even converse with the Greek philosophers in Athens—but Paul says he counted everything but garbage compared to the wonderful knowledge of Jesus Christ. Let me tell you from God's Word three things God wants you to know.

Three Things God Wants You to Know

First, *God wants you to know that He created you and has a plan for your individual life,* but that all of us have eaten that forbidden fruit and filled our lives with the knowledge of guilt and sin and separation from God, and also with death. "All have sinned and come short of the glory of God." "There is not one righteous; no, not one." "The wages of sin is death." So all of us live under the shadow of death. Second, *God wants you to know that He loves you, and sent His son Jesus into this world to suffer and die for our sins.* Even the enemies of Jesus found no sin in him; in his death the just died for the unjust, that he might bring us to God. The third fact God wants you to know is that *through repentance and faith in Jesus as the Son of God and your Lord and Saviour, your sins can be forgiven and your life changed.*

The cross of Jesus is seen as foolishness by the world, by the devil. But it is the power of God, the wisdom of God which leads to salvation for you and me.

The Harvest that Didn't Happen

Jeremiah 8:20; John 4:35; Luke 8:5-8, 11-15

Fall days are a good time to think about the harvest. So let me talk with you about the harvest that didn't happen. When harvests don't happen in the physical realm, people starve to death. When there is no harvest in the spiritual realm, people go to hell. I found myself wondering this week how many of those people suddenly killed in the earthquake, crushed in a twinkling of an eye in the bridge collapse, were prepared for eternity. In how many of those hearts had there been a spiritual harvest?

If we would understand how Jesus saw people, if we would see the great harvest that He saw, and that all too often doesn't happen, turn to John 4.

It was early in Jesus' ministry, He and his disciples were sitting by a community well near the main highway eating their lunch. Jesus had just had a conversation with the Samaritan woman at the well, and

The Harvest that Didn't Happen

she had gone back into the village to tell what had happened. Jesus looked up in the midst of their lunch and commented, "Didn't you say there were still four months until harvest? I say, Lift up your eyes and look on the fields, for they are harvest-white already!" In verse 38 He goes on to say He is sending the disciples to reap where others sowed. Jesus sees the people as precious grain, a ripe harvest, to be gathered into the Father's bosom, a harvest ripened by love and forgiveness and acceptance. He sees a great harvest, He sees the need for workers to gather the harvest.

Now turn to Luke 10. In this chapter Jesus sends out the Seventy and commissions them. Verse 2 tells us: There is a great harvest, the workers are few, and we should pray for more workers in the field. Now turn over to Matthew 9:36-37 where we see how Jesus saw the multitudes as shepherdless sheep and declared to His disciples that the harvest is great, the workers are few, and that we should pray for help in the fields.

The Urgency of the Harvest

There is a sense of urgency in Jesus' vision of the great harvest, the lack of workers, and the need for prayer to the Lord of the Harvest. He knew that He had only a few years; none of us know how long we have. And behind Jesus' words we can hear the melancholy prophet Jeremiah as he wails over his stumbling, misled nation: "The harvest is past, the summer is ended, and we are not saved."

The past few days I have been through our entire file of people we have been visiting, working with, hoping to win to Christ and to His church. Card after card brought back memories; here a young boy and girl led to Jesus by loving members of this church, yet the mother would not even darken the door of the church to see her children baptized; here a couple in their 70's who, after visit after visit, will one day, they say, invite Jesus into their hearts. And on this card the face of a little girl who made a profession of faith in the home, but waits and waits for a mother who says she will rededicate her life as the daughter makes her profession of faith. Two, three years have passed without a move. Here a young couple, needing the care and love of a church, declare they do not want a minister to visit. With card after card I hear the words of the Master: "They are like sheep without a shepherd . . . the harvest truly is plenteous . . .But it did not happen. I hear the words of the prophet: "The harvest is past, the summer is ended, and we are not saved." The harvest that didn't happen.

Why Doesn't the Harvest Happen?

We quote verses about the harvest, we sing about bringing in the sheaves, yet so often there is no harvest, no salvation, no redemption in so many lives. Why? Why is every day a smaller percentage of the world's population marching under the banner of the cross? Why did the Rich Young Ruler turn away from Christ? Why did Demas desert Paul and the faith? Why did Pilate wash his hands of Jesus and His Gospel? Why did Nicodemus not want to be born again? Why did Agrippa put off salvation? Why was there no harvest in their lives?

See the parable of the sower for some answers. Turn to Luke 8:5-8, 11-15. Here are three categories of hearts in which there is no harvest, in which the seed of the Gospel never comes to fruition. First, the wayside heart. Let us get the scene. The sower scatters the seed, some falls on the pathway through the field, pounded hard by many feet. What a picture of the heart of modern man! Pounded hard by every triviality, every lust, every greed, every demand, every schedule, every gadget. So the Gospel lies on the surface of a hard heart, trampled over as a common fruit peel, a dead leaf blown along by the wind, a piece of crumpled paper; of no concern, no interest.

Matthew says of the hardened heart, "he understood it not . . ." And in the parable the birds of the air came and took that seed away. Jesus himself, in a rare personal interpretation of a parable, tells us that by the bird he means the devil. "Lest that person should believe and be saved," the devil takes away the person's awareness, interest, openness to the Gospel. Here is the reason for the lack of a harvest in many lives-lives hardened on the surface by unnatural use of drugs and sex and money, lives of people who will one day die and go to hell without Jesus. Lives that are closed, hardened, unconcerned, worldly . . . my, what a blessing tragedy sometimes becomes when it slows such folks down.

Then there is the shallow heart. Some of the Gospel seed fell on stony ground; that is, not much soil. The seed sprouted quickly, but just as quickly withered under the heat of the sun. Jesus said this represents the person who made a good start, who seemed open to the Gospel, but faded away with testing and temptation. It ends in the same result as the seed in the hard heart; it merely starts differently. How disappointing when someone is apparently so open to the Gospel, so receptive to the Holy Spirit, yet after a few weeks, a few months, they have faded away. Unwilling to pay the price of a reconstructed life, they fall back into darkness. I think of the crowds that followed Jesus for part of His ministry, but turned back when He spoke of discipleship. There is no harvest in that life.

And then the third kind of heart, the choked heart. A life which hears the Gospel, but it is overshadowed by the thorns of cares, the heavy-hanging guilt in their life; the thorn of riches, which choke the Gospel out; the thorn of pleasures, that part of life which in itself is not at all evil or wrong, but which can deafen and blind us to the call of Gospel living.

Personal Responsibility for Harvest

So let us see that part of the reason for a lack of harvest in many lives, in our community, in our world, lies with the heart in which the Gospel seed is sown. Every Sunday thousands of hearts are sown with the seed of the Gospel by this church through the television and radio. The fruition of that seed depends in large part on the person listening. I cannot come into your life and root out the weeds; nobody can put a tenderizer into your heart; nobody can deepen the soil of your life. "Each one shall bear his own burdens . . ." says the Bible, and each of us shall bear some responsibility for his own spiritual harvest. That is why I beg of you who listen to this service to hear me, and to let the admonition of this hour sink into your heart, and by the grace and work of the Holy Spirit, may a wonderful spiritual harvest bloom.

No Harvest Without a Sower

But now let us go back and notice how the parable begins: "a sower went out to sow . . ." Listen! There can be no harvest if there is no seed sown! A sower is essential to a harvest! It matters not how wonderful the Gospel; how burdened down the heart; how open to hearing the Good News of Jesus; there will be no harvest without a sower! Folks, all our piety will not take the place of sowing the seed. There is something pathetic in our prayers in Sunday School and in the Conference Room prayer time when we pray, "that those here today who have never made a profession of faith in come to know Christ as Saviour . . ." when we pray that "the lost in our midst may accept Jesus . . ." knowing that unless we witness to the lost, invite them to church, bring them to church, there won't be any lost people in the service! Wooden pews don't make professions of faith in Jesus! Lost people lovingly cared for, brought to the preaching of the Gospel, put under conviction by the Holy Spirit, do.

This past Sunday, on the way home after Morning Worship, I heard a preacher on the radio ask a congregation, "How beautiful are your feet?" Then I heard him say, "Don't bother looking at your feet!" He went on to say you have beautiful feet if they are used to carry the Gospel to others "How beautiful are the feet of them that preach the gospel of peace, and bring glad tidings of good things!" (Romans 10:9-15). Let me suggest some ways for you to have beautiful feet.

You can take part in the GROW visitation; a group of our church goes out from two locations every Tuesday night to carry the Gospel. You can witness by putting Christian literature in your business office or waiting room. Don't you think God would be honored and situations would be created which could be used by the Holy Spirit if you put copies of the weekly printed sermon in your office; if you put out copies of our doctrinal brochure, *This I Believe*. You can resolve to invite

The Harvest that Didn't Happen

someone each week to attend worship with you. There is every reason in the world for you to do that; at First Baptist we magnify Jesus, we preach the Gospel, we sing the praises of God, not man; we welcome anyone to worship Jesus with us. You can pray daily for a growing evangelistic concern in our church. Pray for more workers for the harvest! You can live a consecrated life before the world. Just this past week I conducted the funeral service of a man who is in heaven today because his employer cared enough to share the Gospel with him.

There's a Place for You

So often the word comes when I speak of evangelism, "What shall I say?" Let me show you what to say by sharing something Dr. Fred Craddock, Professor of Preaching at Emery University, said. In addressing a group of preachers Dr. Craddock said he had brought only two words with him, and wished to talk about one of them. The word was *place*. Simple little word. Common, ordinary word. We often misuse it; make of it a club to beat people with—"They would be all right, if they knew their place . . ." It's a word that can bring a lot of disappointment with it: "I'm sorry, we don't have a place for you . . . Yet it can mean acceptance: "Here, there's a place beside me . . ." It is a word which describes home, too: "We'll soon be home; back at our place . . ." Remember the old song and story of the prisoner coming home? He had written that if he would be accepted back, to tie a yellow ribbon around the old oak tree in the yard . . . and when the bus rounded the bend, every tree in the yard at the old place was decked with a yellow ribbon!

In its highest sense, place means home; love, acceptance, forgiveness, fellowship. Jesus said, "I go to prepare a place for you . . ." So, isn't that what we are to tell the lost and unchurched? There's a place for you; a place of forgiveness; a place at the foot of the cross; a place at the Lord's table, a place in heaven; a place in our church; a place in our heart.

The Haunted House

Matthew 12:43-45

A sermon at Halloween

I think I've told you about the old Drew Mansion. When I was growing up, it was synonymous with Halloween and haunted houses. The Drew Mansion, a few miles out of town on the eastern border of our county, was on the Swannee River. It had been the mansion of the Florida governor during the Civil War. I passed by it a couple of years ago, and barely recognized it, but fifty years ago it was the perfect haunted house. It sat back in a grove of moss-draped oak trees over beyond the railroad track. Great columns graced the front of the mansion, and off to the side you could see the old cemetery.

Inside the house were marble mantles and huge rooms fit for giants with ceilings which dwarfed us. Up in the attic we could look out from portholes from which the inhabitants could fire rifles if attacked. I remember there were tales of a tunnel running a couple hundred yards from the house to the river, but nobody knew where it was.

The Haunted House

Looming in the moonlight, the house was scary, even haunted. Everybody said it was empty, but we kids knew better. Inside the dark and forlorn rooms, beyond the creaky boards and weird slamming noises somewhere upstairs, we knew the house was inhabited. It was inhabited by the spiders who spun the thick webs in the corners; it was inhabited by the 'possums and 'coons who pattered across the attic; it was inhabited by the tramps and vandals and pranksters, and by the memories of what had been a century before. It was a tragic picture of a great house once upon a time, which had been deserted, and now was full of all sorts of dark things. Jesus told a story of a haunted house—it is here in Matthew 12:43-45. Let's read it. Does it say anything to you? Does it speak to much of the emptiness of so many lives?

The Soul Intended To Be Occupied

Jesus is saying in this story that the soul is intended to be occupied. This story is the tragedy of the unoccupied soul, for it is clear that Jesus is talking here about souls, not about houses made of wood or clay or stone. Our soul is that part of us we cannot see, the essence of our life, the real you that can have a relationship to God. The Greek word for soul, *psyche*, is seen in our words psychology, psychic, psychiatry, etc. Our heart, our soul, the real person which continues beyond the body, is meant to be directed, occupied by God.

The story of the fall of Adam and Eve in the garden is essentially the story of the taking over of the soul of mankind by Satan. And ever since the fall, each of us is born with one hand manacled, as it were. We have inherited this tendency toward the slavery of the devil, and even strengthened this unlawful domination by the devil in our lives. We have become like the slaves in the War Between The States who fought the Yankees alongside their masters, the people who enslaved them. They had come to love the enslaver!

Now in the New Testament Jesus clearly teaches that he has invaded the kingdom of darkness, this world, the domain of Satan. And evangelism is the struggle for the souls of men and women and children. This is why the evangelistic question of who sits on the throne of your life is so appropriate—for we are made for God to rule over us and guide us, but we have enslaved ourselves to the devil.

How The Empty Soul Comes About

Here in Jesus' haunted house story we see an unnatural thing: An empty soul. Jesus seems to abruptly begin this story, but I feel it was told against the background of Jesus' ministry of casting out devils and healing the bodies and minds of sick people. Often we read of his casting out devils and not allowing them to speak, and we remember the Gadarene demoniac and the boy Jesus healed at the foot of the Mount of Transfiguration.

So what we have here is a soul which Jesus has rescued, swept clean. This story could begin at the point at which the gospel story of the healing of the demoniac ends—with Jesus sending that man back home to his friends and relatives to tell them how he had been set free. He was sent away to make his freedom, his conversion, complete as he witnesses and takes his public stand for Christ. He departed with a soul swept clean . . . the demons cast out. What happens next is up to him.

So this story begins with an empty soul, an unnatural thing. Neither God nor Satan rules on the throne of that soul. Perhaps in this story the man had an experience of conviction, but it did not progress into conversion. Perhaps it was an experience of remorse, but not repentance. He saw the wickedness of his life, but he was not moved to change. The result was that for a time, a little while, the devil was cast out.

Now, C. S. Lewis draws a vivid picture of demonic presence and influence in his Screwtape Letters, and even though it is fiction, I think that just as there is apparently angelic presence and influence, there is also demonic presence and influence. So here in Jesus' story we see the devil sent packing. Notice that Jesus does not say that the devil was destroyed. We cannot destroy our archenemy; we can only keep him at bay until the end of time when he will be destroyed.

The Haunted House

In common Jewish legend, devils which are cast out of people or animals wander in dry, lonely places. So did the devil in Jesus' Halloween story. He wandered, seeking something or someone to inhabit. But the devil is no fool; finding no new host, after a while this devil determined to go back and check on the man from which he was driven. He came back and found that the man had made only surface changes; he had not invited God to rule his soul! It must have warmed that devil's heart—a life all cleaned up of bad habits, but with no real relationship to God. Rubbing his hands with glee, he hurries off to find other wandering devils, and brings back seven with him. They all moved into this man's soul, and Jesus said the result was worse than the man's original condition!

The Danger Of An Empty Soul

Now we see the danger of an empty house! What happens when a house stands empty? It does not stay empty long. The emptiness draws lower elements, not higher. Mustiness sets in; dust collects over everything; spiders begin to spin their webs and mice begin to run here and there.

But we are not talking about houses here, but souls. What are the particular dangers of an empty soul? A person who has made an effort to clean up their life, to cast Satan out, to lift themselves by their bootstraps without the help of Christ, is a tragic person. Christ is not the Lord of this soul; this person is trying to get by with neither Christ nor the devil in control. Such a person is quite often a judgemental, hypocritical person, filled with a pitiful self-made religion of self-worship.

Spiritual emptiness is tragic and dangerous. We are aware, in the physical realm, of the power of the tornado, a power which is seen in the empty, silent vacuum at the center of the storm. So many of the idols of our time are empty souls, with a terrible vacuum at the center of their souls. There is a book on my shelf by the title of Short Lives, being 31 accounts of famous idols in our culture, folks who were both creative and self-destructive, who took their life at a young age. When the soul is empty, it is a tragic life. It may look cleaned up and swept and garnished on the outside, but if the soul is empty, tragedy is ahead.

Let Us Fill Our Soul With Jesus

Jesus is saying in this story, then: (1) God made the soul to be ruled over by himself, (2) An empty soul is an unnatural thing, (3) An empty soul will be filled with all kinds of evil, and (4) We need to fill our souls with the presence of Jesus.

If we have to sum up this haunted house story in one statement, it would be: It is not enough for our souls to be cleaned out—we must fill our souls with the presence of Jesus. It is not enough to "stop our meanness." That may stop our chewing, smoking, drinking, cussing, dancing, card playing, lying, running around—but if that's all you do, it is pulling up weeds only to see them multiply!

The Christian life, the truly changed life that will stay changed, means having a new tenant. It means not only having our lives cleaned up and cleaned out, but it means having Christ in control, Christ on the throne of our life.

This little story Jesus told is filled with fresh meaning when we remember the verse in Revelation 3:20: "Behold, I stand at the door and knock; if any man will hear my voice and open the door, I will come in and have fellowship with him."

The Five Most Crucial Minutes

Isaiah 6:8; Hebrews 3:8-15; Luke 16:27-31

A sports trivia question: *What professional football team scored 3 times in the last 17 seconds of a game back around 1962?* The Baltimore Colts! It was a Sunday afternoon game and I was a seminary student at Southeastern Seminary. It was an amazing and crucial 17 seconds as the Colts galloped from behind to win a sensational victory! Another question, not a trivial one: *What part, what segment, of our worship service do you feel is the most crucial?*

I expect your answers, if we were to voice them, would range from the choir anthem to the hymns, from the offering to the sermon to the benediction! I wouldn't argue with you on any of them; I would simply point out that the last five minutes of the worship service may well be the most *crucial* for most worshippers.

We know how the "last moments" quality comes into play in the last two minutes of the football game, the last minute of the basketball game. There ought to be that kind of building spiritual excitement, that inner sense that these moments are crucial, as the time of worship draws to a close, as we like Isaiah, feel the need for a response to what God has been saying to us as we worshipped.

For these are decisive moments—the last five minutes may make the difference between heaven and hell; between your leaving this place in spiritual peace or spiritual turmoil; between your spending eternity with or without God. The last five minutes in our worship service is the time of the invitation—when we urge everyone to be sensitive to the leading of the Spirit to make spiritual decisions; for the Christian a decision of deeper commitment in some definite area, and the unsaved person to accept Jesus as Lord and come forward and publicly declare that faith in Jesus.

The Devil And The Invitation

The last five minutes are so crucial that even the devil never leaves early—he stays through to what is for him the bitter end, talking to the Christian and to the non-Christian. He tells the Christian that it doesn't apply to him, so start getting ready to leave: get your coat on, gather up your Bible and Sunday School material, perhaps even leave during the invitation hymn to avoid the benediction rush. The devil misdirects your attention so you may not take the appeal seriously, so you will not pray for the unsaved around you. He speaks to the unsaved in the service, urging them to notice the distractions of people packing up or leaving or yawning, urging them to ignore the small still voice of the Holy Spirit—there's plenty of time.

Now another question: Why does such a drama, so important and invisible, take place in the last five minutes of church each Sunday? Why are these five minutes so important? Why does the devil never miss the invitation? Why are these last minutes so vital to the Gospel message?

The Gospel Is Good News

The invitation is essential to the preaching of the Gospel because the Gospel is good news. The Gospel is more than entertainment or information. It is the answer to the deepest questions you and I ask in the depth of our hearts in the dark of the night—Where is God when this is happening? What shall I do with my life? What shall I do with this present situation, this sin, this guilt, this despair? The Gospel of Jesus is a rope to pull you out of the pit of despair; the one firm fact in the shifting sands of moral relativity; advice more true and helpful than a thousand Ann Landers; a reforming power greater than a thousand prisons.

And many of us came today knowing that we need a new relationship to God, ready to confess our sins, our needs, ready to claim His forgiveness and healing and guidance. And these last five minutes become the testing ground, the decision ground, the holy ground where our need and God's grace can be fused together.

The Gospel Demands A Response

These last moments are vital because the Gospel calls for a response on the part of the hearer. Both our own hearts and the good news demand that we make some sort of response to what we have heard and felt in worship.

> *When I survey the wondrous cross,*
> *On which the Prince of glory died,*
> *My richest gain I count but loss,*
> *And pour contempt on all my pride.*
>
> *Were the whole realm of nature mine,*
> *That were a present far too small;*
> *Love so amazing, so divine,*
> *Demands my soul, my life, my all.*

Look with me at the Gospel in its simplicity and its majesty, calling for a response. Turn to Acts 2:37: "Now when they heard this, they were pierced in their hearts, and said unto Peter and the rest of the apostles, Men and brethren, what shall we do?"

What did they hear? A study of Acts 2, 3 and 4 will reveal the heart of the early preaching: (1) prophecy has been fulfilled, and a new Age has begun, in Jesus. The promises to Abraham and to David are fulfilled in Jesus. (2) Jesus died for our sins according to the Scripture, to deliver us from sin (2:38; 3:18-19). Men need no longer seek the perfect lamb for a sacrifice for our sins; Jesus is the lamb of God, slain before the foundation of the world for our sins. (3) Jesus was buried, raised from the dead, and exalted to the right hand of the Father (2:22-24, 32-33). That is the vision of the dying Stephen. (4) This same Jesus is coming again as Lord of all (2:35). The preaching of these facts and proclaiming of these truths is more than the mere recital of ancient history. For this man Jesus is still alive, and among us! The preaching of the Gospel is good news for sinners; it is full of spiritual power, power that can change lives. For these facts confront each of us with our sin and God's provision for our redemption.

Whenever the Gospel is proclaimed, God's Spirit seeks a verdict, a decision, a commitment from the listener. Remember the old gospel song, *"What Will You Do With Jesus? Neutral you cannot be"* and that is true today for you who have never responded to the Gospel invitation. The verdict, the decision the Holy Spirit seeks from you is to believe in Jesus. That was the answer Paul gave the Philippian jailer (Acts 16:31). To believe in Jesus means to believe in our head—to believe the Biblical facts about Jesus; to believe in our heart—to make a commitment with our emotions; and to believe with our will—to determine to follow, love, and serve Jesus alone through this life.

The Gospel Calls For Public Response

Not only does the preaching of the Gospel call for a decision; it is a public decision that is called for. Jesus seems to have called men publicly, not privately: Peter and Andrew, James and John, the Rich Ruler, Levi, Zaccheus—and Zaccheus is typical. He was a sinner; Jesus gave the invitation to follow—to exchange his old life for a new life and new goals; and Zaccheus responded in full view of the crowd. In the Old Testament we hear the admonition: "Let the redeemed of the Lord say so!" In preaching, Jesus commanded men to confess Him openly (Mt 10:32f).

The whole idea of the Gospel includes the idea of a messenger who has brought Good News, and now stands waiting to know what answer to take back to the One who sent him, and his plea is that of Deuteronomy 30:19: "I have set before you life and death, blessing and cursing: therefore choose life, that both thou and thy seed may live."

The Holy Spirit Is Prompting The Lost

The invitation time is important because this is when the Holy Spirit is speaking to the hearts of the unsaved, prompting them to turn to Jesus: "They were pierced in their hearts." The work of the Spirit during the preaching of the Gospel is to convict and convince the lost person of the need of Jesus. At the invitation time, when the call for decision is given—it is then that the Spirit is speaking to men's hearts to get up, to publicly confess Jesus.

The moments of public call to commitment are a battleground in many a soul between the devil and the Spirit. The devil urges: "Not now!" And many who cannot say "No" to Jesus can say "Not now" forever. None of us knows what a day may bring. On October 8, 1870, the great evangelist D. L. Moody was having a crusade in Chicago. He ended his sermon and urged the people to go home and ponder the message until the next Sunday. Even as he dismissed the crowd, the great Chicago fire was already crackling. That night hundreds were killed; ninety thousand were left homeless in that tragic blaze. Moody called his failure to urge the decision for Christ that night the greatest blunder of his life. God's invitation is always in the present tense—"Today is the day of salvation!"

An Inner Need To Publicly Confess

The invitation time is vital because the man, woman, boy, or girl under conviction needs to express their commitment. The public commitment seals our decision to follow Jesus. As Billy Graham puts it:

"There's something about coming forward that settles it." Jesus pointed out the danger of quenching the Spirit when we do not respond to the Spirit's urging at the time of the invitation—it is like the bird (Satan) in the parable of the sower, who snatches away the Gospel seed planted in the heart (Luke 8:11-12). The public decision aids the transition from spiritual death into life. It tells the world whose side you're on; it begins a life of witness for Jesus. The public decision moves the Christian to evaluate his spiritual health.

More Than Emotion

The invitation time is much more than a time of emotional appeal. No doubt many of us remember the old gospel songs: *Almost Persuaded; Just As I Am; Only Trust Him; Pass Me Not; Softly And Tenderly; Why Not Tonight* . . . Yet these precious moments are much more than emotion—they are the time of the Spirit.

As Billy Graham prepared to have the London Crusade of 1966-67, some British newspapers began to charge him with emotionalism through the hymns sung at the public invitation time. So without telling anyone, Graham decided not to have music at the invitation. He simply preached the Gospel, gave the invitation to make a public decision for Christ, then stepped back and bowed his head in prayer. For a solid month he had no music at the invitation. Sometimes it would be a full thirty seconds of silence before anyone moved. Then you could hear it—the sound of hundreds of people quietly moving in silence to the front—Then the newspapers accused him of using the emotional silence! No, the truth is that the invitation time is the time of the Spirit. We need to recognize that.

Time For The Invitation

And now it is time for the invitation. Time for the simple, powerful, life-changing invitation. Would you take Jesus as your Saviour? Would you say with the hymn-writer, "Just as I am, without one plea, but that thy blood was shed for me. . ." It is an invitation to the banquet of the Great King, for He has told his servants to go out into the highways and invite all who will come.

The Last Temptation of Jesus

Matthew 26:36-56

There is a great deal of concern about the movie *The Last Temptation of Christ*. The Universal Studios film is scheduled for release in September, and is said to depict Christ on the cross having hallucinations about marriage to Mary Magdalene. I am glad to read that the 2,000 United Artists theatres and the 110 Malco theatres will not show the film.

The film is obviously sick in many ways. But all the comment about it recently has served to raise the question in my mind—since the film has no earthly idea what Christ's last temptation really was—just what was the last temptation of Christ? Can we, through studying the Scripture, get an idea of what the last temptation was, and how Jesus handled it? Such a study would provide help, warning, lessons, and strength for us in our own temptations.

What Was Jesus' Last Temptation?

The great scholar A.T. Robertson comments in his **Word Pictures In The New Testament** that in the garden Satan tempted Christ to draw back from the cross, and that Jesus was feeling the worst of all temptations of His earthly life just then. Odd, isn't it. Most of us would never think of Gethsemane as a time of temptation; we rather consider it a trial of God. We think of temptation as temptation to lust; to fleshly sins. But I am convinced that here in the garden we see the last temptation of Jesus.

The character of the last temptation of Jesus was the same as the first temptation experience recorded. In the fourth chapters of Matthew and Luke we have the record of the temptation of Jesus in the desert. The thrusts of these three specific temptations are the same as the garden temptation. First, the temptation to meet his own need (the rocks into bread and the turning away from the cup of crucifixion), then the temptation to use religion to gain a following (jumping from the pinnacle of the temple to be caught by angels and here in the garden the temptation to call down 12 legions of angels), and finally the temptation to gain the whole world (by worshipping the devil and here by refusing the role of sonship as the cross approaches). So, in essence, the first and the last temptations are the same. The devil never gives up!

The Continuous Temptation

After the first temptation, Matthew says the devil left and angels came and ministered to Jesus. Luke gives more detail and insight when he says the devil departed until an opportue time. The devil didn't leave Jesus alone any more than he leaves you and me alone. All through His ministry Jesus struggled with the devil, and now at the close of the ministry He keeps referring to the fact that the "hour is come" and there is a heavy atmosphere of tragedy and doom as He gathers with the twelve for the Passover meal. "One of you will betray me. . .Is it I?" Then, "Be of good cheer, I have overcome the world!" and "Let

The Last Temptation of Jesus

not your hearts be troubled. . ." And in the garden He faces the last and greatest temptation. Sadly, only He knows the depth of the temptation or the weakness of the twelve (verses 30-35).

In Beautiful Gardens

Walk with me through the Gethsemane passage, beginning with verse 36. And perhaps our first lesson is to see what agony and temptation and trial beautiful gardens can hide. Those of you who have been to the Holy Land and seen the old olive trees in Gethsemane have been touched by the scene of peacefulness and beauty. Yet perhaps under those same trees, on that very ground, the Saviour sweated drops of blood, and agonized alone even after pleading with His friends to stay awake and pray. When I ponder such intensity, such inward conflict, such struggle in such a scene of peaceful beauty, I am reminded that none of us knows the struggle that goes on behind the face, the smile, the routine, the life of the person we meet in the aisle after the service, the person who smiles back at us from the choir, the person who takes up the collection, or leads the service.

In verses 37-38 Jesus took the inner circle, Peter, James, and John--the first called--off into the darkness and asked them to pray with Him. In this is our second lesson, we need the help of our friends in our temptations and struggles. Yet notice what happened. What an honor to be one of the small circle to whom the Saviour opened His heart and poured out His turmoil and agony. He needed their love, their support, their understanding, their prayers. But what did they do? They let Him down; they went to sleep! I confess I do not see how they could have done it; but we must remember the devil was right there, and the fact that Jesus came back twice to check on them and ask for their prayers shows how important they were in the struggle--the devil knew that! I wonder how often you and I are used of Satan by not supporting our brothers and sisters in their time of struggle.

In verse 41, when Jesus comes back after the first period of prayer to check on the disciples, He makes an intriguing statement: "Watch and pray, that ye enter not into temptation: the spirit indeed is willing, but the flesh is weak." Here is light on that troubling petition in the Lord's Prayer: "lead us not into temptation." We know God does not lead anyone into temptation (James 1:13f). In light of Jesus' comment we see that we ought to pray that God will not lead us into such a dark garden, a deep valley of trial, such satanic struggle as Jesus underwent, a time when the devil certainly tempts us. We may be ever so committed, as were the disciples, but we must remember Jesus' words--our human spirit is willing, but the flesh (as Paul reminds us so often) is so weak and open to the devil's wiles.

We will come back to the verses on the actual prayer of Jesus; let us consider verses 46-49 and see the depth of the devil's efforts. See how the devil propped up his offer, his temptation, with every means possible. The looming horror of death which Jesus shared with all of us; the sleeping of the inner circle; and now comes Judas, who was a chosen one, who has walked the dusty roads with the Master for three years. The words of David come to mind from Psalm 55:12-14.

The Form of the Temptation

In verse 53 we see the actual temptation, the straw Satan grasped, the door he tried to pry open: twelve bands of angels, something like 100,000 angels. The last temptation was not on the cross; not that of "come down from the cross and save thyself"—those were just bitter taunts from the mouths of men. The last temptation took place in the garden and it was the temptation to push away the cup of death; to save Himself, to call the angels when the soldiers came. It was the same temptation as the first, as I have said, but now we see it more clearly. The temptation to meet his need, to save himself (as with the bread) and surely he could still rescue the world. The temptation to feed on the popular desire for sensationalism in religion—after all, the news would spread like wildfire that angels had destroyed the men sent to arrest Jesus! The temptation to gain the world—the devil would have rejoiced to have Jesus, even after the impact of His ministry.

The Prayer in the Garden

The victory over the devil was already won, however, before the soldiers got to the garden. The decision was made, the cup was accepted.

The Last Temptation of Jesus

The victory was won through prayer most of all; then by the conviction that the Scripture must be fulfilled; and then by the fellowship with those whom He loved and who loved God, even if it be so imperfect. Let us look at verses 39 and 42 to see that victory, and to consider how we may defeat the tempter in our own lives.

So many of us in our trials and temptations do not even end where Jesus started in His prayer. In verse 39 He prays for His heart's desire, to be spared the cross, for He had our natural fear of death. Yet even at that point He acknowledges the Father's will as best. Now in verse 42, after an angel has come and ministered to Jesus, according to Luke 22:43, the second prayer time results in His moving beyond consideration of His will, and focusing entirely on the Father's will.

The Father's will, the sense of Sonship, the holiness of the Scripture, these touchstones which have undergirded Jesus' whole life now give Him strength to reach for the cup if the Father so wills. He embraces the Father's will in confidence that regardless of how it seems, that will is best

Handling Our Own Temptations

Gethsemane was the completion of the temptation in the desert. The devil never gave up on Jesus. And he never gives up on us. The devil uses two ways to tempt us: he offers us sinful pleasures which we know are against the will of God, and he urges us to avoid the hardships to which God calls His people. We understand the first type of temptation far better than the second, and the devil is aware of that, too. Our temptation in a country like ours is to put our wills ahead of God's will for us and for our church; to do the easy thing, the expedient thing, the expected thing. He urges us to leave witnessing to the professional; not to mix our religion and our business. He urges us to count all this talk of the devil as foolishness. I would remind you that Satan is not mentioned in the garden scenes of the Gospel narratives, yet he is surely there!

To understand more clearly what Jesus did to win over His last temptation and to experience even a bit of that same power of Holy victory in our lives, we must model our life, our mind, our heart, our prayers after Him.

(1) Be honest with God. About our trials, our temptations, our sins. "If it be possible, let this cup pass. . ."

(2) Put the Father's will above our own. "Nevertheless."

(3) Lean on our Christian friends, even though they fail us. "Tarry ye here, and watch with me."

(4) Keep the Word of God constantly in our hearts and minds. "That the scriptures might be fulfilled."

(5) Be aware of the devil and his unceasing warfare on God's people. "That ye enter not into temptation . . ."

Getting to Know Jesus as Messiah

Matthew 2:1-4; 26:62-63

Hearing of my intention to preach this series of sermons on getting to know Jesus in terms of the emphasis of each of the four Gospels, one fairly new Christian commented: "I'm so glad! I keep wondering what happened to God between the Old and New Testaments! In the New Testament God is kind, forgiving, loving; in the Old Testament he seems a hard, bloodthirsty God. Why the difference?" Has God changed? Has our understanding of God, both in the Bible and since that time, become clearer?

God and the Parade

One person gives this answer. She says that we, and folks in the Bible, see only a part of God's nature and plan. It's like we're standing on the curb watching a parade go by. We can only see the elephant in front of us; we have no way of knowing that two blocks further along the parade turns and goes in another direction. We don't have the whole picture, and until the entire parade passes we really don't know the full nature and character of the parade. How very true! And in the Old Testament, the people saw only a part of God's character and nature—only the part they could relate to and handle. It is not until the full revelation of God's character in Jesus the Messiah that we see what God truly is like. And in the same way, until the Judgement Day, there is no way we who stand at any given point on the passing parade route can really know all the parade was about or where it was going!

But God knows. Said this person, a little person, I might add: "God is standing on top of one of the buildings along the parade route; he can see the whole parade from start to finish. He can see—all in one glance—the part of the parade that has not yet started to move; the part directly in front of us; the part that has already turned the corner five blocks ahead; and the part that has reached the final destination of the parade."

How Can We Get To Know Jesus?

So the only way you and I can get a fullest grasp of who God really is, and what He is like, and what He is doing in this world is to try to understand Jesus. But Jesus is the man nobody knows! Bruce Barton wrote a book some decades ago about Jesus entitled, The Man Nobody Knows. Albert Schweitzer wrote a very important book in theology titled The Quest for the Historical Jesus in which, in a famous quote, he said that Jesus comes to us as one unknown, as he came to the fisherman along the seashore twenty centuries ago.

The problem about getting to know Jesus, and therefore getting to know God, is we can only meet Jesus and come to know him, in one of four ways. First, through what others say about him. What we read in books, see on television and in movies about Jesus, what TV preachers say, etc. What, then, are you saying about Jesus in your daily life? Second, we learn about Jesus through what we read in the Bible. But so many people don't read the Bible, and so many who do read the Bible read only certain parts and speak to it rather than it speaking to them. Third, we can learn about Jesus through the inner testimony of the Holy Spirit. And fourth, we can learn about Jesus by observing the effect he has on people's lives. So, during this month, the morning sermons will deal with getting to know Jesus through what the four Gospels, the four special and unique accounts of his life and ministry and death and resurrection, tell us about him. Let us begin with Matthew's Gospel.

Matthew: Jesus As Messiah

The Gospel of Matthew is the first of the four Gospels as we have them printed in the New Testament. Matthew was the most widely used in the first centuries of the church, and thus became the first in the lineup of the handwritten and printed Bibles. There is a reason why Matthew's Gospel was widely used and listed first. Matthew explains and emphasizes the connection between the Old Testament and the New Testament; between the old covenant and the new covenant; between what is before, behind the Gospels—the Old Testament— and what comes after and since the Gospels—the church.

The amazing message of the early Christians, the unbelievable assertion, the great stumblingblock to many, the depth of foolishness to others, is that Jesus is the long-promised, long-awaited Messiah. The Christ, the Anointed. And this affirmation that Jesus is the Messiah is a special emphasis of Matthew; we will simply mention a few. Matthew begins his gospel with a genealogy in 3 groups of 14 generations, ending with the Messiah, Jesus. When the Magi come to Jerusalem from the east at Jesus' birth, they ask the whereabouts of the one born king of the Jews. Herod in turn asks the scholars where the Messiah is to be born. At Jesus' trial, the high priest asks him if he is the Messiah. Pilate asks the crowd what he should do with this Jesus called the Messiah. As Jesus hangs on the cross, the mockers call him, in derision, the Messiah. What does Matthew, and the early Christians, mean when they speak of the Messiah? Why was there a need for a Messiah? How could they claim this man was the Messiah? What does that mean for you and me twenty centuries later?

The Hope of the Messiah

The entire Old Testament builds to the expectation of the Messiah. The Old Testament presents some strong theology. We can sum it up in a few statements. (1) God created us for fellowship with him, and revealed guidelines and statutes, laws for our benefit and good.

(2) Beginning with the first people, we have spurned fellowship with God and ignored his good commandments. In pride we have leaned upon ourselves, a broken reed, becoming less than God intends, creating guilt and shame, deserving eternal separation from God. (3) God, in mercy, called out Abraham, and through him and his descendents molded a special people and called them to be his servant people through whom God would bless the world. That special nation, called in Abraham, called forth again from Egypt, called as a special treasure to God, turned away from their calling and refused the destiny God intended for them. (4) A remnant of faithful people and prophets remained even as the nation rejected its calling. They reminded the people of God's purpose and promises, including the promise to give them a king like David and restore the glory of that time. (5) This hope of God's intervention in history to rescue Israel and send an "anointed" one, a king like David (kings were anointed) flourished during the oppression of the Exile and the centuries between the Old and New Testaments. It was the hope under the Assyrians, the Babylonians, Greeks and Romans. The pious looked for a Christ, an anointed one, a king, a material and political saviour, a military hero, a worldly ruler like David. That is why many asked John the Baptist if he were the Christ, with his firebrand approach.

(6) But God had a better thing in mind than an earthly king and earthly kingdom, as some of the prophets realized—Isaiah 53, for example. God chose to come into history himself, not as a passing political ruler, but as a Messiah who would set us free from the power and guilt of our sins and give us a sense of worth, hope, peace with God—things money cannot buy and the passing years and political fortunes cannot take away from us. So the looked-for king, Messiah, Christ, Anointed One was not to be a political, but a spiritual Saviour.

The Stumblingblock

Now, what the early Christians were preaching was that Jesus was the long-awaited Messiah. But this is ridiculous! This man Jesus, this carpenter from Nazareth, no wealth, no political power, no education, no strings to pull, this one who at the age of 33 was executed on the charge of sedition and revolution against Rome—this one is the Messiah? This was a stumblingblock to the Jews; there was no way a common, crucified criminal could be the Messiah they had in mind.

But this is exactly the message of Christianity. Matthew underlines with 60 Old Testament quotations that, unlikely as it may seem, this Jesus is the fulfillment of prophecy. Matthew emphasizes that this man Jesus is the long-awaited Messiah; born of a virgin, the Son of David, the lawgiver who is greater than Moses, above the Old Testament Law, worthy of homage from kings who come from the corners of the earth to worship him at his birth, that he was God in human form and flesh, that he was crucified, suffered and died for our sins, that he was raised from the grave after three days. That all who will accept him as Messiah, as Lord and Saviour, will find peace with God and a full, meaningful life.

A Messiah Who Fulfills

The keynote of Matthew's Gospel is that Jesus, the Messiah, came to fulfill, not to destroy. He came to fulfill the Old Testament, to give us a fuller, clearer picture of the character of God the father. He came to fulfill the intention of God for you and me; he came to fulfill our finest potential. Don't you need a Messiah, a Saviour? All around us we see a world without a Saviour, without a purpose, without a hope. We see all around us violence and crime. There is no respect for life, no self-respect, no demarcation between what is right and wrong, what builds up and what destroys. We desperately need a Messiah. And money, sex, drugs, guns—none of these are Messiahs. None of these can fill the void in our life, the unrealized yearning for forgiveness of sins, for peace with God, for a sense of purpose.

Jesus is the Messiah we need. He is here, in our world, within your reach. Would you accept him as your Messiah? Can you reach out with your heart and mind beyond the stumblingblocks of twenty centuries and claim him as your personal Messiah? Will you accept the forgiveness and peace and possibilities he will bring into your life?

Jesus as the Man of Prayer

Luke 11:1

What is the hardest thing you ever tried to do? Get the attention of that special boy or girl when you were in the seventh grade? Make a speech before a crowd? Lose weight? Stop smoking or drinking? For many Christians, when we really get honest, perhaps the hardest thing we ever tried to do is to develop a deep, ongoing, genuine prayer life.

How much time do you spend in prayer each day? Do you know how to pray? Do you know what prayer is? Have you experienced the power of prayer? Do you know the fellowship, the comfort—and sometimes discomfort of genuine prayer? None of us, in our best moments, can say we are graduates of the school of prayer. Today we look at Jesus as the man of prayer. We should note that Luke has more references to Jesus' prayer life and to Jesus' teaching about prayer than any other gospel. I have made a study of Jesus' practice and teaching of prayer in the four gospels; and I urge that you make such a study.

Teach Us To Pray

Let's turn to Luke 11:1 and put ourselves in the place of the disciples. "And it came to pass, that, as he was praying in a certain place, when he ceased, one of his disciples said unto him, Lord, teach us to pray, as John also taught his disciples." This is an interesting situation. I can easily imagine the disciples asking Jesus to teach them how to turn stones into bread, or how to raise the dead—but we never hear them asking that; rather they ask Jesus to teach them how to pray! They made this request as Jesus was ending a time of prayer one day. What do you suppose prompted this request? Was it something they heard during his prayers? Was it something they saw as they watched him? Had they been talking with the Baptist's disciples? ("Teach us to pray, as John taught his disciples").

In any case, they are right where 99% of us are! Prayer is a vague mystery in our generation, in our society. There are so many definitions of prayer floating around—prayer is talking to yourself, talking to nature, talking to God. Conflicting aims are set forth for the practice of prayer. Is it a tool to get what you want? Or is the purpose of prayer to put you in tune with yourself or God? Is prayer a natural conversation with God, the Creator?

Let us lay aside the muddled New Age views floating around, and go to the Bible itself, and to Jesus, the greatest practitioner of prayer ever to walk this earth. Let's look at two areas: Jesus' own example in prayer; and Jesus' teaching on prayer. As we start, let me position myself by saying that I have seen the power of genuine prayer. I have been there on occasions when I or others truly laid hold on the hem of his garment. But neither I nor anyone else understands all the dynamics of prayer; it is far more powerful than any of us realize. And finally, I know that I want my prayer life deepened; the plea of the disciples is my plea: "Lord, teach me to pray." Perhaps you join me in that plea, so let's look at Jesus' practice and his teaching about prayer.

Jesus' Practice Of Prayer

If we analyze the references in the gospels to the personal prayer life of Jesus, we can put down on paper some helpful guides for our own devotional life. First, he often withdrew to spend time in prayer. He went aside into the desert; he went up into the mountain. All three synoptic gospels mention how he would go away alone, get up before dawn, in order to have time to pray.

This may be the crux of the matter for us. We eagerly rush to sign up for the latest seminar on prayer; to buy the latest book on prayer—but we feel we just haven't got the time for regular, extended prayer times. Are we busier than Jesus? The answer is probably, Yes. But is what we rush around doing more important than what he did? No. I am sure the disciples sometimes found themselves saying, "Where is Jesus now?" "Oh, he's off praying somewhere." No, it's not necessarily Judas who would say that; just someone who knew they needed to be at a certain place that evening, or knew someone was waiting for them . . . You and I let those things that are most pressing and urgent take precedence over those things which are more important. I am personally haunted by two thoughts: the example of Jesus whose secret of power was prayer; and the comment of Martin Luther that unless he spent several hours each day in prayer, he did not have enough time to get everything done.

Jesus Prayed At Meals

Consider some of the specific occasions when we are told Jesus prayed. He prayed at meals, thanking the father for the gift of food. He blessed the food at the feeding of the 5,000 and the 4,000, and even at the last supper when the shadow of betrayal and death fell over the little group, Jesus still remembered to have the blessing for the food. It is such a simple thing—to thank God for the food he has provided; but do you do that in your home?

Jesus Prayed For His Friends

Jesus prayed for his friends when they were in trouble. In Luke 22, as Jesus tells the twelve what is about to happen and Peter makes his rash vow of total support, Jesus then tells Peter "I have prayed for you, that your faith fail not . . ." I think that is the highest compliment ever paid to a mortal man—Jesus telling this bold, brash, stumbling, bumbling,

Jesus as the Man of Prayer

bragging disciple whose walk will never match his talk, that he, the Maker of heaven and earth, is praying specifically for him! If Jesus prayed for his friends in their hour of trial, should you and I not pray more for our friends when we know they are going through a tough time? Let us develop in this church a deep habit of praying for each other in tough times; praying by name and by need.

It is wonderful to see that Jesus prayed not just for his friends around him in the first century, but that he prayed for folks like you and me twenty centuries down the road. Jesus, praying at the last supper, said "I pray not for these [the disciples] alone, but for them who shall believe on me through their word" (John 17:20). Do you and I spend time praying for those who are not Christians today, but will become believers in Jesus and followers of his? If Jesus did it, it is important for us to do. We spend more time praying to keep sick saints out of heaven than we do praying lost people into heaven! Begin this day to pray earnestly and faithfully for someone who is not yet a follower of Christ.

Jesus Prayed In The Good Times

Then we are told Jesus prayed after spiritual victories. After the wonderful miracle of the loaves; after the 70 disciples are sent out two by two and come back with wonderful stories of victory—Jesus prayed and thanked the Father for the victory. Is it not true that most of us pray in the tough times while letting the victories stand on their own, or else we congratulate ourselves!

Jesus Prayed In The Bad Times

Then we see that Jesus prayed in the darkest moments of his life as well as in the joyful times. In the garden of Gethsemane he prayed in great agony with sweat drops like blood. On the cross he prayed—and what prayers they were! He was honest with the Father, and expressed his sense of desolation in prayer: "My God, my God, why have you forsaken me?" From the cross he prayed for his enemies, for they did not know what they were doing, he said. At the end he committed his soul into the hands of the Father and died on the cross. So in hard times, in the garden and on the cross, his prayers radiated honesty, pleas for strength, commitment to the Father's will, forgiveness for his enemies, and at the end, he turned loose of this life in trust and let the Father catch him. May our prayers in our dark hours be the same.

Jesus' Teaching About Prayer

We sing, More like Jesus would I be. One definite step, the most important step, to becoming more like Jesus is to imitate his example in prayer. Now let us turn from his example to his teaching on prayer.

Prayer Is Conversation And Fellowship

First, Jesus emphasized what prayer really is. He said prayer is conversation, communication, clarification and fellowship with the Father. He said prayer is not for show, and urged us to go into our "closet," [a quaint King James idea] which means to go aside to a quiet, undisturbed place for private prayer. But the private prayer will have public results, he says. He warns us that prayer is not a way of persuading or controlling or telling God how good we are. The story of the publican and the pharisee who go up to pray make that clear. Nor will we be heard for our long, repetitious prayers that say the same thing over and over.

Prayer Clarifies Our Commitment

Prayer is conversation with God that clarifies and deepens our commitment to him. Jesus gave the disciples the Lord's Prayer as a model—not necessarily of words, but of the thrust of our prayers. And this model prayer emphasizes our relationship to God, our aim to honor God and seek his will, our relationship to other people, and our trust in God to take care of us. Now some people, when it comes to prayer, simply open their Bibles to verses like Matthew 21:22 "And all things, whatsoever you shall ask in prayer, believing, you shall receive." And they wonder why they didn't get the job, the money, the husband or wife, etc. for which they prayed. Our problem is that we separate the promise of answered prayer from the context out of which answered prayer must come. If we pray out of the relationship to our Father; wanting his will above all else; seeking his kingdom not ours—then, surely, whatever we ask for will be given. We may say that Jesus prayed in the garden to escape the cross, and he did; but that prayer was surrounded by the prayer, "Not my will, but thine."

God Wants To Answer Prayer

The second great emphasis of Jesus' teaching on prayer is that he urges us, over and over, to pray because God wants to answer the prayers of his children. Jesus told several stories about prayer in which he contrasted God's willingness to help us with our unwillingness to help others. In the story of the friend at midnight in Luke 11, Jesus says we answer a friend's plea because it is inconvenient not to do so, but God wants to hear us! In that same chapter he contrasts how even we sinful and evil parents give our kids the food they need—God is good and loving, and wants to give us gifts. In Luke 18, in the story of the unjust judge, Jesus points out how the unjust judge did what was right because of the nagging woman who would not go away—he contrasts that with our heavenly Father who is just and loving!

Jesus tells us God wants to answer our prayers. He wants to give us a full and abundant life. When we stand back and realize God's goodness and love, and his desire to bless us; why wouldn't we pray more? The answer: we would rather try to bless ourselves through our own possessions, through our own busy, overworked and harried efforts than to call on God in a spirit of obedience and trust him to guide our life and bless us. And that attitude is called sin in the Bible.

Jesus came saying our heavenly Father loves us; he wants to bless us. And our Father has gone to the unexplainable and unfathomable extent of Jesus dying on the cross for our sins, in order to bless us. Let's respond to such love by living a life of powerful prayer. And a life of prayer begins with the prayer of confession, as we confess our sins and repent, and invite Jesus of Nazareth to be the Lord of our life.

The Gift of Kindness

Matthew 5:43-48; Ephesians 4:17-32

They tell of the Sunday Phillips Brooks' congregation poured out the doors and folks who had not spoken in years smiled and greeted each other. They discovered it was what they had really wanted to do all along, and were astonished to find out how much they enjoyed doing it! How did this amazing event happen? Well, the part of Brooks' sermon that gets quoted runs like this: "You who are letting miserable misunderstandings run on from year to year . . .you who are keeping wretched quarrels alive because you cannot sacrifice your pride and kill them. . . You who let your friend's heart ache for a word of appreciation or sympathy, which you mean to give someday. . . if you only could know and see and feel, all of a sudden that "the time is short," how it would break the spell! Then you would go instantly and do the thing which you might never have another chance to do." The catalyst for that congregation was the realization that the time we have for love, for kindness, is short. Ralph Waldo Emerson said it this

The Gift of Kindness

way: "You can never do a kindness too soon, for you never know how soon it will be too late."

Why is it that all of us are derelict in doing the kind thing, saying the kind word? We can identify with the comment one Boy Scout said to another: "Do you ever have days when you feel just a little untrustworthy, disloyal, unhelpful, unfriendly, discourteous, unkind, grumpy, wasteful, cowardly, dirty and irreverent?" Most days seem like that! The world has never had too much kindness! George Bush's dream of a kinder, gentler world has always been just that; a dream.

> *So many gods, so many creeds,*
> *So many paths that wind and wind,*
> *While just the art of being kind*
> *Is all the sad world needs.*
>
> Ella Wilcox

And who has not heard these beautiful words: "I shall pass through this world but once. Any good therefore that I can do, or any kindness that I can show to any human being, let me do it now. Let me not defer nor neglect it, for I shall not pass this way again." King George V of England kept it, copied in his own hand, framed on his desk. And Dale Carnegie used to call commitment to kindness one of the basic requirements for happiness in life. Now the reason a world of kindness is only a dream is that the world cannot create kindness; it can only accept it, and pass it on. Kindness is a flower that blooms in the garden of the church, and is passed on to the world. For kindness was born in the heart of God: "With everlasting kindness will I have mercy on thee, saith the Lord thy Redeemer" (Isaiah 54:8).

Paul's Heart-to-Heart Talk on Kindness

There is an interesting and most relevant Scripture on kindness; let us turn to Ephesians 4, verses 17 and following. Here Paul, speaking to the church, talks about kindness. Note the context. In verse 17 he urges them to walk no more as the pagans, in emptiness of mind. In verse 20 Paul reminds them, "You have not so learned Christ." In verse 22 we are told to put off the "old man" and put on the "new man" in Christ. This means, according to the following verses, that we speak truth, let not the sun go down on wrath, give no room for the devil to operate, work so you can give to the needy, speak only what is edifying, don't grieve the Holy Spirit, don't speak bitter, angry, clamoring words, and finally, be kind to each other. There are several truths about kindness in this passage.

Our Kindness is Imitation of God

The very fact that Paul feels the need to remind church members to be kind to one another is a rebuke to all Christians' forgetfulness to be kind! Yet our kindness is part of our imitation of God, to which Jesus calls us in the Sermon on the Mount. In the very next verse after Paul urges us to be kind, he admonishes us to imitate God. Now, our nursery workers see how children imitate their parents all the time; and just so we are to imitate our heavenly Father. Our kindness is not to be based on the Golden Rule: "Do unto others as you would have them do unto you," but rather on the God Rule: "Do unto others as God would do . . ." Pagans can rise above self-interest and be kind, but the spring of their kindness is that self-interest, and so the source of his kindness can dry up. The nature of the kind spirit of the Christian is not so; his kindness is rooted in the kindness of God which we've experienced in Jesus, accepting, forgiving, loving, guiding us.

So Christian kindness is passing on a gift of God, His kindness in the Gospel. This means that our kindness to Christian and non-Christian, like that of God, has no strings attached. Remember what Jesus said in Matthew 5: "For He makes His sun to rise on the evil and on the good, and sends rain on the just and on the unjust." No strings attached. Our kindness is not designed to get us brownie points with God. The church is not a mutual benefit club. This leads me to a growing concern I have about Christians. More and more, Christians seem to be asking the church, "What's in it for me?" If I join the church, if I give my tithe, if I teach Sunday School, if I cooperate with the pastor and

The Gift of Kindness

staff, if I do good deeds, what's in it for me? What a sub-Christian attitude! We are saved to serve, to glorify God, to do the kind thing and say the kind word, not for our gain but because that is our nature as we imitate God!

Kindness and Longsuffering

Now let me point out a linkage between kindness and long-suffering. In the great Love Chapter of 1 Corinthians, Paul says in the same breath, "love suffers long, and is kind . . ." And in 2 Corinthians 6:6 Paul says we show ourselves approved" by pureness, by knowledge, by longsuffering by kindness . . ." Just as not all kindness will be repaid, just so we are not to expect it to be, and we are to be prepared to be patient, and to be misused. Jesus would tell us that if we are commanded to go a mile and we offer to go the second, at the end of that we may be expected to go a third, rather than being thanked! Yet we are still to be kind.

The Power of Kindness

There is, however, great power in passing on the kindness we have received from God. For in the Christian's word or deed of kindness is a bit of God's nature, character, love, and grace. And that is why kindness has the power to put men back on their feet, and give them hope. Oscar Wilde was a renowned author in Victorian England, and his way of life matched his name. He was on one occasion sent to prison and later was converted. He later wrote of a friend who waited in the courtroom corridor, and before the whole crowd of spectators who were hushed by the deed, gravely raised his hat to Oscar as the criminal went by in handcuffs and bowed head. Said Oscar Wilde, ". . . it was in this spirit, and with this mode of love, that the saints knelt down to wash the feet of the poor, or stooped to kiss the leper on the cheek. I have never said one single word to him about what he did. I do not know to the present moment whether he is aware that I was even conscious of his action. I store it in the treasure-house of my heart. I keep it there as a secret debt that I am glad to think I can never possibly repay. When wisdom has been profitless to me, philosophy barren, and the proverbs and phrases of those who have sought to give me consolation as dust and ashes in my mouth, the memory of that little, lovely silent act of love has . . . brought me out of the bitterness of lonely exile."

Wasn't it strange for Wilde to remember that simple act of tipping the hat? Not really, for you and I can pull out of the closet of our memory just such simple deeds and simple words of kindness which at this point or that in our life kept us on our feet, or lifted us up when we had fallen.

Kindness also has the power to mend fences. Distrust, hurt feelings, misunderstandings can melt away with a kind word, a sweet, unexpected deed. And the power to mend hearts that are broken. For instance, at our regular Thursday Bible Luncheon last week, a lady who was not a member of our church was graciously complimenting me for an act of kindness. It had to do with a funeral I had conducted for a relative of hers, a person I did not know. She was very helped and comforted by two facts, she said: I had come to the home immediately after learning of the death, wearing a sport shirt, which made her feel I was very "human," and then at the graveside, since the day was bitterly cold, I had simply said I would be brief, since they should not be out in the cold. Those simple words and actions came across to her as kindness, and indeed, I was trying to imitate our Heavenly Father.

Perhaps it would help us all to remember that our acts of Christian kindness, done with no thought of reimbursement, point to someone behind us. And that One behind us may not be quickly seen, but let us labor on, sowing the seed, and it will bear fruit. For instance, let me share a letter I received in my first pastorate at Marianna, Florida, over 20 years ago:

Dear Brother:

Why does it take 28 years to do something that should be done? This is something I have intended to do for a long, long time. Perhaps it

The Gift of Kindness

will stir your memory. In January, 1941, I was hitch-hiking through Marianna, a young fellow 21 years old. I was stranded and broke, and not knowing what else to do, sought the Baptist church. You and your wife very generously gave me a place to sleep, and breakfast the next morning. Your labor was not in vain in the Lord. I was not a Christian at that time, but on Easter Sunday, 1943 I received the Lord Jesus Christ as my personal Saviour. God has graciously allowed me to be used of Him in witnessing, writing, and speaking, and has given me a wonderful helpmate.

God bless you and your wife, wherever you are ministering now. Your name may be forgotten, but your kindness is not. Your practical commentary on the Scripture, "As we have therefore opportunity, let us do good unto all men," was greater than a sermon of words.

> *Sincerely in Christ,*
> *Carter Bundy*
> *April 16, 1969*

How Can We Show Kindness?

It sounds so simple, but kindness has to be worked at. We say kindness ought to be "second nature," and that's exactly right and that's why kindness is so scarce! Our first nature is to be self-serving, and our second nature is to act like Jesus, and that is not always easy for us. Go back to our Scripture text in Ephesians 4. Again, let us notice that Paul is talking to the church. How can we start showing kindness to our fellow church-members? We can speak the truth to our fellow church members (25). We can refuse to let the devil have any opportunity to use differences of opinion (26-27). We show kindness by refusing to gossip (31) just as earlier we refuse to lie (25). We can "minister grace" to each other by speaking encouraging and upbuilding words. We can be tender-hearted toward one another (32), which means being emotionally positive about each other. We can show kindness by accepting people as they are, and loving them anyway!

That's what Jesus did. And last, we can forgive one another (32). Is that asking a lot? It is only asking that we imitate Jesus!

Remember that little poem:

> *Drop a pebble in the water,*
> *And its ripples reach out far;*
> *And the sunbeams dancing on them*
> *May reflect them to a star.*
>
> *Give a smile to someone passing,*
> *Thereby making his morning glad;*
> *It may greet you in the evening*
> *When your own heart may be sad.*
>
> *Do a deed of simple kindness;*
> *Though its end you may not see,*
> *It may reach, like widening ripples,*
> *down a long eternity.*
>
> Joseph Norris

But don't wait too long to give that smile or speak that kind word or do that deed of simple kindness. A group of ladies were discussing the philosophy of "Live each day as if it were your last." "Well," said the sweetest old lady of the group, "that's a fine saying, but for 20 years I've been using a philosophy that's a little different. It's this: "Treat all the people you meet each day as though it were their last day on earth." Why not try that, seriously and consciously, just for this coming week?

The kindness we share is a kindness we echo from God. We read in Holy Scripture and we sing the truth that "in loving kindness Jesus came, my soul in mercy to reclaim . . . " And He is here today in kindness and mercy to call you from darkness to light, from wrong to right, from death to life.

The Law of the Echo

Malachi 3:7-10; Luke 6:38

Theft and robbery is a growing problem in our nation and in our city. The US Chamber of Commerce says industry loses $40 billion a year through white collar crime. That's the kind of theft you do without a gun. In Memphis there is a robbery every two and one-half hours.

Theft: Memphis Style

A bit of research turned up some unusual robberies last year in our city. For example, ten huge historical markers were stolen; whatever for? And then there was the man arrested by the FBI in Memphis for stealing secrets and trying to sell them to Russia. And there was the theft of the gorilla from behind the wheel of a yellow VW! The imitation ape was regularly parked by a novelty shop to get attention. And then there was the theft of a Barbecue cooker—not your everyday backyard type, mind you; this one took three years to build, weighed 3500 lbs, and the thieves must have hooked it up to a truck and hauled it off! The upset owner, Greg Gang, lamented "I just don't see how anybody could enjoy having a good barbecue on a stolen cooker." Said Deanie Parker, Marketing Director of Memphis in May, "That really gets to a man's soul, messing with his cooker!"

Theft: Church Style

No, Deanie, there's another kind of theft that really gets to a man's soul; it's the theft that goes on in churches. But I don't mean the stealing of VCRs and purses from unguarded rooms; though we have plenty of that. In 1989 we had 146 church burglaries in Memphis. John Bennett, administrative assistant to Memphis Police Director Ivy said, "There's no longer anything sacred about religious institutions. The sad reality is that burglars no longer respect the sanctity of a church. Today, a church is just another house." Shucks, Mr. Bennett, the Bible has been telling us for 2500 years that some folks will steal from the church! Police Director Ivy says, "Our goal [in crime prevention seminars] is to make religious leaders more aware of crime and how to prevent it. Then, they can pass this on to their congregations."

Well, that's exactly what I want to talk about with you who are members of First Baptist Church: how to prevent church theft because more theft goes on between 11 o'clock and noon in our churches than all the other theft in town put together!

Theft As Malachi Sees It

Remember the last children's sermon when I asked the children the question in our text: Will a man rob God? Were you as touched by their swift response as I was? With one small voice they all answered, "No-o-o!" The little children in one family asked their parents on the way home about that verse again; it was shocking to them that people would rob God! Yet our text tells us many folks do just that! Now Malachi 3:10 is more than a springboard for a sermon on tithing. Consider the context of the verse, for it is a symptom of a far greater spiritual problem.

Malachi was the last of the writing prophets; his message is the seal, the signature, the caboose of the Old Testament. Yet we know very

The Law of the Echo

little about the prophet. We are not even sure the word Malachi is a proper name; it literally means messenger, and may merely mean that instead of a person's name. What final message did he hurl into that 300 year silence between the Old and the New Testaments?

He begins his message with the assurance of God's love. Indeed, this affirmation is his very first words. But the love of God is treated by God's people as dirt under their feet! They dare question God Himself!

How have you loved us? How have we despised your name? How have we polluted your house? How have we wearied you? How have we robbed you? What have we said against you? Why don't you accept the offering we do bring? Such "backtalk" to God, scattered throughout the Book, is sheer blasphemy!

The prophet sketches their religious practices and habits: (1) you offer polluted sacrifices. They brought the sick, the blind, the lame animals to offer God as a sacrifice (1:7-8). Try offering that to the IRS, says the prophet! (2) You say it is a drag to serve the Lord. It wasn't exciting to their carnal spirit to serve and worship God (1:13). (3) You cast aside the sacred bond of marriage Divorce was a way of life for many of God's people (2:10f). (4) You weary God with your empty words. Apparently they made many promises and vows to God which they had no intention of keeping (2:17). (5) You say God really won't judge us. They felt God was non-resident; that He was looking the other way and did not see them (2:17). (6) You say it isn't worthwhile to serve God. There's no future in it! (3:14).

But the final insult to God and the prophet's rebuke to the people involves their dishonesty with the tithe (3:7f). And if you put all this in the light of 1:6-7, we see where the prophet is coming from: these are not folks from off the street; these are chosen children of God the Father! And where is the obedience and reverence and honor to which He is entitled? Malachi stresses a simple truth that blesses us wonderfully when we take it seriously: God honors those who honor Him.

Many of us were moved and blessed by the movie about Eric Liddell, Chariots of Fire, relating his religious faith and his magnificent win in the 1924 Olympics. Just before he went onto the track for the 400 metres final, he was given a note by the masseur of the British team. It simply said, "In the Old Book it says, 'He that honors me will I honor.' Wishing you the best of success always." The reference is to 1 Samuel 2:30. And it is so very true: God honors those who honor Him. If you will honor God, the echo comes back! That's what Malachi is saying to his people, and that's what I want to say to you today.

Malachi's Challenge

Malachi, on behalf of God, issues to the people a challenge. You know, the prophets were often doing that. We suck in our breath when Elijah, on Mount Carmel, issues to the people gathered there a challenge: call down fire on the sacrifice and the altar! We lift our eyebrows when he has water poured on his offering to soak it, then calls down lightning from the sky! But folks, here in Malachi 3:10 we find an equally tremendous challenge, and this time it is to the people of God!

A command is attached to Malachi's challenge: bring ye all the tithes into the storehouse. Unless we are willing to do this, we cannot receive the fullness of His blessing. First, *notice that it is the tithe Malachi commands we bring.* Literally, the text says the whole tithe, and most scholars feel the prophet is calling for the proper spirit behind the tithe. The tithe is one tenth of our income. It is proportionate; everyone can do it, from the widow to the millionaire. Our problem is that too many of God's children use the same principle in figuring the tithe that they use in paying their taxes: to give as little as possible. But the tithe is a response of joy, love, and gratitude. A person who tithes from gratitude does not see how far he can whittle down his income before figuring the tithe!

I remember the story of the young man who knelt with his pastor and promised to honor God with the tithe of his income. At the time he was making very little money. But the years passed, he prospered, and one day he came back to the pastor with a problem: the amount of his tithe was simply more than he felt he could give to the church! What could be done? The pastor told him there was no way to change the Biblical command to tithe, but they could get on their knees and ask God to reduce his income to a figure that he could comfortably tithe again!

Second, *Malachi commands us to bring the tithe into the storehouse, the church.* The tithe of your income belongs to God through the local church of which you are a member. I want to testify to the worthiness of the programs and ministries of this local church; I urge upon you the need of this church; sometimes I feel deeply the old adage that the shoemaker's children have no shoes, when I discover how you support so many fine Christian endeavors outside the church and let your own staff ministers labour without adequate funds for programs and ministries. I believe that as a member of this church, you have a responsibility to give the tithe here. If we are not honest in the support of this storehouse by the tithe, we will not long remain able to stand strong amid the darkness at home, nor send spiritual food around the globe.

Third, *let us notice the challenge, or the proposition Malachi puts to us. The prophet urges the people to test God!* Now, we know the Scripture tells us not to test our God, but here we have the prophet doing that, and I believe this is an area in which God would be pleased if you tested Him, too. For in light of the context of this challenge, we see that the prophet is urging the people to enlarge their view of God. And that is what tithing is all about: the reality of God in our life. No man ever feels deeply about the reality and presence of God in his life and yet refuses to tithe. The man to whom God is real as His Saviour, Lord, and Benefactor has no problem with the tithe, once he understands it is commanded in Scripture.

Now, if Malachi's challenge to tithe sounds legalistic, remember a couple of things: (1) refusal to give the tithe to the Lord is a symptom of a spiritual problem, i.e. the reality of God in his life. And (2) There is no more practical way to show our return to God, and the reality of God in our life, than by tithing.

Can you see the prophet hurling out this challenge to tithe to the complacent congregation gathered before him? Folks who had a spiritual problem: God was not real to them. Folks who desperately needed to return to God. I would do the same today. I would dare you, challenge you, urge you, plead with you to test God by giving the tithe to Him through this storehouse.

Finally note the promise attached to the challenge. It is described three ways: I will open the windows of heaven. Remember that heaven's windows, as G. Campbell Morgan says, swing on love's hinges. God wants to open the windows of heaven! Second, I will pour you out a blessing. Who this morning does not desire, need, want a blessing from God! Is not that part of the reason we are here? And third, there will not be enough room to receive it! My, how that reminds me of Luke 6:38: "Give, and it shall be given unto you; good measure, pressed down, and shaken together, and running over, shall men give into your bosom. For with the same measure that ye mete withal it shall be measured to you again." And Psalm 37:25: "I have been young, and now am old; yet have I not seen the righteous forsaken, nor his seed begging bread."

Brethren, I am trying to persuade you who do not tithe to begin to do so today. Do it as an act of love and gratitude, and as surely as night follows day there will be a spiritual echo of blessing! God wants to bless us! Let Him do it!

A Lion on a Leash

I Peter 5:8-9

I'd like to scare you to death in the sermon this morning, so to speak. I'd like to have you go away this morning realizing that the Devil is more real than you think, more powerful and deadly than you think, more involved in our society and our individual lives than you think, and more vulnerable than you think. One of our secretaries summed it up pretty well when she looked at the title of the sermon, A Lion on a Leash, and asked me, Is that the same as a Tiger by the Tail? I reckon that's about it!

Images of the Devil

To get a picture of the Devil we must start at the end of the Bible, not at the front. In the book of Revelation we see the Devil as an enraged dragon, seeking to devour the brothers and sisters of Christ. That's you and me. He is called the slanderer. Ever been slandered? Hurts. Paul says we must put on spiritual armor to against the Devil and his hosts, for this is a spiritual battle. Peter says the Devil is a roaring lion, pacing and stalking, seeking whom he may destroy. The Devil even sought to lead Jesus astray, so why on earth would any of us think the Devil is afraid of us? In the parable of the tares, Jesus says the Devil sows the sons of the Devil. In the parable of the sower, Jesus says the Devil takes away the seed of faith from people's hearts. Jesus tells us that hell itself was prepared as a final disposal for the Devil and his followers. Judas shows us how the Devil puts things into our hearts, and Paul warns us on several occasions not to give the Devil an opportunity to control us. Paul speaks of the snares of the Devil, and Jesus even saw Satan in Simon Peter. Peter shows us how Satan gets into churches and church members when he accuses Ananias of letting Satan use him in the early church. This world, we read, is the kingdom, the dominion of Satan. And we also read that Jesus, dying on the cross, broke the power of the Devil, who holds us all bondage in fear of death. And James urges us to resist the Devil, and he will flee from us.

Folks, just think of someone who dislikes you, who is very angry at you, who wants to do you in—at work, at church, perhaps even in the family? It's not a light thing, is it? Then how come we do not take the Devil seriously? For he is like that person multiplied by a thousand.

Through these past twenty centuries the reality of the Devil has been apparent. St. Anthony out in the desert experienced how the Devil could tempt him and come to him in the form of a young woman. In the Middle Ages there was great emphasis on the final effort the Devil would make when a person was on their death bed, to secure the lost soul. And the Devil's victory was seen in the macabre Dance of Death depicted in paintings, as the Devil, leading his captives, wound their way over the hills to hell. Martin Luther could see the Devil in his study, and he even threw the inkwell at him one time. Most of us are familiar with Goethe's *Faustus*, the story of a man who sold his soul to the devil. But in the last couple of centuries the reality of the Devil has faded. Folks take the idea of the soul lightly, and even try to auction it off on the Internet. That's right, I read of a case in which a man tried to auction his soul on e-bay. The folks behind e-bay withdrew that auction on the grounds that if the soul doesn't exist, it cannot be auctioned, and if it does exit, then it comes under that site's prohibition of auctioning body parts!

Our problem as we stand in the doorway of the 21st century, is that the rise of the scientific view and the psychological approach has cast out the Devil. He has been debunked by scholars and relegated to being the mascot of football teams. And the Devil laughs. We are more religious than ever before; we create our own concept of God, a kind, loving deity who looks like us, has our values and bless what we bless. And the Devil laughs. We create our own moral system; nothing is right or wrong in itself—right and wrong depend on whether it clashes with my thinking. And the Devil laughs. We have redefined sin; it has nothing to do with God and his moral law. Sin is to be politically incorrect, to draw a line on what a moral person should tolerate, and to refuse to embrace all religions as equal. And the Devil laughs.

And so the first point I want to make is now made: the Devil is real. And his energy and his force is directed against the Christian and against the church. Luther was fond of saying that God builds the church and the Devil builds the chapel. The term Church Militant is not an empty phrase. The church is in constant spiritual warfare against the Devil. He is not spending his energy on those who already smirk at the law of God, those who already scorn the narrow way. They are already his. Our biggest danger is to take the Devil lightly. I read just this past week of a pet tiger that bit the arm off of a little boy. Just when you think the Devil is tame, he'll bite your arm off. Listen to Peter on this and believe him!

How the Devil Works

Let me say a word about how the Devil works, remembering that he has only the power in our lives that we give him. I see him at work in three clear ways. *First, he twists our thinking.* It is the Devil who urges church members to focus on our individual rights, to guard legalism, to fall back in the face of enthusiasm. It is the Devil that tells us in the school and the marketplace that if nobody sees it; it isn't wrong. It is the Devil who says just a little bit won't make a difference. It is the Devil who plants the idea in our head that the worse sin is to not tolerate as equal every squirrelly religion.

Second, the Devil uses things that happen to us as a church family and as individuals. He will try to get us to interpret things that happen in the way most contrary to God's will. He will always try to make us negative and blame God for things that happen to us.

The third way the Devil gets to us is to appeal to our self-interests. It is the Devil who tells us to look out for number one; he tells us to insist on our way. He appeals to our greed and lust. These are a fire which he feeds. It's the Devil who always tells us we need a little more.

Let me give you some ways to tell if the Devil is in something you want to do. *First, when it looks good and feels good, but is against the law of God. Second, when it affects your spiritual growth in a negative way. Third, when it does not build up the church. Fourth, when the result will not be a positive witness to Jesus.* Look through those lenses when you have an opportunity to cheat on a test or on your wife, to do drugs and sex, to gamble away the paycheck, to gossip and slander other folks, to draw back from the challenge of faith, to water down your biblical convictions to be in style with the gang.

Hear it again: the Devil is deadly serious about destroying you (physically and spiritually), destroying your Christian witness, destroying your church. And he will do it by twisting your thinking, by using things that happen to you, and by appealing to your self-interest. You may say this thing is against the will and law of God, and the Devil will have your friend say, But isn't it fun. It won't hurt anybody.

Withstanding the Devil

But I must hurry on and speak of how we as Christians can withstand the snare, the wiles, the strategy, the fiery darts of the Devil. Look first at Ephesians 6 and the image of the armor of God. All the parts of the

A Lion on a Leash

armor—salvation, God's Word, faith—these are all part and parcel of our total relationship with God. What he is saying is that if we are to successfully do battle with Satan, we must have *a genuine relationship with God* and use it in our spiritual fight with Satan. Stand always, like the little child who stands between his father's knees and looks out at the stranger; with our back to God (and close to him) and our face toward the enemy.

Second, we resist the Devil by *remembering that the attacks of the Devil are a common experience of all Christians.* (1 Peter 5:9). In fact, this is one of the reasons we ought to take off our masks in small groups of fellow believers and in other appropriate settings and gain strength from each other in our struggle with temptation.

Third, our resistance to the Devil will be strengthened by *remembering that Jesus is praying for us.* Remember how Jesus told Peter at the last supper that Satan wanted to grind Peter up, but that Jesus was praying for Peter. What a powerful image that is! The battle is serious and fierce, and Jesus is praying for you and me. Do we pray for each other like we should? If Jesus prays for us in our struggle with the Devil, shouldn't we pray for each other? Fourth, we will fight the Devil more successfully if we keep our eyes on Jesus, and remember that he is stronger than Satan. As Luther says, a mighty fortress is our God! And last, we must remember that Christians are "overcomers." All through the book of Revelation the Christians are called the conquerors, the "overcomers" who have defeated the Devil. Our destiny is to be victorious in the spiritual battle. Along this line we ought to read again Pilgrim's Progress.

Now I must close by speaking a word about the future of the Devil. The simple truth is that he doesn't have a future. That's why he is so angry—the book of Revelation says that the Devil is so angry because he know his time is running out. A good analogy to the Devil is seen, I think, in Hitler in the last days of the Second World War. There he was, in his cage of a bunker underground in Berlin. The ring was closing, the lion was surrounded, yet he breathed out slaughterings and death to innocent people, terrible in his insane fury. I think that's the way the Devil is in these days. And no matter how long the world will stand, we are in those last days in which the Devil, crazed with rage and fear of God and hatred for the church, does his worst.

The Bible says that at the end of this world the Devil will be thrown into a lake of fire and destroyed. That day cannot come too soon! For the Devil turns family member against family member, church member against church member; the Devil lures people to eternal punishment in hell.

One of the stock gestures in horror movies with vampires, etc. is the holding of a cross before the evil one. That's the way to final victory over the Devil. Can you hold the cross before the Devil? Is Jesus the Crucified your Lord?

The Naming of a Mystery

I Corinthians 11:23-26

A Communion Sermon

My early memories of the Lord's Supper—for so it was called in my little Baptist world—are of a pastor in a dark suit standing by the side of the table in front of the pulpit. Sitting at the side of the table was an obviously uncomfortable layman, the deacon chairman. The organ is playing *Here At Thy Table, Lord*, and now the two men rise and begin to lift and fold the snowy white linen cloth that has been covering the trays of grape juice and the plates of broken pieces of hard cracker. The entire congregation watches this procedure as if it were a part of the sacred story.

It was only later that I came to realize this ritual of folding the cloth—and indeed, the using of the white cloth over the elements—was related to the flies that used to be a pest before air-conditioning and window screens and not to the gospel!

Then came the solemn words by the pastor, and then the passing of the trays and plates by the deacons. Maybe you can imagine a boy's chief fear on those occasions: What if you dropped one of those plates! Then came the lifting of the bread and later the tiny cups in unison. Everybody looked so solemn. I hesitate to mention one of the most enduring segments of these memories—the inevitable clatter as everyone, again in unison, deposited their little plastic glass in the holder on the pew in front of them.

Perhaps your memories are a bit different: the pastor in clerical robes, the scene dominated by a large gold cross, people quietly moving to the front of the church to kneel and receive the wafer and the cup, the hushed tones of the pastor speaking the formula, the wiping of the common cup. For some of you, maybe the scene which has come to your mind is a priest lifting high the chalice and speaking the words of institution.

All these memories are different paths by which we come to the Lord's Table, and they hark back to the one and same event—the Passover celebration meal of Jesus and his followers, their last meal together before his crucifixion.

Earliest Description

Paul gives us the earliest description of that meal, telling us what was done and said and meant. It is found in Paul's first letter to the church at Corinth, in chapter 11, beginning with verse 23. Notice that Paul said he received from the Lord this account which he is delivering to the readers of this letter. Does he mean that he received this knowledge in a vision, or does he mean God gave it to him through listening to those in Christ before him?

First, Jesus took bread. Paul does not indicate the bread is anything but common, everyday, ordinary bread. The Gospel writers, in describing this last meal, say it was a Passover feast with unleavened bread. This is my body, for you. The oldest texts do not say given. Let us understand what the simple phrase, This is my body, for you is saying. Jesus' body, the very idea and act in incarnation, is for us. For we who are stuck in sin, wounded by sin, slaves to sin. It was for us

The Naming of a Mystery

he took upon himself human flesh, a human body, and walked among us and went even to the cross.

My body, given for you. Surely that addition of given is also correct, for he who first decided to take on the confinements of flesh also decided to remain in the flesh even to the painful death on the cross. That body was given for us on the cross, around which the yapping hounds of hell gathered to gloat in the misguided hope of victory over God's love.

This do in remembrance of me. Eat this bread thinking of me, thinking of the cross. As the Jews think of their freedom from the torments of Egypt as they eat the Passover break, so let the Christian reflect on the price of our salvation.

And after the meal, he took the cup. A cup of ordinary wine, one of several cups of wine in the Passover ritual. This cup is the new covenant in my blood. The old covenant was made at the mountain; it was a covenant of rules, of law, of works; futile and external and unable to bring peace of mind and soul and salvation. This is the new covenant, a covenant of grace and forgiveness and peace and acceptance into the throne room and heaven of God. It is a covenant made in the blood of the Son of God. Drink it thinking of me. Thinking of the one who has made, in his blood, this new covenant, this new relationship with God, possible.

For as often as you eat this bread and drink this cup, you do show forth the Lord's death until he comes again. That means that whenever you come to the Lord's Table and eat the bread and drink the cup, you are taking your stand beneath the cross of Jesus, showing that he is your Lord and Saviour. It means you are setting forth your faith, hope, expectation that Jesus will surely return to this earth.

Our Names For The Mystery

So much is the actual background for what we are doing as we come to this time that some of us call the Lord's Supper, others call Holy Communion, and others call the Eucharist. It is difficult to name a mystery; something none of us can fully understand. Even so, why do we have these—and still other—names for this coming to the Table of the Lord?

Some of us call it the Lord's Supper. The biblical text doesn't actually use the word "supper," unless you count the headings at the top of the page! The word translated supped, etc. is also translated in places as dinner, feast, banquet. It is simply a reference to the main meal of the day in Palestinian homes. Apparently that main meal in King James England was the supper! Most Baptists use the term Lord's Supper, and what we think of, and were brought up thinking about, was the simple meal at the close of the day with friends and family. A time of relaxing after a long, hard day. A time to enjoy one another. It's a good way to describe what we are doing this morning at we come to the Lord's Table. For here we ought to experience that feeling of love for each other, that trust and joy in the knowledge that we walk this pilgrim road together. That feeling of family is a part of the experience of the Lord's Table.

Some of us call this meaningful time Holy Communion. Perhaps this idea comes from the use of that term in 1 Corinthians 10:16, in which Paul says that the cup and the bread is the communion of the body and blood of Christ. Here the emphasis is vertical, on our communion, our fellowship with Christ and on the realization that Christ is in our midst. The emphasis here is a worshipping emphasis, for in the stillness of this solemn moment we see ourselves as sinners brought near to God by the blood, and we kneel at the throne of the father.

Some of us call this time the Eucharist. This is simply the Greek word for thanksgiving. It springs from the memory of the Gospel writers of Jesus giving thanks, saying the blessing, even over the bread and cup which symbolized his death, on the evening before his crucifixion. The emphasis is on our thanksgiving, our gratitude for what God has done for us in Christ.

The Meaning, Not the Name

The name of the mystery, however, is not important. What we experience at the Table of the Lord is important. We ought to go away with

The Naming of a Mystery

a deep sense of fellowship. We should leave this place with a renewed commitment to each other in Christ; a commitment to love, to forgive, to encourage, to believe the best, to trust, and to serve one another. For each one of us in whose life Christ is Lord becomes a part of that circle at the table that night when Jesus said, "You are those who have continued with me in my trials, and I give to you a kingdom. . ." A great moment of my life was to stand in the church at Wittenberg, Germany and realize that a few feet away under the pavement rested the earthly remains of Martin Luther. The great renaissance painter, Lucas Cranach, painted a picture of the last supper for the altar of that church. The interesting thing is that he put 13 disciples around the table—he painted his friend Martin Luther among the Twelve! The spirit of the painting is absolutely correct! There is fellowship at the Lord's Supper.

There is another element we ought to experience at the Lord's Table, the understanding of how God's heart is broken with our sins. In the solemn moments of Holy Communion we commune with God Almighty, we confess our sins, we repent, we depart with a deep desire to serve him better. The prayer of Richard of Chichester says it well:

These three things we pray, Grant we may
See thee more clearly;
Love thee more dearly;
Follow thee more nearly. Amen.
That is the result of Holy Communion.

There ought to be the third element, that of Thanksgiving. A sense of praise, thanksgiving and joy over the wonderful fact that God loves us; God forgives us; God guides us—and Jesus is coming again!

The Lord's Supper as a Symbol

Luke 22:14-20, 28-30

First Celebration at Trinity Baptist Church

As We Gather to celebrate the Lord's Supper, Holy Communion, for the first time as members of the Trinity Baptist Church, consider the character of the Last Supper of Jesus and his disciples.

The biblical accounts are filled with pathos; with the gathering shadows of doom; with the pounding of the heartbeat of destiny. Mark draws a picture of the strong Son of God striding toward the cross, knowing that he lays down his life as a ransom for many. Luke writes with a lump in the throat and a mist in the eye, as he speaks of the dream in Jesus' heart concerning the kingdom: "I give to you a kingdom, even as the father has given to me a kingdom. . ." In John's account of this last supper we can almost see the pharisees' squinted eyes and tight lips and stroked beards as the net of wickedness tightens. John tells us the last straw for the pharisees was the raising of Lazarus; from that day on they determined to put Jesus to death.

From Last Supper to Lord's Supper

But now turn to the account of the last supper in chapter eleven of Paul's first letter to the Corinthians. Here we see that the Last Supper has become the Lord's Supper as it is celebrated in the churches. That last meal of Jesus and his disciples has become a symbol of belief and hope and a reminder for Christians much like the Passover feast had become for Jews. And when we from time to time reenact that supper by taking the bread and grape juice, we stir up and bring to life again the deepest hopes and beliefs of every Christian. Since this is the first time Trinity Baptist Church has celebrated the Lord's Supper, it is a good time to remind us all of the deep meaning of this ordinance—an ordinance being something we are commanded to do by Scripture.

Saving Grace or Symbol?

Granted, equally committed Christians may have differing views of the significance of Holy Communion, or as we Baptists say, the Lord's Supper. The Roman Catholic Church believes that the elements—the bread and wine—actually turn into the body and blood of the Lord in the celebration of the Mass. This is called transubstantiation, the changing of the elements. In the Middle Ages the elements of communion were referred to as the "food of immortality."

Lutherans believe that the bread is both actual bread and the body of Christ. This is called consubstantiation, both the body and the bread existing together. Now we Baptists reject any saving power in the elements, and, indeed, we have sometimes so stressed that both baptism and the Lord's Supper are merely symbols, that we have made these celebrations poverty-stricken in some way. I would say to you that both baptism and the Lord's Supper are more than empty symbol; there is a mystical quality about the experience of baptism; there is a mystical quality about these moments when we take the bread and the grape juice that goes beyond mere symbol.

Perhaps I ought to say a word about the grape juice. Baptists use grape juice not because Jesus and his disciples drank grape juice at the Last

Supper; rather they drank the ordinary wine of the time. And it was fermented, for there are references to getting drunk in the Old Testament. Many denominations today use wine in communion services, and that is perfectly all right. Nor is there anything wrong in the fact that we Baptists use grape juice, either. Our use of grape juice is not based on direct theological grounds, but because it is important to say to our community and nation that alcoholic beverages are a curse to our society and that to partake of alcohol is a betrayal of our Christian witness.

The Lord's Supper as Symbol and Pointer

In one sense the Lord's Supper is a symbol, like the liberty bell or a wedding ring. It reminds us of a relationship—we see the liberty bell and we are proud to be Americans; we see a wedding ring on someone's finger and it says they are taken; they belong to someone and someone belongs to them. The Lord's Supper is also a pointer; it points beyond the bare facts of a meal 2000 years ago to the eternal promises made at that table that night and sealed at the cross. The Lord's Supper speaks to both the church and to the world about those things which are important to the church.

The Lord's Supper Speaks of Unity

To the church the Lord's Supper speaks of unity. Turn to 1 Corinthians 10:16-17. We should note that Paul's comments about the Lord's Supper are the earliest report we have about the Last Supper; earlier even than the Gospel accounts. And we would not have this letter of Paul and these inspired comments he made were it not for the fact that the church in Corinth was terribly divided over many things, and even the Lord's Supper was being dishonored. So Paul had to remind these folks that the Lord's Supper was a symbol of unity.

The situation in Corinth was that the church met usually at night after the members got off from work, and some of the folks were probably slaves. It seems that in the Corinthian church, Holy Communion followed a fellowship meal much like we will have next Sunday, where the members bring covered dishes, etc. At Corinth, those who came early apparently ate all the food and drank all the wine, and the feast turned into something of a drunken party. Those who came late not only missed out on supper, but had no bread or wine with which to celebrate the deepest meaning of the church. So Paul is writing to denounce their humiliation of the poor and their focusing on themselves.

So Paul writes: The cup of blessing which we bless, is it not the communion of the blood of Christ? The bread which we break, is it not the communion of the body of Christ? We being many are one bread, and one body: for we are all partakers of that one bread" (1 Cor. 10:16-17).

The Lord's Supper celebrates that essential unity of all Christians; we are all one loaf. That is why here at Trinity we will invite any and all Christians to take Holy Communion with us. This is the "table of the Lord," not the table of this or any local church. I have taken the Lord's Supper in churches where I could not understand the language; I have taken the Lord's Supper in the grandeur of Westminster Abbey; I have taken the Lord's Supper in tiny country churches—and felt in every case the eternal tie that binds us all together as Christians.

A Symbol of the Church's Humanity

The Lord's Supper speaks of the humanity of the church. It ought to be and is a time of deep soul-searching. The Last Supper was just such a time of deep soul-searching and recognition of sin, as each man in turn around the table asked, "Is it I?" And each of us knows how thin is the layer of commitment in our life. In 1 Corinthian 11:27-28 it seems at first glance that Paul is saying that we ought not to take the Lord's Supper if we are unworthy. None of us are worthy to accept the blood and body of Jesus for our sins. But this passage is still focusing on the shabby way the Corinthian church handled the Lord's Supper. Paul is saying to them, and to us, that we are to come to this time with sober minds and repentant hearts. We are not to come to the Lord's table flippantly or irreverently. We are to reflect on the meaning of this moment and take it seriously.

A Symbol of Jesus' Death

The Lord's Supper speaks of Jesus' death for us. Most likely Jesus was moved to make his comments at the Last Supper as he saw how blood-red the wine was, and mused upon the broken bread that night. When we take the grape juice and the bread, we remember that we are one side of a new covenant with God made in the blood of Jesus. A covenant which takes away our sins and grants us salvation and peace with God through the death of Jesus. The Lord's Supper always points us to the cross. And in our heart we ought to be saying the words of the great old hymn, When I Survey the Wondrous Cross.

A Symbol of Jesus' Return

The Lord's Supper reminds us of Jesus' triumphant return. Paul stresses this in 1 Corinthians 11:26, as he tells them that "as often as you eat this bread, and drink this cup, you do show the Lord's death until he comes." We need to live as if Jesus were going to return today, for he just might. We do not worship a dead man, no matter how good he was; we worship a risen Saviour, Almighty God in human flesh, who said he was coming back one day to this earth and take his people home. Paul thought, without a doubt, that Jesus would be returning in his time. The early Christians, they say, used to look down the road each way at every crossroad, to see if Jesus were coming down the road. They were expecting Jesus, and we should be looking for him, too.

The Lord's Supper Speaks to the World

But the Lord's Supper speaks not just to the church; it speaks a word to the world. To those among us who are not professing Christians, those who have not asked Jesus to be your Lord and Saviour, the Lord's Supper speaks if you will listen. It is deep calling unto deep . . . The supper says that all of us are sinners. All of us need a Saviour. When we lift the cup, we say that the blood of Jesus, shed for every person who ever has lived or ever will live, is sufficient to wash away your sins.

The Lord's Supper as a Symbol 167

All of us realize the need to change our lives; to become better people than we are. I read of a Japanese man who had dreamed of becoming a policeman, and finally passed all the requirements except one: he was just too short! He tried everything, including having himself stretched on the rack, but to no avail! The Supper proclaims that Jesus can change your life; that he and only he can grant you salvation. We can give money; we can give misery—but only Jesus can give salvation.

In some way that none of us can fully understand, the death of Jesus bridges the gap between us and God; a gap made by the hideous strength of our sins. God in Jesus has worked in the midst of this gap, sending Jesus to die in our place for our sins. And every time we lift the Lord's cup, and break the Lord's bread together, we proclaim his death for our sins, and his resurrection for our new life.

If you are not a Christian, you ought to respond to the Gospel today; you need to respond today. The Bible says you will be unhappy in this life and the next if you neglect so great a salvation. If not here, where will you make that life-changing decision? If not now, when will you make it? When will there be a better time? If not Jesus as your Saviour, then who will it be? There is no other name under heaven whereby men may be saved, except the name of Jesus.

Love Beyond

Ephesians 3:14-21

Ephesians 3 is packed with superlatives as Paul reaches out of sight for an adequate way to express God's love. He is overwhelmed by the reality of the calling, the grace and love and power of God, and speaks of the unsearchable riches of Christ, the many-splendored wisdom of God, the Christian being strengthened according to Christ's riches, the striving to comprehend the breadth, the length, the height, the depth of Christ's love, and of being filled with all the fullness of God. In such efforts to describe God there is no adequate vocabulary! Nobody has a "verbal advantage" in this area; nor will the latest edition of the Oxford English Dictionary help!

Have you ever felt overwhelmed by God's calling of you to salvation, by God's love and forgiveness of your sins? Here is a man overwhelmed by the grace of God! Most of us have never been overwhelmed with a sense of God's great love; never fumbled for words like Paul does here. And there are many reasons for that; some of us

Love Beyond

grew up in an atmosphere of thanking God for His love. Not long ago one of our church families had a wedding in which all the little children of the family, all the little nieces and nephews, came in together after the musical portion of the service. I found myself reflecting that these children would never know anything but the love of God; they would grow up in the church! So it is with many of us; there was no traumatic conversion experience like that of Paul; God and His great love has always been there, like grandparents or a spinster aunt who lives with you. And so there is a danger that our faith and our gratitude to God will become a dull throb rather than a raging fever, and we shall never be overwhelmed by the reality of His love.

For others, our Christian identity is merely a part of our culture, so that we march through life as a church member surrounded by friends who are all church members, until we have woven a cocoon of habit and comfortable routine which means no more than a club membership and costs no more. For still others, vaguely Christian but not even involved in a church, religion is on the edge of life; God is not even related to the ups and downs of life.

And Paul is here writing to a church whose members apparently aren't overwhelmed by a sense of God's great love, either. Perhaps they, and we, are not even fully aware of the impact of the indescribable love of God on our lives, or of the great task we as Christians have.

Unsearchable Riches of Christ

In Ephesians 3:8 Paul reflects on his calling. He cannot get over the fact that he—the one who once persecuted and killed Christians; the one who is surely the least among the saints, the most unworthy to serve Christ—has been called to preach the unsearchable riches of Christ. What a word this unsearchable is in Greek! It appears only once more in the New Testament, in Romans 11:33, where in reference to the future of the Jewish people, Paul speaks of the unsearchable judgments of God. In the Greek writers such as Homer the word is used to describe a situation in which you are trying to track down a person or an animal, and there is no track, footstep, or clue; nothing even for the dogs to sniff out. Paul is saying the limits of the riches of Christ are absolutely untrackable; there is no clue to the limits.

That wonderful preacher of the early part of this century, John Henry Jowett, one day was reading this verse (8), and glanced out his window to see a bee exploring the wealth of a flower. He thought of all the flowers in his garden, and all those in the neighborhood, and all those by the roadside, and all those in the country, and all the flowers in the tropics, and all the flowers in the world; there was no way the bee could ever comprehend such a wealth of flowers! Unsearchable, unfathomable, untraceable, exhaustless, endless, incalculable—that's the Gospel of Christ!

Now the unsearchable riches of Christ, the Gospel, the Good News of Jesus, is that He has the power, which no other human being has ever had, to forgive, to give a new start, to take our punishment for our sins, to grant us peace with God and our past, to grant us strength for the present and the future, to push death aside and bring us to life again after we breathe our last breath here on earth. And He is able because behind the man Jesus is an unsearchable, unfathomable, untraceable, exhaustless, endless, incalculable wealth of divine love and power. Will you right now let that reality sink into your heart and mind, and into your situation? Now matter how difficult things are, the greatest wealth and the most powerful force in the universe, the Gospel of Jesus, is available for your life.

God's Many-Splendored Wisdom

Paul says that this unsearchable Gospel is what he is called to preach. But in verse 10 he points out that there is an even more far-reaching reason for proclaiming the Gospel than individual salvation: that the many-splendored wisdom of God might now in his time and ours be made known both to the temporal rulers and the dark spiritual powers through the church (10).

Bear with me a bit: what is it that Paul says God wants to communicate to the "powers that be" through the church? The many-splendored wisdom of God in sending Jesus: in the incarnation, the suffering, the cross, the resurrection. 1 Corinthians 1 and 2 are very helpful here. Paul says " . . . we preach Christ crucified, to Jews a stumbling block, and to Gentiles foolishness" (1 Cor 1:23; see also 2:6-9). Here again, when Paul tries to describe the wisdom of God in this plan of the ages for our salvation, he simply hasn't the words to do it! He takes the word usually translated in KJV as "divers" as in "divers diseases," meaning various, and adds a "much" before it. In secular Greek the term is used to describe a beautiful piece of cloth or tapestry with a great variety of intricate designs. God's wisdom, says Paul, is like a many-splendored tapestry. Just to let the mind range back and forth in the Bible, the written record of God's wisdom, shows how varied and splendid is His wisdom! Only the wisdom of God could build our salvation around a cross!

The Dimensions of His Love

So Paul is saying he is called to preach the unsearchable riches of Christ so that the many-splendored wisdom of God may be known both to the kings of the earch and to the evil spiritual powers of this world, and that this wisdom is to be made known through the church. But in order for the church—any church, although Paul had the Ephesian church especially in mind—to make known to the "powers that be" the many-splendored wisdom of God, three things must happen. And Paul now, in verse 14, leads in a prayer for these things to happen in the lives of the church members at Ephesus.

They must be strengthened in the inner man first of all (verse 16). The outer "man" may be growing weaker and older; but we speak of the inner, the spiritual, person. Just as the Scripture speaks of conversion bringing about a "new" man, so conversion calls to life the "inner" man of the heart. Brethren, this strengthening must take place, and the Christian must keep on growing stronger and stronger in the Lord as the years go by. Secondly, *each Christian must comprehend the breadth, length, height, and depth of Christ's love* (verse 17). And that only begins to happen when we are growing in the inner man, when

Christ dwells in our hearts, when we are rooted and grounded in love. Then we begin to comprehend; then we begin, like Paul, to be overwhelmed by God's love!

What does Paul mean by these four dimensions of the love of Jesus? Again, it is a way of trying to express the inexpressible! Paul says we must try to comprehend Christ's love backward and forward, up and down. Some scholars think he was referring to the 4 arms of the cross, other scholars see other schemes: Jerome thought the height was for the angels, the depth for the demons, the breadth for those on the broad way leading to destruction, and the length for those on the upward path. Others say the height refers to Jesus' ascension, the depth to His descent into Hades, the breadth to the invitation to everyone to be saved, and the length to the salvation stretching back to eternity.

Most likely Paul's terms are simply to say that we need to be overwhelmed by the love of Christ, which did indeed begin in the heights of glory and then came down to the depths of human flesh; which does reach out everywhere, and will seek out sinful man down the lengths of the years to the end of time. The love of Christ is greater far than pen or tongue can ever tell. From the best, cleanest life to the most shameful, Christ's love is adequate. From the youngest child who asks who Jesus is to the oldest, white-headed sinner, the love of Christ is sufficient.

And the third essential for the church at Ephesus is that *they be filled with all the fullness of God.* That is done only by opening our lives, in whatever shape they are, to the Gospel. I am quite sure those most filled with the fullness of God do not even know it. They simply live close to Jesus, trusting Him to forgive them as they forgive others, to love them as they love others.

That the World May Know

Now remember that Paul prays that each member of the church of Ephesus might be strengthened in the inner man, be able to comprehend the love of Christ, and be filled with the fullness of God for a

Love Beyond

purpose: so they can reveal to the world the wisdom of God in the cross. Brethren, pharisees can't do that. Hypocrites can't do it, either. Nor can cultural Christianity, and half-hearted disciples without a vision can't reveal to the world the wisdom of God in the cross, either.

It can only be done by those whose past, present, and future are hidden in Jesus; those who are overwhelmed by the love of Jesus, and will take up their cross and follow Him. Those who have felt the forgiveness He offers, and the love He imparts. For the love of God is greater far than pen or tongue can ever tell; it goes beyond the highest star, and reaches to the lowest hell.

Neither Sand Nor Beast

Matthew 16:13-18

We are celebrating our 150th birthday as a church. These days are full of drama, pageantry, displays and history which paint a portrait of the church we have been and are; a portrait of which we can be justly proud; a portrait which is a fair likeness of the Biblical concept of the church. Yet there are those today who see any local church as either a lifeless sack of sand, unable or unwilling to do those things which remind this wicked world of Christ, or as a cage of wild beasts, fighting and quarreling among ourselves. There is more, much more.

There are four aspects of the Biblical picture of the church I want to present to you today: *the church as the guardian of tradition; as the invader of hell; as the possessor of gifts; and as the proclaimer of the Gospel.*

The Guardian Of Tradition

For many folks our sesquicentennial is a celebration of tradition. Now, there are two kinds of tradition. First, there is the empty, prideful, useless tradition that Jesus condemned, the traditions of the pharisees. A life rooted in a dead past which God has left behind. I have read how one of the Russian Czars just before the turn of the century was walking in the royal rose garden soon after taking the throne, and noticed a soldier standing in the middle of the garden. He inquired of the soldier why he was stationed in the middle of the flower garden. The man knew only that he was commanded to stand there by his officer. The Czar decided to follow this interesting incident, and asked the Captain of the Guard why the soldier was stationed there. He, too, was ignorant; it had been done all the decades he had been a soldier. The Czar had the archives searched, and found that Catherine the Great had planted a rose bush at that spot in the garden centuries before, and to keep it from being trampled, had ordered that a soldier always be stationed at that spot! So it was done through the years--empty tradition!

And church tradition can be dark, grey, paralyzing—if we think only of inscribed marble slabs on the wall and effigies on the floor with the noses long since worn off by the tramping of tourists; or candles and priests and relics from the past, whether they be bones of St. Mark, the chains of St. Peter, or a bit of the true cross! One of the most melancholy churches in the world is the Capuchin Church in Vienna, in the crypt of which you can see 140 coffins of the Hapsburg emperors stacked like so much firewood.

There is another kind of tradition—tradition which points the way into a meaningful future. The Lord's Supper is an example of this kind of tradition. Anything from the past which calls forth the best in us is a worthy heritage and tradition. Anything from the past which reminds us of a great invisible company of saints who surround us, and who truly love us and this body of believers, who cheer us on and want us never to be timid or faint-hearted or hide in the past, and spur us on to greater deeds, is good. Rich, meaningful traditions have a reason for their existence. They call us back to the roots of our faith, and urge us forward. So enjoy the heritage and traditions of our church which bid us rejoice in a faithful past, and call us forward to new and exciting adventures for Christ. Our forefathers were pioneers; let us follow in their train.

The Invader Of Hell

Examine Matthew 16:15-18. We Baptists are famous for our insistence that the rock upon which Jesus promised to build His church is the faith of Peter, not the man himself. We have paid little attention to the rest of the verse, and acted as if it guaranteed hell would never break into the church. In fact, what the verse says is that hell will not be able to hold out against the church! The picture is not that of a weak, mealy-mouthed church full of children and women huddling in fear that Satan is pounding the door down! The picture is of the church as a mighty army with banners waving invading hell!

True, it is a strange image in a time when most churches are more concerned with the 500 foot law about closeness of liquor stores to churches than they are about invading hell, and some folks are uncomfortable with the militant image of the church. Yet the Biblical image of the church is more like the Salvation Army than monks talking to flowers.

To march against hell the church must have self-consciousness, as did Peter and John when they healed the man on their way to worship at the temple. We must know who we are (the redeemed soldiers of Christ), what it is we have to give the prisoners of hell (the Gospel of freedom in Christ), and why they can be set free (because Jesus died for their release from sin). We must realize that the essence of hell is characterized by separation from God, by the rule and will of Satan, and tens of thousands of people in Memphis live in hell, live under Satan's rule. They are married, they are single. They are rich, they are poor. They live in midtown, they live out east. And all of them need Christ!

If we intend to invade hell, we must also have a self-commitment. A willingness to commit not just our money, not just our occasional, casual attendance, but ourselves to the invasion of hell. In that light it was exciting to see over 100 of us out last Saturday, going to nearly 7000 doors, covering 25 square miles as we worked toward our satellite services out east. But this sense of commitment came home to me last Sunday when two beautiful little girls said to me, "We had planned to get a picture of you in your robe and us in our Easter dresses, because this is the last Easter we will worship here since our parents are working out East." It is not easy to leave the comfortable nest; there must be a sense of commitment, if we invade hell.

The Possessor Of Gifts

Turn to 1 Corinthians 12:14-17 with me. Here we see a clear and simple analogy of the church as a body. A body that is alive, full of life and purpose. It is not a heavy, lifeless bag of sand, nor a snarling cage of beasts, but a living, functioning body. The church, like the body, is composed of many parts, yet it functions as one. In wintertime we see the beautiful flocks of geese hurtling overhead, made up of separate birds, but so sensitive and cooperative that they function as one as they dip and turn and change course.

The church is also a finely tuned, beautiful creation of God. A special creation, a tool with which God invades hell in these days. The church is different from any civic or social club; it is composed of redeemed, recreated people. And each of us as a part, a member of the church has our own place in the body. I feel the greatest tragedy of the church in our time is our failure to recognize, and appreciate, and use our spiritual gifts as part of the Body, the Church. You see, it is impossible for either the church or the individual Christian to fulfill Christ's intention without each other. The New Testament never dreams of a lone christian; the New Testament is the story of the church, the body with all its parts working together.

According to 1 Corinthians 12, the basic question for the Christian is, "How do I, with my spiritual gift, fit into the broader work of this particular church of which I am a part?" Every Christian who ignores his spiritual gift, or fails to use it for the upbuilding of the church, or withholds it in disagreement with the church, cripples that church and is like an anchor dragging. To fail to use our gift is clearly and definitely a sin.

A further word about our gifts. Every Christian is given at least one spiritual gift to use for the building up of the church of which he is a member. The gifts vary greatly, and are not to ranked in importance, although some are more useful in public worship and others in private. The most important spiritual gift is not faith, nor prayer, nor tongues, nor preaching, but Christian love! And in his stating of this fact, Paul penned the lovely poem on Christian love, 1 Corinthian 13.

The Proclaimer Of The Gospel

The glory of the church, the glory of this particular church, the First Baptist Church of Memphis, for 150 years, is that it is a proclaimer of the Gospel.

A Gospel wrapped in the finest tradition; yet it is the same, simple Gospel that every man needs. And when this or any church invades hell, the weapon we take is still the same, simple Gospel. And when redeemed people pour their spiritual gifts into the fellowship and ministry of this church, it is because they have been redeemed by the hearing of the old, old story; the same, simple Gospel.

The Gospel that gives a meaning for life,
>   that erases our sin and guilt
>> that tells us of God's love
>>> that says there's a man on
>>>> the cross.

A Gospel bigger than sin
> more real than guilt
>> more lasting than the stars.

A few years ago in Berlin I visited a famous church in West Berlin, the Kaiser Wilhelm Memorial church, with its bombed out spire still standing, floodlit and stark, against the sky—as if to say that all the evil in the world couldn't destroy the church. I crossed over into East Berlin and visited the old Berliner Dom, the old city cathedral, which was a museum for years and only now is being opened again. I noticed the twin inscriptions in German on the façade of that church: "Behold, I am with you every day, until the end of the world." "Our faith is the victory which has overcome the world." As I read those words, I wondered what Hitler must have thought as he read them, passing that church on the main street so many times. Today I wonder what you, as a part of this body of Christ, think of them. "Our faith is the victory which has overcome the world."

Never Before . . . Never Again

Deuteronomy 17:16; Joshua 3:4
A Sermon for the New Year

This morning let us take two statements from the history of Israel and apply them to our own lives. The first statement comes from Moses' speech to the children of Israel at the edge of the Promised Land. In that speech, one of several Moses made as they camped on the other side of Jordan opposite Jericho, Moses talks of many things-laws, punishments, cities of refuge, the portions due the Levites, the Sabbatical rules, and often reviews the past-but a theme which looms large in all he said about the past and future is this: You shall not pass this way again. He underlines this theme in all kinds of situations; here in our text he speaks of the process should they decide to select a king.

Our second scripture is a statement made by Joshua only a few months after Moses' speeches about remembering. In the meantime Moses has died, and the scene surrounding our text is a stirring one. For a month they have sat in their tents grieving for Moses. Now early one morning the man appointed by Moses as his successor, Joshua, calls the leaders of the people to his tent, and commands them to go through the camp with this message: Prepare provisions! For within three days we will cross over Jordan! Joshua also reminded those tribes who had already settled in the land east of the Jordan that they had a responsibility to help the rest of the children of Israel win the Promised Land. Joshua sent two men to spy out the land, especially Jericho. It was these two men who hid on the roof of Rahab's house.

So all the people made ready to journey over Jordan. When they got to the river, Joshua gave further orders. He ordered the people to consecrate themselves, and told them they were to follow the Ark of the Covenant, which would be carried by twelve men, one from each tribe, about a half-mile ahead of the main group of the people. They were to follow the Ark, and then our text: for you have not passed this way before.

From these two occasions I would focus on two phrases, one from Moses and one from Joshua: never again that way, and never before this way.

Never That Way Again

We all know the meaning of Moses' words, never that way again. It is a law of life; with each setting sun there closes a door on the day. We cannot go back and undo or do better or pour more energy or change the direction of that day; it is past. It is a law which we see forced upon us at every turn in the road of life: as we leave high school; as we leave college; as get married; as the first child is born; as the last child leaves home; who does not hear the voice of Moses: never that way again.

Sometimes in traveling in a foreign country I get that feeling, as I look out over a particularly beautiful setting, or glance down a dark alley, or see two old men playing chess; I shall never see that particular scene again . . . never this way again. And the same is true as we stand at the close of a year and look back. We shall never go back to this year after today . . . never this way again. So let us look at some of the lessons which come with that fact.

First, a realization. *We made it what it was.* Consider the past year in your life, in your family's life, in the life of your church. God had a plan, a vision, an intention, a blueprint for our life, our family, our church. But we cannot blame God for the way things turned out, for we made the year what it was. To the extent we let Christ dwell in our lives, this past year was what God intended. If you were to sit down later this day and consider the past year, it would be like a patchwork quilt. Some events which would come rushing into your mind would be painful; some would be warm and comforting; others would be refreshing; yet others would reproach us for sins-sins of omission and of commission.

We made it what it was by our goals, our dreams, our desires, by the set of our sails in life. Have you heard that radio ad for a very fine and popular national newspaper which sums things up this way: . . .faster, tougher, smarter-it could be you! When we get to that place in life when we spend more time looking back at our journey through life, I really do not think that "faster, tougher, smarter" is what will warm our heart and make us proud to have lived, but rather the reflection of Christ in us that brought joy, help, peace, and hope to others that will make us glad. —And that's why I keep a file of letters I have received through the years, letters of love and appreciation, letters that essentially say, "I saw a reflection of Christ in you the other day," and one day many, many years from now I shall sit on the front porch overlooking the mountain range and listen to the birds and the wind in the trees and read them and be glad that I passed that way.

So, first there is the realization that we made the year what it was. Then, an evaluation. Did we learn the lessons and do the work God intended? Are you the same person you were when 1989 began? Obviously not, physically. Some folks have more white hair; some have less hair! But what has happened to you spiritually? Have you grown or regressed? Did you plan to grow? Perhaps nothing has happened spiritually, and you didn't particularly plan for anything to happen. None of us are spiritually mature; all of us need to keep on growing. If you did not change any of your theology, any of your understanding of the church and its work-then I humbly submit to you that you ought not be proud but rather grieved; for God has fresh light to give us from and upon His word with each passing day and year.

You know, I had some excellent help on this sermon. Brother Aubry Byrn dropped by the house the other day while I was working on it, and as we chatted about the topic, he reminded me of an anonymous little poem entitled, "I Shall Not Pass This Way Again":

> *Through this world, alas!*
> *Once and only once I pass;*
> *If a kindness I may show,*
> *If a good deed I may do*
> *To a suffering fellow man,*
> *Let me do it while I can.*
> *No delay, for it is plain*
> *I shall not pass this way again.*

Since we shall not pass this way again, *we must also set down the truth that we must let the past go.* What's done is done in so many matters. We cannot go back:

> *The Moving Finger writes; and having writ, moves on: nor all your Piety nor Wit shall lure it back to cancel half a Line, Nor all your Tears wash out a Word of it.*

In many things about the year—and years gone by—we must say, "let the dead bury the dead," and turn our faces forward. Man does not live by the past alone. It was trying to go "that way again" that spelled the doom of Lot's wife. Let us then learn from the past, give it our best when it is the present, and then let it go.

Never This Way Before

Now consider for a moment Joshua's words: for you have never passed this way before. None of us have ever been in this coming year. Not even the greatest among us; the politicians with golden promises, the scientists who with their telescopes probe the outer reaches of the heavens, the explorers who walk on the moon—none of these have ever set foot in the year ahead of us. H.G. Wells' time traveler didn't even get there. Next year holds tremendous changes for many of us. Marriages, changes of jobs, births of children, deaths-nearly 50 of our members died last year; 100 of us had a family member to die. A new year is a strange land of surprises. And none of us is capable by ourselves of dealing with what this next year—1990— will bring.

Look again at Joshua's commands to the children of Israel as they go where they have never been before. First, he commanded that they sanctify themselves. We do not know all that meant in that situation, but we know that when the Bible speaks of sanctification it means a setting apart of a person or an object as belonging to God. If you and I are to go into 1990 prepared to meet the challenges and surprises there, we must first sanctify ourselves. It means we must realize our special relationship to God in Jesus Christ; it means we must accept that relationship and rejoice in it-so many Christians seem to want to hide their salvation, their relationship to Jesus from the world-and it also means we need to rededicate ourselves to do the will of God, not man.

Second, notice the guiding Ark of God. Now the Ark was a chest, about 4 x 2½ feet in size, completely covered with gold. In it were kept the tablets of the Law, the rod of Aaron, and a pot of manna. The Ark was the meeting place between God and man; the Ark was God's throne; the Ark was the symbol of God's presence and God's Law. And they were to follow the Ark, as it was carried over Jordan and into the Promised Land.

Now folks, I do not think it pressing the case to apply this image to our relationship with Christ. Jesus is the meeting place between God and man; He is the symbol of God's presence, forgiveness, blessing, and law. And if we will follow Him into the New Year, we too shall be safe. So many folks will begin 1990 with revelry and booze and a spirit of indifference and rebellion toward God. But you are God's people, called as sanctified people to follow the Ark into the future.

True, never this way before. But that only applies to you and me. God has trod the paths of 1990; the new year is a creation of His hand. And in 1990 He has put some wonderful blessings for those who love Him. As Paul says in Ephesians 2:10, "For we are His workmanship, created in Christ Jesus for good works, which God prepared beforehand, that we should walk in them." 1990 also means a fresh start; another chance. Not to go back and change the past, but to make of the future what it ought to be; what perhaps the past should have been. And that's what the cross is all about!

And I said to the man who stood at the gate of the year:
Give me a light, that I may tread safely into the unknown!

And he replied:

Go out into the darkness and put your hand into the Hand of God. That shall be to you better than light and safer than a known way.

Full Armor for Fierce Battle

Ephesians 6:10-18

There is almost an epidemic— if that word can be used in a good sense—an epidemic of patriotism sweeping our nation in these days. No doubt it springs in part from our feelings of guilt for the way we ignored our Vietnam veterans, but in any case we are more aware of our fighting men and women than at any time since the Second World War. As civilians we probably have more knowledge about our military weapons, with half-page spreads in the papers during the recent Gulf war, than any people in history. We have mobilized—and demobilized—a half million soldiers in record time. And now most of the troops are back home, and it is time to reflect on patriotism.

Perhaps the most profound and stimulating statement I heard this holiday weekend was made by Arthur Schlesinger on the MacNeil/Lehrer news program. Asked to define patriotism, Schlesinger said patriotism is helping your nation to be the very best nation it can be. Patriotism is usually seen in terms of war, of military action. And, indeed, the willingness to lay down your life in behalf of your country is an inspiring demonstration of patriotism. But it is also patriotism when a man or woman labors quietly in a classroom for forty years, developing young minds which will enrich this nation. Patriotism is seen in the efforts to raise the moral level of our society. In fact, I do not understand why a large segment of the military forces of this nation are not devoted to patrolling the borders of our country and stopping the tremendous infiltration of drugs into our society.

Indeed, to be engaged in combating the forces which would destroy the moral fiber of our society is to do battle with an enemy more threatening than an enemy army equipped with tanks, planes, missiles and chemical weapons. Listen, wars on the national, military level come and go; but there is a deeper, darker, more sinister war which continues. Every Christian is in an ongoing spiritual war against one who wishes to destroy the nation from within. An ongoing spiritual battle fought not in the desert, but in the lap of luxury; not with weapons of the latest technology but with spiritual weapons. And the stakes are even higher than in Desert Storm, or Vietnam , or Korea, or WWII. In these wars the outcome could mean loss of democracy, perhaps physical slavery, even death. But the battle in which every Christian patriot is engaged daily is a battle in which a nation's soul, and the souls of her citizens, are at stake.

And so this morning I want to us remember with gratitude those who risked their lives and gave their lives for our national freedom; and I want to remind every Christian that you are a soldier in a desperate, spiritual war. Look with me at Ephesians 6. Here, in the same context with teaching about marriage, home, relationships between employers and employees, we find the admonition to realize we are soldiers, and to stand firm in the battle against an evil power dedicated to destroying us.

Be Strong!

For the time that remains, says Paul, be strong! He is writing to the first generation of Christians, but the admonition is valid whether it is for a generation or for thousands of years—be strong! But that's part of our problem. We get an army and we feel strong; we get loaded with booze and we think we're strong; we shoot up with drugs and we can lick the world. The person strong in his own strength is no match for the evil powers which would destroy our society. Be strong in the Lord. That is, be strong in the spiritual life through prayer and devotion, by keeping an up-to-date witness. Be strong in the Lord and in the power of his strength. Three different Greek words are used here for "power," but the important thing is that we are to be strong in His strength. The strength of the Lord is seen in the power that created this world; the power of storms; the power of the lightning—but above all in the power that raised a dead man from the grave and gave Him life again, in the resurrection of Jesus. Paul says that same power is available in our lives to combat the evil forces against us. And listen, even when we are strong, we still face a battle.

The Enemy and the Battle

In verses 11-12 we see a vivid description of the struggle and the enemy we face. As I read through these verses, notice the images. And remember that Paul is probably being closely guarded, perhaps even chained to, a Roman soldier of the Praetorian guard. Put on the full armor of God; avail yourself of all the protection available! What soldier would have gone off to Desert Storm without his or her helmet, or gas mask, or rifle, or even boots? Notice that our armor is the armor of God; not of men. It is spiritual armor, unseen to the world, but most effective. That you may be able to stand; that is, stand in the battle-line and take part in the struggle. Against the wiles [methods] of the devil. Methods, yes! The devil is cunning, methodical, organized, and powerful. And here we see that our adversary is more devious and cunning and powerful than any Hitler or Stalin or Saddam Hussein. The name for the devil here is *diabolou*, to "throw across," as if casting a net or a lasso. So he uses slander and lies.

Because our battle [hand-to-hand struggle] is not against blood and flesh. The word here for battle means a fierce hand-to-hand struggle; some of you veterans have probably experienced what I think would

Full Armor for Fierce Battle

be a most chilling command, to fix bayonets for hand-to-hand combat. No long distance bombing, this! And the battle is not against flesh and blood, but against cosmic powers, governments and powers and world rulers of this darkness. These seem to be levels of power in the dark hierarchy. That is to say, we struggle in this spiritual war with the overlords of this dark world, against spiritual hosts of evil. Yes, Paul is saying that governments can be infiltrated and influenced by the devil. A good comparison can be made by thinking of the demons mentioned in the Gospels which attacked individuals; only here we see spiritual forces in the world which attack the structure of society, the home, the family, the church, the community values. And so it is because of these things mentioned in verses 11 and 12, the methods of the devil, the realization that it is not a flesh and blood fight, and the realization that we face a tremendous network of evil throughout time and space, that we are urged to put on God's armor and take our place in the battle line. Verse 13 adds another reason to take up this spiritual armor: so that you may be able to withstand in the evil time. The "evil day or time" may refer to the lifelong struggle with the devil, or the judgement day, or a day of especially heavy temptation, or even the day of our death, as it was interpreted so often in the middle ages.

The Armor

It might be good to read the description of the armor of Goliath, the Philistine giant, in I Samuel 17:4-7. Now notice in verses 14 and following the description of this spiritual armor for the Christian. Again remember, the armor is another way of describing the power of God. There are six pieces of armor. The sword is the only aggressive weapon; the other pieces are defensive. These pieces of armor are God's weapons, God's defense. They were given at first to only one person on the earth, the Messiah, according to Isaiah 11 and 59. But now they are given to every Christian in order to do battle with the devil.

Girded about the waist with truth (14). There were three different kinds of belts worn by Roman soldiers: the leather apron of the common soldier, the sword-belt which held up the sword, and the special sash denoting that one was an officer. Perhaps Paul refers to the officer's sash here. The belt is truth. The truth that Jesus is Lord; the truth as a mark of the relationship of one Christian with another; the truth always spoken in love; the truth as opposed to the lies of the devil. Without truth, there is no belt on which to hang the sword of God; there is no honorable sash to mark the Christian as an officer of Jesus.

Having put on the breastplate of righteousness (14). The righteousness of God protects our heart. Never, ever go forth to fight the devil on the basis of your own righteousness and goodness. We see, even in the examination of Judge Thomas for the Supreme Court, how everything is sifted in order to compromise the candidate's own righteousness. That's child's play compared to how the devil will twist your goodness, slander and use your good intentions if you dare fight him in your own moral strength.

Having the Gospel of peace bound under your feet for steadfastness (15). Standing on the Gospel, the good news, the firm foundation—with no danger of slipping, the soldier can do battle effectively. In all of this, take up the shield of faith (16). The shield Paul speaks of here, seen so often by him, was probably a shield made of wood and layers of leather, attached to an iron frame. The shield would be soaked in water before a battle, and thus would quench the fiery darts of the evil one. What is meant here by the burning arrows? Our doubts, our misunderstandings, temptations—all missiles hurled at us by the devil.

Take the helmet of salvation (17). Here salvation is associated with the head, because full salvation includes the heart and the head; the emotions, the will, and the intellect. The sword of the Spirit, which is the Word of God (17). This sword is the only offensive weapon we Christians have. But the Book of Hebrews says the Word of God is sharper than any two-edged sword. Although we should see this as a reference to the New Testament, in Paul's thinking, this Word of God was not the New Testament as we know it, for it was not yet written when Paul wrote this letter. He had in mind God's Word in the Old Testament promises, God's Word embodied in the everlasting Yes of

Full Armor for Fierce Battle

God to men through Jesus, God's Word of conviction in the sinner's heart, a spiritual sword in the hand of the Holy Spirit, leading us to see our sin and guilt.

Vigilance: the Price of Freedom

Paul sums up this picture of the Christian soldier preparing to do battle by urging vigilance in prayer. In verse 18 Paul uses the word all four times: we ought to engage in all kinds of prayer; we ought to pray in all the seasons of life, good or bad; we ought to pray with all perseverance and determination; and we ought to pray for all the saints.

I wish that you and I, and all Christians, could clearly see the spiritual battle going on around us; I wish we could be stirred with the emotions we feel about our national army these days; for the battle is for even higher stakes. Let me share with you the description of this unearthly battle between every Christian and the overlord of evil as it was felt by John Bunyan in his book Pilgrim's Progress. He describes the fight between Christian, who is on the road to heaven, and Apollyon, the devil and the destroyer.

Christian: *Apollyon, beware what you do, for I am in the King's highway, the way of holiness; therefore take heed to yourself.*

Apolyon: *Then Apollyon straddled quite over the whole breadth of the way, and said, I am void of fear in this matter. Prepare thyself to die; for I swear by my infernal den, that thou shalt go no further: here will I spill thy soul. And he threw a flaming dart at his breast; but Christian had a shield in his hand, with which he caught it, and so prevented the danger of that.*

Then did Christian draw, for he saw it was time to bestir him; and Apollyon as fast made at him, throwing darts as thick as hail; by the which, notwithstanding all that Christian could do to avoid it, Apollyon wounded him in his head, his hand, and foot. This made Christian give a little back, Apollyon therefore followed his work amain, and Christian again took courage, and resisted as manfully as he could.

This sore combat lasted for above half a day, even till Christian was almost quite spent: for you must know that Christian, by reason of his wounds, must needs grow weaker and weaker.

Then Apollyon, espying his opportunity, began to gather up close to Christian, and wrestling with him, gave him a dreadful fall; and with that Christian's sword flew out of his hand. Then said Apollyon, I am sure of thee now: and with that he had almost pressed him to death, so that Christian began to despair of life. But as God would have it, while Apollyon was fetching his last blow, thereby to make a full end of this good man, Christian nimbly reached out his hand for his sword, and caught it, saying, Rejoice not against me, O mine enemy: when I fall, I shall arise. Nay, in all these things we are more than conquerors through him that loved us. And with that Apollyon spread forth his dragon wings, and sped him away, that Christian saw him no more.

Every human being is in the midst of a battlefield. Even when we are strong in the Lord, we need his righteous armor. Remember there is no armor for the back. Would you be a soldier of the cross? We receive this armor only at the cross of Christ.

The Power of Positive Giving

I Chronicles 29:5-17

The very title of this sermon has, no doubt, caused some folks to mutter a "Bah, Humbug! A dollar in the offering plate is a dollar in the plate—whether the giver is a grouch or not!" Dollars don't frown or smile! The preacher doesn't care how I feel about giving it; so long as I give my money! You couldn't be more wrong.

What Is Positive Giving? It's the opposite of negative giving. Let me illustrate from my experience the negative giver—just one, and then we shall let even him slip quietly off into the darkness.

Once upon a time there was a churchman—he may at one point have been very active in the Sunday School; it is possible that he once served as a deacon. But now he took great joy in saying, "I give my check to the church a couple of times a year—and then I tell them how to spend it!" That is negative giving—and it didn't do much for the man or the church.

Now the Bible really doesn't say much about negative giving—it focuses on positive, joyful giving. Let me characterize positive giving for you. Notice its motive: positive giving is giving because we want to; not because we have to. Positive giving springs from a sense of gratitude, not a spirit of obligation. For a beautiful example, see John 12:1-8, and refer to John 11:2, to see the spirit of gratitude which motivated Mary to do this beautiful deed. The aim of positive giving: it looks toward a high purpose. Our text story is a fine illustration of joyful giving toward a purpose. The character of positive giving: it is free from stinginess or regret. The challenging story of Zaccheus and his free giving shows this character. Positive giving has a touch of daring, in that it is giving from the heart in faith, not always according to the purse. The widow who gave only a mite— all she had—pictures that challenge for us.

The Bible is full of illustrations of positive giving to the Lord. And it is evident that positive giving isn't little, it isn't green, it isn't sour, and it isn't bent out of shape. It is big, bubbly, and joyful. I just love the story in our text about the building of the temple. David first tells what he is going to do, and challenges the rest to follow. After David challenged the people, they followed—read verses 6-9. Notice verse 9: "Then the people rejoiced because these had given willingly, for with a whole heart they had offered freely to the Lord; David the king also rejoiced greatly."

Now, folks, each of us has to decide whether our own giving is negative or positive. The character of your giving depends not on the make-up of the budget; I seriously doubt if everybody got their special interests designed into the temple, either—but they still gave joyfully. The flavor of your giving does not depend on the economy or how much you earn—not all the people in the text story gave an equal amount; they just all gave in the same spirit, because the basis of their giving was bigger than any other aspect of it.

The Power of Positive Giving

Since negative giving hasn't near the power of positive giving in your own life, or to God, what is the power of positive giving?

The Power of Positive Giving 195

First, It breaks the bonds of a fearful, negative spirit. Many Christians are unhappy with their approach to financial stewardship, but are afraid that if they tithe, there won't be enough money to go around to meet family needs. So they are not radiant, joyful Christians—they are filled with guilt. They are uncomfortable with their own faith stance in this matter, and often they find fault with whoever and whatever is being done at church. I had a fine man sit in my car late one night not long ago here in the church parking lot and say that he was filled with guilt and remorse, had become irregular in his church interest and work—because he had gotten into a financial squeeze and had stopped tithing.

My friends, the primary reason for the Biblical teaching on tithing is to increase our faith. God doesn't need our money! He could make hundred dollar bills out of every green tree leaf if that were needed! Tithing, with its measure of risk, on the foundation of faith, leads God's child to constantly grow in assurance of God's provision. What blessings many of God's children miss by not joyfully, gratefully, gladly putting our faith in God through the tithe. In 1 Kings 17 God told Elijah, when he was starving in the drought, to get up and go to Zarephath, where God had told a widow to feed him. That widow had already been impressed by the Lord to use her meagre, remaining resources to feed the prophet—but she almost missed out on the blessing! But God is faithful who has promised, and the jar of meal and the cruse of oil failed not until the drought broke. More than that—because she had faith, later on her dead son was brought back to life by Elijah.

Second, positive giving enhances our gift and enlarges its meaning. Giving from a heart that wants to give adds great value to a gift. I am often given a drawing of myself, or the church—usually drawn during the service—by preschoolers. They may never get into the Louvre, but those pictures are very meaningful to me, and I have a batch of them in a desk drawer! I think God feels the same about us—it is the motive, the faith involved, that gives value to our gift to Him. In 1813, Emperor Frederick III of Prussia needed gold for the wars of the empire, so he sent out a plea for the gold jewelry of the women of the realm. In return for their gold he gave each woman a cross of iron with the inscription: "I gave gold for iron." They treasured the iron as much as they loved the gold because of the love behind it.

Third, positive giving creates a positive attitude in other areas of life. Our lives revolve around money. Jesus said that where a man's treasure is, there is his heart also. When we give positively, generously, gratefully to God—other areas of our lives fall into proper place. Such giving turns our hearts toward spiritual things.

Fourth, positive giving leads from gratitude to gratitude and builds a grateful church. Positive giving means we've settled the issue of ownership. We don't have to decide every Sunday all over again whether we are going to tithe—we've settled that! Years ago my daughter made a little cameo in Vacation Bible School with the motto on it: "We can give without loving; but we cannot love without giving." Our love for God, our gratitude to God, dictates that we give back to Him. And the longer we walk with God, the more we want to give. The committed Christian wants to give more and more to God, the older he gets. The spirit of positive giving becomes a lifestyle that is never abandoned.

The Old Apple Tree

Some years ago in a seminar with Norman Vincent Peale I heard him tell an experience from his own life which demonstrates well the power of positive giving. Just a year earlier Peale, getting older and trying to decide whether he should "hang it up," was out walking in the back field of his Dutchess County farm. He said he walked up to the top of a windy hill and stood there thinking about himself and his future, then noticed an old friend, an old apple tree. Long ago he had cut down the other apple trees, and now this one seemed on its "last legs." Old and diseased, full of termite holes and woodpecker pecks, the tree seemed finished, it was apparently good for nothing. But as Peale leaned against the tree in a rather pessimistic mood, he began to notice other things, too, about the tree. It had a lot of leaves, and more than that, the old tree was making a valiant effort at apples. In fact, if it kept going, it would have the finest crop in years! So Peale began to talk to the old apple tree.

"Old apple tree, why are you still working so hard in your old age? Why are you still giving and giving and giving? Why don't you give up and quit? You're tired, old, worn-out..." And, old apple tree, I feel just like you!

And the old apple tree responded: "Norman, you and I are alike. True, we're old and worn-out, but we've both got a little more in us. Let's keep on giving; let's do the best we can, the very best we possibly can! Because God's been good to both on us!"

"Thank you, old apple tree," said Peale as he turned to go back down the hill. True, perhaps the old apple tree had only one more year—but it still had a giving, grateful heart!

The Greatest Positive Giver

Our Heavenly Father is the greatest positive giver of all time. In spite of all our sin, all our rebellion in every life, God sent Jesus to die for our sins, to make us right with God. And God was glad to send Jesus, and Jesus came joyfully seeking the lost. That is positive giving. Will you respond to such positive divine giving today?

The Priority of Evangelism

II Kings 7:3-9

It is a distortion to say that the church has but one purpose, for the church exists to do many things: to worship God, to impact our society for God, to flavor the world as a spiritual salt, to promote religious education, to help the needy with the cup of cold water, and to enjoy the fellowship of like-minded folks who love God, to name only a few.

But there is no doubt that the task of evangelism stands head and shoulders above all I have mentioned. All these other aspects of church life must lead to evangelism, undergird evangelism, result in evangelism, or they become invalid, a reproach and an insult to God. For failure to make evangelism our priority is brazen disobedience to God and shows a colossal indifference to both the love and the pain in the heart of our Redeemer.

The Priority of Evangelism

But what do you think it means to make evangelism a priority for yourself and the church? And do you agree with the assessment that evangelism ought to have such a commanding place in the work of the church?

Priority is what you give those bills you pay each month while holding others back; priority is what you give your child when you drop whatever you are doing and run out into the back yard when you hear the child scream—even if it turns out to be only a fight over the tricycle! I raise a question here to myself, to you as individuals, and to our church as a whole: to what are we giving priority? We must give priority to the same concerns which moved the hand of God in the Old Testament, and focused the ministry of Jesus in the New Testament.

The Priority of Evangelism

Evangelism—the salvation of mankind for fellowship with God both here and hereafter—was a priority with God before there even was a Bible! Before men were ever led to put their understanding of God and His will on paper, God was working to reclaim errant old Adam and his children! God was calling out Abraham, recalling Jacob, confronting Moses from the bush, forming a nation which was to be His servant people through whom God would embrace all mankind. The priority of evangelism is the priority of God the Father.

Evangelism was a priority with God before we ever had an Old Testament; it was His priority throughout the Old Testament; evangelism was a priority with Jesus when God became flesh and dwelt among us. Just listen to Jesus' own words in the synagogue, Luke 4:18, and His comment to the disciples in Mark 1:38, and Jesus' response to the change in Zaccheus, Luke 19:10, and Jesus' statement of the Father's work, His own work, and our work, in John 4:34-35.

Evangelism was a priority with God in the Old Testament, evangelism was a priority with Jesus in His ministry, and evangelism was a priority with the early church. In Acts 8 we find that in its darkest moment, when the fellowship was torn with persecution and fleeing for their lives, they that "were scattered abroad went everywhere, preaching the Word." When the early Christians were converted, they came out of the waters of baptism preaching! Paul confounded the Jews at Damascus just days after his conversion—see Acts 9:17-22. Evangelism was the priority of Peter, of Paul, of Stephen, of Philip.

Evangelism is God's priority, Christ's priority, the church's priority through the ages, and this church's priority. Last year, church year 1987-88, we ranked 25th among the nearly 3000 Baptist churches in Tennessee in baptisms, as we baptized 84 persons into Christ. But I must raise the disturbing question: Is evangelism still our priority?

Is Evangelism Our Priority?

I must confess that I am not sure evangelism is the priority of this church just now. When we ranked 25th in our state in baptisms, we did it in large part because I was visiting, witnessing five nights a week, taking a different deacon with me each night. I slowed down last summer, because nobody can keep up that pace year in and year out. It is sad that there has not been the continuation of lay visitation there should have been. Not many deacons have been willing to take another deacon and go visiting one night a week; not many folks are willing to go out one night every two weeks; and not many more are willing to go out one night a month! I do not say these things to shame you; it is partly my fault, and I intend to start back on a rigorous evening visitation program. But we must realize that the devil's goal is to divert our attention from the task of evangelism, the blessed work of reaching the lost and unchurched. Now, we can make excuses: we have no Minister of Education right now, we have been focusing on our heritage for the past few months, we have differences of opinion on the direction our church should take in the future, we are just too busy—but that's all those things are—excuses! And the devil loves our excuses. In a time when the average church member has heard 4,000 sermons, 8,000 public prayers, sung 20,000 hymns in his church "career"—and has won nobody to Christ, it is a victory for the devil.

I bring this concern about evangelism in light of the fact that summer is approaching, the days are longer with more daylight for church

The Priority of Evangelism

visitation; in light of the fact that I have asked our deacons to lead out in a visitation of young parents out east—some 3000—next Monday night; in light of the fact that the Sunday School will lead out in a similar visitation of young parents in midtown—over 1000—a week from this Monday night, on May 8; in light of the fact that we have just mailed a brochure describing the ministries of our church to 10,000 families in midtown, and will knock on possibly 7,000 doors in midtown on Saturday, June 3. But all those efforts will be crippled unless evangelism becomes a priority for this church, and for you as a member. We stand at the door of a remarkable opportunity in these days, but we must all have the same priorities and same visions of reaching the lost. We do not wish to be like the boy whose family visited the Grand Canyon on vacation. Now the father had given each child a notebook in which to record the memorable sights. On the day of the visit to the Grand Canyon with all its magnificence and grandeur, the little boy ran over to the edge, leaned over the rail and spit. His parents were scared out of their wits and scolded him good! That night the father noticed the boy's journal, and this was his comment after visiting the Grand Canyon: "Today I spit two miles!"

Do you ever get the feeling that in your Christian life you've missed the real point, got the priorities wrong? As we look at the fields, both in midtown and out east, we must have the same goals. Unless evangelism becomes your personal priority, it will be just another church program; just another emphasis by the church staff. Another beautiful idea incomplete and greatly diminished in value because you were not a part of it. A huge department store had a sign in the window:

Jigsaw Puzzle Bargain
Was $39.95 — Now $2.95
(3 pieces missing; 8,997 still here)

How Do You Make Evangelism a Priority?

First, pray about it. Ask for forgiveness for your lack of involvement in this blessed ministry, for our church's tendency to hire somebody to do it, to expect television to do it, to expect somebody else to do it. Ask for a fresh and deep commitment to witnessing. *Second, read about evangelism in the Bible.* Warm your spiritual life by that fire. You will be moved by the Spirit. *Third, talk about evangelism* in your Bible Study class, with deacons, help us set church goals in this area. *Fourth, encourage each other.* Say a good word to those you know are out knocking on doors, and offer to go with them. *Fifth, increase your giving to this church* that there may be funds for materials for outreach. *Sixth, become personally involved in evangelism.* A man once told the great evangelist Dwight L. Moody: "I don't like the way you do evangelism." To that Moody responded, "I don't always like the way I do evangelism, either. How do you do it?" The critic replied, "Oh, I don't do evangelism," to which Moody said, "I like my way better!" We must get involved; any way of witnessing is better than no way at all!

Here are some practical suggestions for your involvement in witnessing. Put the weekly printed sermons in your offices and waiting rooms; that is certainly not too much to ask of you as a church member. Everybody needs to keep a few brochures about our church in your car. Call a staff member or a deacon and offer to go visiting with them one night soon. Call the Church Office and ask for the name of a family you can phone or visit. Bring somebody to church with you. Howard Lee, who greets folks in his inimitable way at the back door each Sunday, can testify to the fact that far too many of us come to church alone!

Let Us Not Tarry

Our text tells the story of four lepers who approached the city of Samaria during a siege. The city was surrounded and the people were starving to death within. Said one beggar to the rest, "If we go into the city we will starve with the rest; if we sit here at the gate we will likewise perish; let us go and surrender to the Syrian army surrounding the city; if they let us live, very well; if they kill us, we shall but die." But when they rose up in the twilight to go to the Syrians, they found no army there! The Lord had caused that army to hear a noise of chariots and horses, and they had all fled in the dusk. So now in growing darkness, the lepers went from tent to tent, eating and drinking, and taking all manner of treasure and hiding it during the night. Now look at verse 9: "We do not well: this day is a day of good tidings, and we hold our peace: if we tarry till the morning light, some mischief will come upon us: now therefore come, that we may go and tell the king's household."

They were but lepers; they did not have all the answers as to why the enemy fled; but they did realize the pressing priority of sharing the good news they possessed! We are like them—after all, evangelism is merely one beggar telling another beggar about the spiritual bread he has found, isn't it?

Listening to the Wrong Voice

Genesis 3:1-5; Matthew 4:1-11; Isaiah 30:21

Morality and Family Values have become a drum to beat for both political parties in this election year; but even so, I appreciate Attorney General William Barr's recent comment: "We are in the midst of a great moral crisis." He focused on the alley-cat antics of entertainer Woody Allen with his step-daughter. Allen seems surprised by all the fuss. "After all," he said, "the heart wants what the heart wants." In those seven words all morality, all integrity, all decency is cast out. Barr said those seven words capture contemporary moral philosophy.

What is Happening?

He is right. There seems to be no moral restraints in our society; the heart of darkness is found on every hand. I am simply speechless in the face of the wave of child abuse which is surfacing in our society, and I cannot fathom the charges of moral failure against ministers that I read about practically every day in the news. As we struggle to seek ways to get a handle on the racism in our city, as we grapple with the overload of TV violence and homosexuality and the rage of those who demand abortion be the standard, I find myself mumbling, What on earth is happening to us all?

The Voice of the Devil

And then I realize that I know full well what is happening; our society is responding to a voice—the wrong voice, too. As the shapers of our society slough off the moral constraints of 3000 years of Biblical ethics, it is in response to a voice in the air and in the ear—the voice of the devil. Perhaps those who proudly seek to pull down the edifice of Biblical ethics do not know they are following the urging of the devil; after all, our bent nature wants to take credit even when we should be ashamed and alarmed and afraid.

What the devil whispers into the ears of those who control the moral tone of our society, including those who control and produce our television programs and pour them into the minds of our children for several hours each day, always appeals to the lowest level. The devil appeals to our pride, our self-preservation, the "me first" attitude. He appeals to our comfort, our complacency, our culture. He appeals to the greed in us; to the lust and violence, to the herd instinct in us. And I tell you the air is ringing with his words; he is behind the moral dilemma, the crisis which we as a society face. The devil is behind the belittling of the sacredness of life. He is behind the divisive racial self-interest that always crops up in our city; he is behind the current trend for the churches of our land to be entertainment centers.

Here are sobering truths: *(1) the devil is real.* Funny how we who say we believe in the Bible refuse to take it seriously about the devil! It tells us the devil tried to destroy Jesus; that the devil's children are scattered in the church like the tares among the wheat (Matt 13:39); that the devil scoops up the gospel word from the heart of the lost person (Luke 8:12). Jesus realized that even though he himself chose the disciples, one of them was a devil (John 6:70)! The devil filled Judas' heart to betray Jesus (John 13:2). The devil fills even church members' hearts with rebellion against God (Acts 5:3). Paul warns us not to give any room to the devil; that the devil seeks an advantage—it is a wrestling metaphor.

(2) The devil is dedicated to the destruction of all that is godly in our world, our churches and in our society. *(3) He is bent on your destruction*—here and hereafter—don't relegate the devil just to hell—spiritually, morally, physically. And he doesn't care if you are a Christian or not. We take his work as "progress" and "expression of freedom" and all the while he is there, covering himself, appearing as an angel of light, the voice of reason, as ministers, politicians, TV directors and toy makers.

What is He Saying?

We find the devil talking to man at the very beginning of both Old and New Testaments, and what he said then to Adam and Eve is what he says to us today. And just what is that? What does he say that can persuade folks to wreck their own society as we are doing? Turn to Genesis 3 and examine what the devil told the first man and the first woman.

God Is Real But Not Relevant

The devil tells us that God is real but not relevant. What a mistake to think the devil wants to turn everybody into an atheist! No, he just wants each of us to think like, act like, live like there is no God. In the very first words to Eve, the devil acknowledges the reality of God.

God Isn't Honest With Us

The second thing the devil says to us is that God doesn't really want us to enjoy life. Look at verses 1 and 4 and 5. You and I have not met a talking snake on hind legs like Eve did, telling us that it is ridiculous, small and childish of God, to deny us the fruit of that one tree. But the prohibition of that tree is simply another way of describing God's moral law. The devil whispers to us that the moral law of God in the Bible, the 10 commandments, really isn't in our best interests. A few days ago one of our members handed me a newspaper article about a new book in which the author, a woman herself, maintained that adultery was good for folks; it helped women, especially, feel good about themselves. The author spoke with the voice of the devil. God says such behavior will destroy you.

The Devil Can Satisfy You

The third thing the devil says is that his devilish way will satisfy your desires and needs. Eve's musings on the "apple" shows how the devil seduces us—she rationalized the breaking of God's good command by saying the fruit looked good; the fruit surely was good to eat; and, after all, everyone wants to be smart. Eating the fruit, said the devil, would meet her needs. And the devil knows exactly what the human desires and needs are. Turn to another scripture, Matthew 4:1-11. Here we see the New Testament parallel to the temptation of Adam as the devil tempts Jesus. The devil appeals to the human tendency to want to be "Mr. Big." Buy the people's loyalty with bread. Jump off the steeple; when angels catch you they'll know you're a big shot. And finally the devil suggests Jesus throw all sense of integrity, all relationship with God to the winds, and worship the devil. In return the devil will deliver this world to him. The devil said he could meet the human needs of even Jesus. I doubt you would have seen the devil making those offers if you had been there; the devil's much too clever for that. He plants his ideas in the mind.

There's Nothing Special About Jesus

A fourth word of the devil: there's nothing special about Jesus. "One religion is as good as another." "It's enough to tip your hat at a divine being." Television is big on this. When religion is mentioned, when the name of God is mentioned outside of a profanity context—which is seldom—the emphasis is on vagueness, all-religions-are-created-equal stance. And the more weird the sample of religion is, the better. The Bible tells us in 1 John that the one who denies the divinity of Jesus does not know God, but is of the devil.

Never Deny Yourself

And the fifth word the devil whispers in your ear: you need never deny self for service to God. This is where the devil is most at work among Christians. Look with me at the Matthew 16. Here we have what is called the Great Confession. Jesus asked his disciples who folks were saying he was, and they replied that some folks said Jesus was a prophet, some said he was John the Baptist come back—but Peter declared that Jesus was the Messiah, the Son of the Living God. Jesus compliments Peter and assures him that this realization is of God. Jesus then begins to speak of the need for his suffering and death on the cross, but he is interrupted by Peter, who rebukes him for even thinking of such things!

And then we have the strange spectacle of Jesus—who only minutes before has complimented Peter on his spiritual understanding—now accusing Peter of being Satan! "Get thee behind me, Satan, for you speak not out of the things of God, but from the heart of men." This passage comes right to the heart of what Satan is whispering into the heart of Christians in our times. The devil seems to be saying to many people, Go on to church; just be sure you have your priorities right—go for entertainment, go to see what they can do for you, go to see how the church can fit into your plans for a secular life.

I fear that many church folks in these last years of the twentieth century are listening, unconsciously, to the devil more than to the Spirit of God. Like Peter, we cringe when the idea of sacrifice is mentioned. We would change sacrifice to convenience. We would use the church, rather than letting God use us through the church. It is as grave a misunderstanding of the Christian life as Peter's rebuke of Christ.

The Results of Listening to the Devil

The results of our listening to the devil are obvious. Over half the births in our County are out of wedlock; over half of all marriages end in divorce; grade school kids pack guns and metal detectors are being installed in area schools; drugs and alcoholism are a way of life; shopping centers are putting up guard towers; gambling gallops through our society taking bread from the mouths of children; and racism—by both black and white—continues to divide our city. There is great personal unrest and a continued undermining of the family and faith. This would be a sad world if the voice of the devil were the only voice speaking to us.

Another Voice

But there is another voice in this world. It is the voice of the Holy Spirit. We do not usually hear it or heed it until a crisis turns us from the clamor of the devil's voice. Some cannot hear the voice of God until they reach the depth of despair and failure. Often it takes a tragedy in our life before we hear God's voice. Sometimes we hear it, hauntingly, in a time of quietness in worship. Sometimes it is through the influence of a friend that we hear the voice of God. And what we hear is not of this world—it is not the voice of deceit, or destruction or delusion. It is the voice of the One who created us. Isaiah described that voice in Isaiah 31:21 "And your ears shall hear a word behind you saying, This is the way, walk in it; when you turn to the right hand and when you turn to the left." It is the voice of the Spirit of God. The voice of rest and fulfillment: "Come unto me, all ye that labor and are heavy laden, and I will give you rest." It is the voice of forgiveness, saying "Neither do I condemn you; go and sin no more." It is the voice of moral guidance: "If you love me, you will keep my commandments." It is the voice of love: "God so loved the world that he gave his only begotten son, that whosoever believeth in him should not perish but have everlasting life." It is a voice from beyond this world calling us to focus on that which will outlive this brief life. Things more lasting than a new car, new clothes, a new house or great wealth.

Why I Am A Christian

None of us listens only to one of the these two voices, that of the God or the devil. All of us have from time to time obeyed both. As I move through life and mark various milestones, I sometimes evaluate what I have done with my life and what I am doing with it. Is being a Christian the best way to spend your life? Why not eat and drink and be merry; why not cast morality and integrity to the winds? Many folks do. I keep coming back to these truths: I am a follower of Jesus Christ because in Him I have found what every human being craves: forgiveness; peace with God. It isn't just the Lee Atwaters who feel the need for forgiveness. I have never buried a single person who didn't feel the need at some point to "get right with God." There is a built-in hunger for a communion with God.

The second thing the Christian faith gives me is a perspective on this world. On the radio one day this week I heard of the couple who mowed their yard, cleaned the house, left notes all around, then committed suicide. They couldn't make sense of this world. But even when I can't make sense of it all, when everything goes wrong, I am still persuaded deep down that I am engaged in a work of eternal consequences. Too many people live apart from any personal relationship to Jesus, and always leaning over them is the realization that when they retire at 65 or 70, they will look in the mirror and realize that they have been no more than a cog in a machine; a program in the company computer. What was life all about? Was it different than the life of an animal—gathering food, fighting with other animals for sex, shelter, status? Most of us are smart enough to know that when we die, we don't take any money, any cars, any houses to wherever it is that folks go. The person who lives out of a relationship to Jesus has the deep satisfaction that whatever you do for a living is caught up in His great plan.

If your life is to have any ultimate meaning, you have to hitch your wagon to a star that survives your death. The only person who has ever tamed death is Jesus. Hundreds saw him die; a handful of those who loved him most carried him to his tomb. They were not expecting a resurrection—but he rose from the grave and is alive today. No other religion has a crucified, resurrected Saviour as its head.

So I am a Christian, I seek to walk with God, I seek to listen to His voice because He fulfills my deepest needs as a human being; in Him I find forgiveness, a sense of purpose, and I look forward to the life beyond this world.

The Sin of Overwork

I Kings 20:38-43

Occasionally we preachers preach on sins of the body such as sexual sins and occasionally even meddle into gluttony! We preach on the sins of the spirit such as worry, hate, and hypocrisy. That being so, should we not warn folks about the sin which touches both body and spirit such as the sin of overwork? And isn't Labor Day weekend an appropriate time? Yet several folks have said to me after seeing the sermon title,"Do you really think overwork is a problem in our society?" Well, there's no doubt we still have people who love work and who can watch it for hours! Folks like the old mountaineer and his son. They sat before the fire all evening, slowly rocking and crossing and uncrossing their legs. Finally the father said to the son, "Go outside and see if it's raining." Not even looking up, the boy replied, "Aw, Pa, why don't ye jest call in the dog and see if he's wet?" So, when I speak of the sin of overwork this morning, I'm not speaking of lazy people, or those who dread to go to boring jobs. I speak of those who love their work, and spend day and night on it, and in so doing sin against Almighty God in their work.

The story in 1 Kings 20 is a parable told by an unknown prophet to rebuke king Ahab for being too busy about the wrong things, for working too hard at the wrong job! During the heat of battle a man was given charge of a prisoner; told to guard him with his life. At first the man carefully guarded his prisoner, but in the confusion he slipped away for a few moments to wield his sword, and while he was gone- "busy here and there" by his own admission the prisoner also slipped away!

This is not only a parable in the Old Testament, it is a parable of our lives, too. That man rushing into the frenzy of battle is a mirror of modern life. Too many irons in the fire, seeking to serve too many masters, busy here and there, we often find the most important thing we are supposed to do has gotten away from us. We fight the battle of the clock, rushing here and there. Our schedules are as tight as our collars. A trip to Nashville for our grandfather was a trip of days; now if I fly over in the morning on church work I always try to hop an earlier plane home than scheduled so as to get in a half-day's work after I get back! I remarked to my wife Friday that I had risen during the 5 o'clock hour 4 mornings this past week to get work done. One morning I rose at 4:30 a.m. to return from a meeting of Moderate Baptists in Virginia, in order to get here in time to visit the hospitals and then prepare to lead the midweek prayer meeting. A while back I watched a friend who missed a trans-Atlantic flight get all uptight over a delay of a few hours at mostyet Columbus took over two months to make the trip! In church you can hear several watches alarming on the hour at noon! The battle of the hourglass.

Work Is Not A Sin

Now as we explore this business of the sin of overwork, let me give credit to Dr. Robert McCracken, successor to Fosdick at Riverside Church, for some of the thoughts, and let us mark first that work is not a sin, nor evil. It is true that the toilsome aspect of some work springs from our sinful nature, shown first in Adam's rebellion, and repeated in us (Gen 3:17f). But the commandment "Six days shalt thou labor, and do all thy work . . ." and other scriptures speak of work as our proper activity. "Let him that stole steal no more: but rather let him labor, working with his hands the thing which is good, that he may have to give to him that needeth." (Eph 4:28). And Jesus said, "I must work the works of him that sent me, while it is day: the night cometh, when no man can work" (Jn 9:4). God intends that men work, and in our work be a partner with Him in continuing His creative work in this world. That was Adam's task even before the fall; to be a partner with God by keeping the garden.

Work is the salt of life, building character. I love the story of the old man who was dictating his will to his lawyer, a long-time friend. "To my son John $25,000; to my son Bill $25,000; to my daughter Mary $25,000; to my grandchildren $10,000 each; to. . ." "Whoa," said the lawyer, "Your estate is only $50,000; just how are these beneficiaries going to get this money?" The old man sat up in bed in indignation. "Git it?" he shouted. "Let 'em work for it, same as I did!" Work is the salt of life, preserving it and giving zest. Lots of folks say they're through with work when they retire, but the folks who have no work, nothing to do in retirement, soon decline and fade away. We are made for creative, rewarding work, and will most likely experience that joy in heaven. As Kipling puts it:

> *When Earth's last picture is painted,*
> *And the tubes are twisted and dried,*
> *When the oldest colors have faded,*
> *And the youngest critic has died,*
> *We shall rest, and, faith, we shall need it*
> *Lie down for an aeon or two,*
> *Till the Master of All Good Workmen*
> *Shall put us to work anew.*

And those that were good shall be happy:
They shall sit in a golden chair;
They shall splash at a ten-league canvas
With brushes of comet's hair;
They shall find real saints to draw from
Magdalene, Peter, and Paul;
They shall work for an age at a sitting,
And never be tired at all!
And only the Master shall praise us,
And only the Master shall blame;
And no one shall work for money,
And no one shall work for fame;
But each for the joy of the working,
And, each, in his separate star,
Shall draw the Thing as he sees It
For the God of Things as They are.

Overwork Shortchanges Life

Work is no sin, but overwork is, because it results in shabby work. The text shows the result of "biting off more than we can chew." It is better to do a bit less and do it well! Nobody is a credit to himself, God, or his employer when he does shabby work. Overwork is a sin because it sacrifices your health. Often we are so busy we ignore our body's need for exercise, we get overweight, flabby, have heart attacks (I'm preaching to myself now). No doubt we have time, but we think we don't. Often the overworked person doesn't sleep well, and may not eat right. And it is not only the physical health we sacrifice, but the emotional health as well. Too much pressure strains the mind and the emotions, and we get irritable, tempers flare up, we get depressed. Then we go home and take it out on the wife, or husband, who takes it out on the kids, who take it out on the dog, who takes it out on the cat, which is why our cat is neurotic! Or you may begin to lean on alcohol or drugs to "get on top of things." Work is no sin, but overwork is, because it shortchanges the family. A husband's death or divorce is not the only kind of "absentee father" children experience. The pun in which the child asks, "who's that man?" when Dad comes home has grim truth in it for too many homes. Gone in the morning before the kids are up, and never home until past their bedtime.

Yet we all have some control over our time. I make a plea for two things: first, make sure you have some leisure time. Life is meant to have rhythm to it, a rhythm of the stress of toil, and the release of rest. It is true that the bow always bent will have no power when it is needed. This is a beautiful world; slow down and smell the roses! I remember seeing, during my seminary days, the respected New Testament professor Dr. E. A. McDowell standing by a tree one day between classes, totally absorbed in watching a squirrel up in the tree. When was the last time you really noticed a bird, a squirrel, or a flower? We rush and rush as if the company, the church, the job cannot do without us; yet I've buried a lot of people in the midst of their working career; some dead through overwork, and their companies went right on without them.

Overwork Shortchanges God

My second plea is that we recover a sense of spiritual perspective, because overwork shortchanges God. William Temple, in an address at Oxford, said the world is like a shop into which someone came during the night and changed all the price tags around. The cheap items were priced high, and the precious items were tagged cheap! That's the way this world is, and my plea is for recognition of the true values Jesus taught. And we will only do that by making room for a relationship to God. I've got enough sense to know that if I only impress on you the sin of overwork, I'll have a line of teachers waiting to resign their Sunday School classes! When I tell folks to slow down, the first thing many people cut out is their church work! No, listen: spend your life on the supreme values Jesus taught. Your relationship to God; your relationship to His Church; the building of your family; these are most important! We must pick and choose in life. Some things we shouldn't have time for! Some things we should make time for. Ask yourself, "What am I here, in this world, for? The work you do to feed your family is only a part of why God put you here. The point of this sermon is simply this: the soldier in our text fell down on his job; the king fell down on his job; and too many of us, like them, are "busy here and there," even overworked, while neglecting that which God wants us to do and sent us to do.

"As the Father hath sent me, so send I you," said Jesus. He sends us to do a special task that no one else in the world can do. And that leads me to say that God has a work, a plan for the life of each person. Surely the Wonderful Father who sent His Son to die for our sins, the Great Creator who so guides the flight of the geese and clothes the duck with such glorious colors—just last week I received from the taxidermist a beautiful wood duck I bagged this past winter, and what colors! Surely the God who so provides for the rest of creation has a marvelous and meaningful plan for each life. Our problem is that too many of us have forgotten God's plan for our lives. We are like the boy whose schoolteacher had asked him to bring his birth certificate to school the next day. Naturally, he forgot to bring it, and confessed when asked about it, "I forgot to bring my excuse for being born." There is a divine reason for the birth, the life, of each of us.

On the coronation day of King George V in 1910 a businessman sat in his London office window to watch the parade go by below. He began noticing a teen-aged boy hanging precariously from a lamp post, and finally went down to invite him up to the office to a better perch. As the king's royal coach drew near, the boy stared at it in pride and admiration, and when it passed, he turned to the businessman and said over and over, "Did you see those lamps? Didn't they shine!" He told the man how he worked in a coach manufacturing plant and his job had been to shine the lamps of this particular carriage to be used for the coronation. He was proud of his work, and rightly so.

Take time to evaluate your relationship to God; to ponder the meaning of the death of Jesus; and to respond to the Living Christ. Remember the parable Jesus told of the wedding feast, and the excuses? I don't know all that lay behind each man's excuse; they were all legitimate endeavours: the purchase of the farm, the five oxen deal, and the third had gotten married! "As thy servant was busy here and there, he was gone..."

Retire From Church? Never!

Galatians 6:8-9; Titus 2:1-5

A Sermon for Senior Adults

This is a sermon for retired folks. The rest of you can leave if you're sure you will never grow old, never reach the "Golden Years," never need Medicaid or Medicare, never be called a "Senior Citizen."

I am accustomed to folks retiring from their business, whether that is repairing clocks or hearts, teaching or preaching, or selling shoes or booze. People retire.

But I have never gotten used to seeing people retire from church! My first experience with that phenomenon came as a ripe old college senior, 20 years old and brand new pastor of the Cassia Baptist Church between DeLand and Eustis, Florida. My church field was a haven for sand fleas, palmettos, yellow flies, scrub oaks, mosquitoes, rattlesnakes, and Yankees. We had 13 members. I beat the bushes as only a starry-eyed student who doesn't know it can't be done will do and yet the answer was the same: "Young man, I came here to retire from everything!"

Not all the elderly couples felt that way; some took their religion and the young pastor in stride. I still remember the Sunday night our van broke down on the lonely stretch of road between the church field and college. We had started a revival that morning; it was late, so the preacher and I just slept in the van that night, after we pushed it off the pavement. All night long there was the humming of mosquitoes, broken only at intervals by the increasing sound of a automobile, which would crescendo in a "whoosh" as it passed, leaving our van rocking, and the mosquitoes humming. About 4 o'clock we gave it up, and set out walking to the nearest church member's home, a couple of miles away. We sat on their front porch until dawn, and shortly thereafter, we heard folks stirring inside, and the door opened. An impish, bald-headed old Yankee just looked at us as if he found preachers on his doorstep every morning, and hollered back inside the house: "Mom, put on some more pancakes; here's two hungry boys!"

That old couple was a real blessing to many lives in that community and that church. As I said, the church had 13 members when I came; upon my graduating less than a year later, the church had 56 members—due to the hard work of the retired folks. That's the way God wants it.

The Church and Senior Adults

This is not a sermon on "Life Begins At Forty," or "How To Live All Your Life," but it is a sermon probing the relationship between retirement and your church involvement. Here are some things I believe about older folks and the church:

1. There are a lot of retired folks in this church.

2. Our church cannot and ought not carry out its mission apart from them

3. Every retired member ought to find a ministry he can do in the church.

4. The church must recognize the value of older members.

Is that Biblically based? Is it true? Let's look at the reality of older folks. As a nation we've had a one-track mind for a good while, focusing entirely on youth. Watching TV ads would make you wonder if our country has any citizens over 25! And churches have followed this lead by emphasizing areas such as youth, pre-school, children—which we should have done, but we have largely ignored the long gray line, the invisible senior adults. I think we will soon realize that older people exist, too: In 1900 only 4% of the U.S. population was over age 65; today 10% is over 65; by 2000 13% will be over 65. The retirees are coming!

This rise in the number of elderly folks is due in large part to higher standards of living and better health care. Which means we need to lay aside the myth that all older people are in poor health.

"On an average, old people spend less than fifteen days a year in bed due to illness. ... 80% of all aged say their health is excellent, good, or fair..."[1]

In our own church, there are many folks who are retired. Our long range study showed that 40% of our members are age 60 or over. Can I level with you? This church cannot grow, it cannot even maintain itself in the future unless our older people become more involved. There are simply not enough couples in their twenties and thirties to staff a Sunday School of over 1000. Right now we are needing teachers in the younger areas and so many children need that grandparent touch. With the elderly population growing, who can better lead in ministries and outreach to this group than senior adults themselves? Your church needs you!

The Bible and Senior Adults

Now, what picture does the Bible give of older members of the Family of God? Obviously, there is Abraham and Sarah, who started trusting God in their younger days and found God able to make them fruitful in their nineties! We think of Moses, who at the age of 80 led the people out of Egypt. In connection with that, turn to Numbers 11:16-17 and

Hebrews 11:2; here are the more ordinary older folks of God's people. We remember Samuel, who in old age was still guiding and rebuking kings.

Witness to the Messiah is given by Simeon and Anna when Jesus is only days old and Anna is 84 years old! At Pentecost Peter quotes Joel 2:27-28 (Acts 2:16f) about the pouring out of God's Spirit on His people and the visions of the future. James urges the sick to call the elders (James 5:14) surely a term reflecting the fact that mature years and leadership were not separated. And Paul, in Titus 2:1-5, gives advice to the older people in the church.

The Pattern for Senior Adults

Summing up all this evidence, we find that older Christians are to be wise, caring, burden-bearers, full of faith. What a beautiful personality that describes! Secondly, they are to be leaders. Full of dreams for the future; out in front in planning and promoting the Kingdom. Look at Caleb in Joshua 14. We are familiar with Caleb I, the first segment of Caleb's story here in Numbers is Caleb II, the second part of his story. You remember how in the first part he and Joshua differed with the report of the other ten spies concerning the Promised Land. Because of the cowardice of the ten, the tribes wandered for 40 years, and all adults save Joshua and Caleb died. Now hear the second part, the conclusion of Caleb's story. The Promised Land has been divided up among the tribes, and in verses 7 through 12 Caleb comes to Joshua saying: "Give me that hard part; the mountains full of giants I can handle it!" His views at 85 were an extension of his forward stance at 40!

The older saints are to be examples to the others. Listen, you who are older can never really know how much the younger people watch you and unconsciously model their faith and church relationship after you. You may think the youth see you only as old fogeys who cast a baleful eye on their whispering and note-passing . . . but they see more. They will never forget you! I still remember vividly the Junior department in Sunday School, the teachers and the contests and the verses we learned! I still see in my mind's eye older folks in their pews, serving as deacons, praying in church services, visiting in the community.

We Need You

It is true in our own church. Just to call up names of some of our departed saints brings back a rush of beautiful memories: Mertie Chapman, Tarwanda Garabedian, Dr. Hamilton... and some still with us: Ruth Young, Frank and Marian Quinn, Aubrey Byrn, Fred Strain, Roy Talley. We need examples in how to love and worship God. Your presence here in old age speaks of the abiding values of your life. We need examples in how to serve God. Do you know who has done more visiting than anybody else in this church in recent years? He just turned 80 this past week—Roy Talley! He reminds me of that article in the most recent issue of Royal Service which describes a prayer group of 16 ladies between the ages of 73 and 89. But the article says they send cards, carry on a shut-in ministry, prepare prison kits, help migrants.

We do not all enjoy excellent health, whether we are young or old, but regardless of health, there are ministries we can do. Try on these suggestions:

> *You can be enthusiastic about your church.*
> *You can teach Sunday School.*
> *You can encourage staff, deacons, teachers.*
> *You can sing in the Senior Adult choir.*
> *You can send birthday cards to members.*
> *You can call or visit for the church.*
> *You can do a religious survey of your neighborhood.*
> *You can distribute the printed sermons in waiting rooms,*
>   *beauty and barbershops, etc.*
> *You can help check out requests for help, such as the*
>   *Thanksgiving baskets, etc.*

. . . that's enough to get you thinking.

We need examples in how to be grateful to God. Your example of stewardship is a model for all the rest of the congregation. You can be an example both during your life, by tithing, and after you are gone, through your will as you remember the church.

We need your example in how to grow old. For all of us will grow old if God lets us live. The world does not teach us how to grow old; in fact, the unpardonable sin in our society is not AIDS, or Adultery, or murder—but to grow old! Our culture denies the reality of aging in every possible way. So you must be our Enoch . . . walking with God and showing us the way, and someday we will say of you, "He walked with God, and he was not, for God took him." We need to hear you saying with dignity and love and grace and faith:

> *Grow old along with me!*
> *The best is yet to be,*
> *The last of life, for which the first was made:*
> *Our times are in His hand*
> *Who saith "A whole I planned,*
> *Youth shows but half; trust God: see all, nor be afraid!"*[2]

We need you. But are you willing to be the leaders the Bible calls you to be? The example? The teacher of faith? Are you willing to shoulder that responsibility? Your motivation must be, first of all, gratitude to God for His blessings. Then, a love for the Church, the Body of Christ. The choice is yours. You have more time to devote to church work than most young couples in the midst of raising a family and making a living. You need the blessed work of serving God in these retirement years. You need the joy of contributing to other lives for God.

We often think how sad it would be to have no children on the streets, as reflected in the song *"The King Is Coming."* Just as sad would be the lack of older people standing tall in the churchvisiting, encouraging, praying, worshipping!

Your young men shall see visions, and your old men shall dream dreams . . . " And both shall be used of God to build His Kingdom!

[1]Statistics given by J. Winston Pearce in his delightful little book, **Ten Good Things I Know About Retirement.**

[2]The first verse of Robert Browning's poem, *"Rabbi Ben Ezra."*

Stones

I Peter 2:1-10

The Holy Land is a land of stones. Until I visited Israel I had no idea how rocky that place is. There are rabbinic legends of how God sent out two angels at the time of creation, each with a sack of rocks to scatter over all the earth; one poor angel's sack of stones split open above the land of Israel, and half the world's rocks were dumped right there! So it is not surprising that all through the Bible we keep reading about stones—altar stones, remembrance stones, stones for pillows, stones in fields, stones in slings, even stoning as a way to execute criminals.

Stones

When Jacob lay a'dying down in Egypt land, his thoughts went back to his rocky homeland, and that strange night when he used a stone for a pillow, and how the Lord was good to him. And as he called in his sons and blessed each of them, he reminded them of the mighty "Stone of Israel," the Great Shepherd.

When Solomon set his hand to build the magnificent temple, we are told that he declared there would be no sound of hammer and mallet at the building site. And so it is that at the north side of Jerusalem you may yet see Solomon's quarries, caves that tunnel beneath the holy city. In these caves Solomon's engineers quarried the magnificent stone for the temples. Josephus describes the Temple for us and the glory of the stones. He tells us some of the stones were 60 feet long, 18 feet high, 12 feet wide—magnificent, huge stones. There is a legend about one of those stones; a huge stone was quarried, dragged to the temple site, put into place, but it would not fit. They turned it this way and that to no avail. Finally the builders rejected that stone, saying "it doesn't fit anywhere!" They dragged it over to the side, and the grass grew over it. But then as the temple neared completion, a certain stone was needed, of a definite size and cut in a particular way. After a long search, the rejected stone was found to be the one needed. Perhaps that legend is behind Psalm 118:22, where the writer tells us that the stone the builders rejected has become the cornerstone.

When Isaiah confronted those leaders of Israel who had a covenant with death, he said God was laying in Zion for a foundation stone a tried stone, a precious corner stone, a sure foundation (28:16). When Daniel wrote in exile he used the stone as a symbol of the kingdom of the Messiah. He describes pagan kingdoms as a statue made of brass, clay and iron which is destroyed when a stone uncut by human hands suddenly rises up and smashes the statue.

God's word is rich with the symbolism of stones, reaching its most striking use in Jesus' comments as he told the parable of the Vineyard in Matthew 21. The tenants of the master's vineyard refuse to give the owner's portion to his messengers, and when he sends his son, they kill him. Jesus summed up the story with these words: "Have you never read in the Scriptures the very stone which the builders rejected has become the head of the corner?"

Perhaps that was the first time Simon Peter had ever heard the idea of a person being the "Stone of Israel." But now Peter began to understand that Jesus is the cornerstone of all that God is doing. And in Acts 4, when Peter and other disciples are arrested for preaching the gospel, he declares that Jesus is the cornerstone which was rejected by the builders (10-11). The Messiah as the living stone, the cornerstone of all God's intentions for mankind, comes to the front again when Peter, as an elderly man, writes to the church in the shadow of persecution. Let us turn to 1 Peter 2 and see how he speaks of stones.

The Living Stone

He begins by calling Christ the "living stone." Peter reminds the Christians that when they believed in the gospel, they came to Christ as "unto a living stone, disallowed indeed by men, but chosen by God, and precious" (verse 4). Remember again that rock cut out of the quarry below the city of Jerusalem, hauled up to the site of the building of the Temple, rejected by the builders, lying there off to the side—this is the picture with which Simon Peter begins. But see that particular one, laid over to the side. Peter says it was a living stone. It refused to be forgotten. It refused to be cast aside; although grass grew upon it, it refused to die—it was a living stone. And when Peter brings all the prophecies of God to bear upon that living stone, he is saying in the first place that God's eternal plan for the ages is embodied in this person Jesus. He is the living stone.

He is saying in the second place that this living stone, though rejected by the builders, has been declared choice and precious by God. Therefore, God's choice is a reversal of human judgment. And he is saying in the third place that though men may reject the corner stone, yet it remains unaltered through the ages as God's chosen cornerstone.

The Living Stones

That living stone draws us as the magnet draws the filings, and we become part of it, drawn to him. We partake of his life. We partake of his calling. We partake of his destiny. He is the living stone, and our dead lives become living stones, as he points out in verse 5. Living stones for a beautiful purpose. Just think on the imagery Peter uses here. Many of the Christians were of Jewish background in these first decades of the church and would understand his symbols. He says we are living stones, building blocks in a spiritual temple.

I suppose that when Peter wrote these words the temple was still standing. Now for centuries the Jews had a beautiful and awe-inspiring temple there in Jerusalem; remember how impressed the disciples were, calling Jesus' attention to the huge stones. But in god's sight was the building the true temple? Obviously not, for as God said to David and Solomon when the temple was being planned and as Stephen reemphasized in his sermon just before he was stoned (!) to death, God's delight is in his people, not in a building, the work of men's hands.

A few days ago I was showing my grandson, Alexander, this community center and told him this was our new church. He glanced around at the building and promptly asked, "Where's the steeple?" I told him the told chimney would have to be our steeple for awhile! The building is not nearly so important as the real church, the people! When God looks at the Trinity Baptist Church He does not see this community center, a charming but old school building; rather He sees the group gathered here this morning to offer worship and praise to our Living Christ. The people are the church!

Each individual church has its spiritual and invisible counterpart, the spiritual temple which those who are members of that particular church are building. Like the temple in Jesus' day, the spiritual temple is in the process of being built but not yet complete and always changing. Our lives together make up the church, the spiritual temple in the process of being built. And if our attitude is right, if our commitment is there, if our hearts are right, then that spiritual temple which you and I are building together for the glory of God is a beautiful thing.

The quality of the spiritual temple, the quality of the spiritual worship depends upon the living stones. I remember how touched I was to read the diary of David Livingstone after visiting his home in Scotland. He spent his life in Africa for the Lord, dying on his knees in prayer one morning. Those men to whom he had preached, with whom he had lived and prayed and died, took his body thousands of miles to the coast where the British took the body back to England to be received in great honor and be buried in Westminster Abbey. A secular magazine, Punch, said, "David Livingstone was buried today in Westminster Abbey amidst all the marble and the fine stone. Let other stone crumble—this is Living Stone." So he was and is; so we are.

The CornerStone

But Peter goes on—he has spoken of the living stone, and then of the living stones, but now in verse 6 he quotes from Isaiah 28 to speak of the cornerstone: "Behold, saith the Lord, I will lay in Zion a stone, chosen, precious, a cornerstone." A cornerstone means community, cooperation, unity, a cornerstone demands working together. A cornerstone implies the kind of fellowship we had the other night when we gathered to take down the wall which divided this area in which we worship—a lot of folks came too late to do much work, but we all sat around and ate pizza and had a grand fellowship! It is possible to have an isolated, solitary tombstone, but a cornerstone demands cooperation. In the old days the cornerstone was the starting place, the place from which all the rest of the building got its soundness. In the church the cornerstone of the spiritual temple we are building is Jesus—not any other person, not a past, not a program, but Jesus. The intention of God is that on Jesus, the cornerstone, our lives be built into a temple to God, ministering in his name, reaching the lost in his name, and worshiping him in his name. That's what we are to do. And for every inactive member of any church, there is a gaping hole, missing stones, in the spiritual temple each church as God sees it.

The Stumbling Stone

Simon Peter goes on to speak of another stone in verses 6-8, the stumbling stone. Jesus is at the same time both the cornerstone of the spiritual temple and the stone of stumbling in the pathway of those who do not believe. It is not true to say that you can either take or leave Jesus and his claims upon you. The Bible says that Jesus is going to be like the rock in the path and you will keep on meeting him when you don't expect it and you will stumble over him. Jesus, you see, has a relationship to everybody—he is either the cornerstone or the stumbling stone to every single individual in this world.

To some Jesus is the cornerstone—the cornerstone of faith, the cornerstone of life, the cornerstone of fellowship here in the church, the cornerstone of his hope beyond the grave. Such people are rich in faith and hope and love. But if the man in our town who is richest in material goods does not have a relationship to Christ, he will find Jesus not to be the cornerstone, but to be the stumbling stone. And he will stumble on Jesus all his days. And verse 8 says that such are destined to stumble—stumble in this life, and keep on stumbling through eternity.

Precious Stones

I point you to one other kind of stone we find in this passage. In a time of persecution Peter dares claim for this little band of believers all that the rabbis claim for the nation of Israel throughout the centuries. The church—in its universal and invisible sense and in its local sense—is special to God. The church is a chosen group, a group of royal priests, a holy group, a special people. This same idea is expressed so beautifully in Malachi 3:16-17, where we are called God's jewels. The key in this present passage to understanding how special we are to God is in verse 9, in KJV English, God's "peculiar" people. The Greek word there is a word used to speak of a little child's favorite toys: marbles, his sling, his choice pebbles, maybe a bit of glass that he had picked up (only the rich had things made of glass), a piece of candle that had melted down in a beautiful way in his eyes—little treasures that wouldn't mean anything to anybody else, but to the little boy meant a great deal. That's the word used here to speak of you and of me as God's own special treasures.

And we have a special work to do. We are called to do the work of a priest, something not even the king could do in the Old Testament—

remember how King Uzziah decided to act the part of a priest and offered sacrifices, even going into the Holy of Holies over the protests of the priests. He was suddenly stricken with leprosy and fled from the Holy Place to live in isolation the rest of his days and his son took his place as king. The king shall not be priest , but you, my friend, and I are called to be priests; royal priests, for we are children of the King. What are the spiritual sacrifices that we, who are part of the spiritual temple, are to be giving to God? The only sacrifice you and I can really give to God is the sacrifice of our lives in his service in praise.

Peter ends this passage with a beautiful statement: You who once were nobody, you are now somebody. You who once had received no mercy, now you have mercy. For we are God's precious jewels Why do women wear beautiful jewelry? To give glory to the person, to bring out the beauty, to compliment them. So you and I, says this passage, are the beautiful stones of God, the precious jewels of God. We are to show forth the mighty deeds of him who called us out of darkness into his marvelous light. My, what a privilege it is to be a Christian, to be able to be a part of that great company who are living stones of God. Your life can be a living stone too, through him who is the Living Stone, Jesus Christ. Through him who is the cornerstone, laid in Zion for your peace.

The Career of the Soul

Text for sermon

The writer of psalm 49 makes an interesting and keen observation in his closing verse when he says some men are like animals. What is the difference between man and the rest of God's creation? Granted we often act like animals; but there is a tremendous difference! Most of us would say without hesitation: the difference is that man has a soul! But exactly what is a soul? Have you ever seen a soul? Touched a soul?

What is the Soul?

I realize that I am not talking to New Testament scholars who debate the difference between body, soul, and spirit, and I hate to dabble in Greek in a sermon, but it might be helpful to you to know that when your New Testament speaks of a person's life or soul, the Greek word most often used is a little word pronounced *Sue-Kay*. Just think of a beautiful Mississippi girl with one of those double first names, Sue-Kay, and you have the word translated both life and soul. This little word is the root and inspiration for our English words like psychology and psychiatry, and when we say a person is psychic . . .

The Meaning of Sue-Kay

The first use of this word, sue-kay, is to designate individual, personal life. In the Sermon on the Mount Jesus urges us to "take no thought for your life" (sue-kay). In John 15:13 we read that "greater love than this hath no man, that a man lay down his life for his friends." (sue-kay).

But there is a higher use of this little word when we translate it as "soul," a term sprinkled all through the Bible. In Genesis we read that God breathed into Adam and he became "a living soul." Jesus in Matthew 11:29 bids us take His yoke upon us . . . and find rest for our souls. And when the Greeks come to Jesus, he comments, "Now is my soul troubled." It means more than just your life; it means your life as lived in the presence of God, before the face of God. It means life with a dimension none other of the animal creation has: life with the possibility of an eternal relationship to God. It means life filled with a spiritual dimension as opposed to life lived on the natural levelwhere men spend their energy getting and begetting, taking and being overtaken by misfortune and death. We are born into this world and into time, we live and die in ticking time, but our having a soul means we have the possibility of a dimension of life not confined to time and this world; but opening onto eternity and heaven. In brief, our soul is our awareness of God and our relationship with Him. Our soul gives us the possibility of living our physical life as God intended, and receiving eternal life in His presence as a gift.

Does every person have a soul? Yes, every one of us; the good and the mean, the bad and the ugly, the rich and the poor, the wise and the foolish, the religious and the irreligious, has a soul. Each human being stands before God, both in this world and the next, and each of us fashions our soul, our relationship to God, and are responsible for it.

Can the Soul be Lost?

Does that mean we can lose our soul? Indeed, we can lose our soul. Turn to Matthew 10:28 for a striking illustration of the soul as our relationship to God which God can destroy and terminate. "And fear not them which kill the body, but are not able to kill the soul: but rather fear him which is able to destroy both soul and body in hell." We see clearly that the soul is more than the body, and cannot be destroyed by men. But we ought to notice that God may reject our soul, our relationship to Him, if it is unworthy of His presence or if we have used it carelessly and made it an enemy of God.

Not only can God destroy our soul, but we ourselves can cast it away. Look with me at Mark 8:34-37. Here is how many people lose their souls. Notice that verse 34 is a call to follow Jesus: "Whosoever will come after me, let him deny himself, and take up his cross, and follow me." But what is the meaning of verse 35-37? "For whosoever will save his life will lose it; but whosoever shall lose his life for my sake and the gospel's, the same shall save it." Turn with me to Psalm 49, especially verses 6-7, 9-15, 20. The Psalmist has realized that the man who desperately seizes and hangs onto the booty of this world may collect houses and lands called by their name, they may be praised by their descendants but none of them can redeem his brother from the grave that he should live forever, or pay God a ransom for him! Now read Mark 8:36-37! What Jesus is saying here is plain: the man whose heart and mind is focused on this world, on the providing of a comfortable and easy existence, will lose his deeper soul, his sue-kay. Only the one who is willing to lose, to give up his grip, on this material world will in the long run save his soul. And what this losing of this worldly life consists of is clear: he must follow Jesus.

A tragic illustration of gaining this world's goods and losing one's soul is seen in the story of the Rich Fool in Luke 12. This man even talks to himself, to his spiritual side, his soul. And he tries to feed his soul on the things of this world. But he ignored the fact that the soul is not just a standard piece of equipment that comes with a car or an appliance.

The soul is more like that new baby with tiny hands and feet and wet diapers and wailing; the soul is fed, and grows, through a realization of the spiritual nature of life.

How is Your Soul Doing?

And now we come to the question of the sermon. Is your soul growing? We often speak of a person's career. We say, "Joe, how's the medical career, or the law or marketing career coming along?" And perhaps here at the beginning of a new year it is appropriate to ask each other: How is the career of your soul coming along? It would be wonderful if every pastor could write to his church people as the writer of III John did, and assume the health and prosperity of their soul: "Beloved, I wish above all things that thou mayest prosper and be in health, even as thy soul prospereth." Has there been any change in your soul during this past year of 1990? Is your soul poorer or richer spiritually?

Have you ever thought about your soul growing and changing? Many good people, church-going, Bible-believing, baptized folks see their soul as a static, unchangeable, once-for-all possession given at birth. They are anxious for the soul to be acknowledged, the transaction to be made with Christ, the church to be joined. But that is the end. To them the saving of the soul is a transaction, not a relationship.

Jesus described such folks when he talked about the man who started building the house and only got as far as the foundation! Some folks are content for their souls to live in basements all their lives. If our souls do not grow, we run the risk of losing our souls to this world; of our having our traitorous souls condemned at the Judgment Day.

A study of the Bible will reveal that those we deem most spiritual, most mature, took seriously the need for their soul to grow and develop. For instance, here is Simon Peter, waiting on the rooftop in Joppa for lunch. I feel certain he has been pondering what for him was a real problem: Does God love everybody equally? In Acts 8 we see Philip organizing a church in Samaria, of all places. Peter is sent up from Jerusalem to make sure it is "kosher," and in verse 25 we read that he preached all the way back to Jerusalem! Through the same Samaritan villages which refused to give hospitality to Jesus, and on which James and John wanted to call down fire! Those unclean Samaritans! But now it seems God is doing a strange and wonderful work in that same area; how can this be? Does God accept Samaritans? I feel sure that Peter is still wrestling with this matter of inviting anyone of any race and color to worship and serve God with him, as he meditates and ponders on the rooftop in Joppa. You know the story; the sheet appeared from the sky; whether it is a dream or a wide-awake vision is not important, he saw the scene and heard the voice of God declaring that whatever God called clean was clean regardless of what Peter thought. Then the knock on the door, and the Gentile soldier Cornelius' request. And Peter went, and preached to them, and then defended them before the entire church. What a step of growth for the soul of Peter! But a careful reading shows how he was struggling as he grew.

Or see Paul in Philippians 3, as he writes to the church in Philippi, telling them that he is not complacent, not satisfied with the spiritual development he has reached. Pick it up with verse 7, and hear him as he says he has flung all his past, all his worldly goals and dreams, behind him so that he might, if possible, be found in the Judgment Day in such a close relationship to Christ that he knows the fellowship of suffering with Christ, and may be worthy of the resurrection. And then in verse 12: "not as though I had already attained, either were already perfect: but I follow after, if that I may apprehend that for which also I am apprehended of Christ Jesus. . . . this one thing I do, forgetting those things which are behind, and reaching forth unto those things which are before, I press toward the mark for the prize of the high calling of God in Jesus Christ." Those we count closest to Christ kept on encouraging their soul to grow.

Helping the Soul to Grow

So by what means does the soul grow? What can you, I, any person, do to help our soul develop? Here are some suggestions for the grow-

The Career of the Soul

ing soul in the New Year. *Let us be constantly mindful of the vast spiritual realm.* Samuel Miller, late Dean of the Harvard Divinity School, tells of an old custom of the Puritan settlers. Each day they went down from the town to the sea and gazed long into its vastness, thinking the deep thoughts of those who have sought a new country and have left the security of an old one. But as time went on, the sea was taken for granted, and the settlers got more and more immersed in the busyness of their lives. And there grew up along the edge of the sea warehouses, piers, and walls until even if they had been inclined to go down to the sea and gaze into its vastness again and think the deep thoughts of pilgrims, they could not have easily seen it.

Could that be a parable of our lives? Do we get lured away by the discoveries of our scientific world until we have walled off the vast spiritual world? Are our worship opportunities and experiences merely the result of long habit? Did you come to this place today, or turn on your radio or television, with the expectation of drawing closer to God, of experiencing a spiritual adventure?

Another suggestion is to let your spiritual life be pliable, flexible in this year. If we want our souls to grow, we must be like Simon Peter, and try to break out of old molds, old wineskins, both in our personal spiritual life and in the corporate life of our church. Be willing to try new approaches in worship, in witnessing, in ministry. Let Peter be our model.

A third suggestion: let us stop protecting our souls. Spiritual growth, growth of the soul, can be a scarey, painful, lonely pilgrimage, but in this year let us dare to do those things which bring spiritual growth. Like Peter, let us dare to respond to the leading of the Spirit in our lives. And I am not talking of earthshaking deeds in the eye of the world; I am talking about adventures in changing of attitude and deeds that perhaps only you and God will notice. If the Spirit bids you re-dedicate your life, then do it. If you feel led to kneel and pray at the altar at the close of the service, do it. If you feel like standing up and saying, "Hallelujah!" at the close of a choir song or a hymn or in the middle of the sermon, then do it! If you feel led to speak to someone about their relationship to Jesus but you're afraid you may appear foolish, never mind that, just do it! If you feel convicted to tithe your income, but you don't see how you can, do it anyway! Do you see what I am saying? Let us in this year untie our souls, let them find new and fresh adventures. And then let us share in testimonies from time to time the growth of our souls.

Somebody's soul may be reaching out this very morning to Jesus as Lord and Saviour. For Jesus died to redeem us, body and soul.

Now may our benediction be that of Paul to the Thessalonians: "And the very God of peace sanctify you wholly; and I pray God your whole spirit and soul and body be preserved blameless unto the coming of our Lord Jesus Christ" (1 Thessalonians 5:23).

The Gospel Truth

I Peter 3:18-22

One of the biggest problems I wrestle with in my spiritual life is my understanding of suffering, especially the suffering of the innocent. It has haunted me ever since I was in the fifth or sixth grade, in that handful of years just after WWII. I saw in a library book one day a photo of a trench with people lined up on the other side, and a soldier was shooting them one at a time in the back of the head. Little children and mothers and fathers. And it chilled me to think that someone stood on "my" side of the trench and from my perspective had the heart—or lack of it—to take such photographs of such a terrible thing. Questions come to mind like *Where was God?* Where is he in such times? Why do these things happen?

The most satisfying answer we will ever get to such questions is in God's Word. Turn to the third chapter of 1 Peter. Here he has been talking about suffering. Who among us hasn't suffered? He talks about suffering unjustly. And as Peter gives hope and comfort to suffering Christians, he is reminded of the suffering and death of Christ. Look at verses 18-22. While this is one of the most controversial passages in the Bible, it is also one of the most glorious and hope-filled passages. Peter turns to the suffering of Christ and makes three points: Jesus suffered and died for our sins, Jesus won a total and complete victory, and Jesus rose again and reigns on high and is coming again.

We almost need a chorus, like the Greek chorus in the children's film Hercules, a chorus that chants as they did, "That's the gospel truth!" Now in Hercules, the chorus underlined the hard-nosed, hard-boiled, hard-edged facts by saying, "that's the gospel truth!" There wasn't any hope in the truth, just the facts. But here Peter is giving us the real Gospel truth, full of hope and glory for each of us who will listen to the Gospel and accept it for our lives.

Truth #1: Christ Died For Our Sins

What I am about to tell you ought to come into your ears as an amazing thing. Those who are not Christians have every right to burst out laughing and walk away shaking their heads. It is a symptom of our complacency and lukewarmness as Christians that the Gospel story does not stir us. Christ also has suffered (died in the oldest manuscripts) for sins once for all, the just for the unjust, that he might bring us to God.

To calmly accept that a man could die 2000 years ago and affect our daily life, put us right with God, and cause us to rise up from the dead at the end of the world is astounding! As Paul said in 1 Corinthians 15, we Christians are the most blessed people in the world, and ought to have a sense of urgency about sharing this tremendous, world-shaking Gospel, or else we are the biggest fools the universe has ever seen. Even Paul put it that way!

Look at what this verse is saying about Jesus' death. First, the innocent died for the guilty. The just/righteous/perfect man died for you and

The Gospel Truth

me, who are sinners. The innocent died for the guilty! If you want to try to put this in terms you can get your arms around, think of the tragedy of the shooting of the innocent people this past week—a deputy stops to help a woman who is waving him down, and he is shot in cold blood before he even gets the full picture. A couple of minutes later, as the dead deputy is still sitting in his car which has gone over into the next yard, the firemen come rushing up, expecting to perhaps find children in this burning home. Before they know what hits them, two are gunned down. These three are folks who are trying to help others and pay for it with their lives. We can get this—our hearts pound, we are filled with grief at the craziness of it all.

Raise that in some way to a higher level and conceive of the perfect man, Jesus, somehow dying for all mankind. The innocent for the guilty. The Bible says that Jesus did not die because he was finally caught up with; bound and brought before the authorities and sentenced to death in spite of his protests. Jesus' intent was to rescue us, to die in our place for our sins. He suffered and died of his own will and choice: No one takes it from me, but I lay it down of my own accord (John 10:18).

Notice that this self-sacrifice is more than a good man, even a perfect man, dying for other men. This one is both God and man, rolled into one package, divine nature in human flesh. If you believe this, really believe this—then never again will you wonder in your heart, doubt in your mind that God is good, that God is for you and with you in the blackest darkness. For God has already come into the depths of our individual sins and died for us, even while we were running the other way and denying his love.

Notice also about the death of Jesus: It is once for all. That is very different from "once upon a time" Christ died. There is a finality to Jesus' death on the cross. In his suffering something was done, done once, done forever. On that particular day, and it is a day on a calendar if we knew which one, Jesus died under a hot Judean sun on a trash dump hill for the sins of folks living in Cordova in the year 2000. Do you really believe that? It's fantastic! Let me point out that, contrary to much of today's preaching, none of the New Testament writers stress the physical aspects of Jesus' suffering by describing it at great length. But Peter, and the whole New Testament, is adamant that the Gospel account is not a "once upon a time" event, a fairy tale, but hard, solid, saving facts. It happened once, will never happen again, and in that death and resurrection of Jesus lies all our hope of salvation.

I must go further on this first point, that Jesus died for us. Why did this amazing thing happen? If you can swallow that this man's death 2000 years ago does indeed impact the world today, How and why does it affect us? Thousands of folks died daily in the world at that time, and thousands of folks were crucified back in the first century. What does this man's death do that other deaths cannot do?

Our text says Jesus died for us to bring us to God.

That means we are separated from God. Mankind has, through the ages, expressed that separation in many ways. From the pathetic efforts to fight off "evil spirits" to the forlorn hope of bribing whatever powers there may be, to the vain hope of becoming gods ourselves, to the sense of dis-ease that modern people feel—there is a sense of brokenness, of separation, of alienation, of futility, loss of meaning in life, of fear of death and the beyond in our lives.

The Bible says what is wrong is us is sin. It goes further to speak of how we inherited this bent attitude toward God, this desire to rebel against God and lean on ourselves. We have been injected with sin, so to speak. By ourselves, we have a lot of weird stuff in our gene pool, but the Bible says it is worse than that. If you try to figure up how many ancestors you have in just the last 500 years, some math professor with two much time says in 21 generations you have over 2 million ancestors, all of whom muddied up your gene pool. But the Bible says that worse than your great-grandpa who went to prison is the influence of the devil in your life. That what happened to Adam and

The Gospel Truth

Eve has happened to each of us. We have been deceived by the devil into believing we are as smart, as powerful, as divine as God. And our heads and hearts and hands are filled with sin. As one guy said, My heart has committed sins that my hands haven't gotten around to yet.

I read of an 80 year-old woman who was resisting going to live with her daughter. The daughter kept on insisting, and the mother would bring up how such an arrangement would bring tensions, quarrels, etc. The daughter said, "But you're different, mother." "I know, I know," said the mother, "but you're not!" Human nature is infected with sin and self-interest! William Golding wrote a book a generation ago titled Lord of the Flies, in which a group of English schoolboys were stranded by a plane crash on a deserted island. The veneer of culture soon disappeared, and the ugly head of sin and self-interest brought suffering and death to the group.

You know, I read about all the "bleeding heart" movie stars trying to raise money for AIDs research, and sometimes I get teed off. I say to myself, They tell us that 1 of 3 of us will die of cancer, but I don't hear a great cry for speeding up research. And I think about how the great majority of AIDs cases are the result of behavior that flies in the face of biblical teaching, and I resent the misplacement of our research efforts. (Now I know I will hear from some folks on this, but I am illustrating a point). And just as I feel resentment about all this emphasis on research to cure a disease brought on by sinful behavior while a greater disease is ravaging our population, I hear the Bible saying that Jesus determined to come and die, the innocent for the guilty, to die for us while we were still running the other way. What I cannot feel in my heart, he has felt in his heart for sinners like you and me.

Truth #2: Jesus' Death Means Total Victory

The second truth of this passage is briefly stated: Jesus' death means total victory. We haven't time to go into all the interpretations of this passage, but it seems to say that when Jesus died, he went in his spirit to preach to the imprisoned spirits, those who were disobedient in Noah's time. I'll deal with the interpretations another time. But the heart of that statement is this: Jesus' death means complete and total victory of Jesus over sin. He is lord in this world, in the world of the dead, and in the world above. That's what is important, not some particular interpretation of who those folks were, or what this says about a second chance, or about hell, etc. By virtue of his death on the cross for you and me, Jesus is Lord. Somehow, someway, in his death Satan has lost his power forever.

Truth #3: Jesus Rules Today

Verse 22 says that Jesus has gone into heaven, and is at the right hand of God, receiving the praise and worship of angels, authorities and powers. That scene, Jesus in authority in heaven, has a most practical side to it. What I have said this morning about Jesus is fantastic, ridiculous, unbelievable—unless you are a Christian. And the question that needs to be asked is this: *What difference would it make in my life if I accepted what Peter is saying about Jesus? What does Peter want me to do as I read this scripture?* It might mean that both you and I need to take the unseen presence of Jesus seriously; that Jesus needs to be the unseen partner in our businesses; the unseen guest at our dinner table. It might mean that we change some of the way we live simply because we are aware that Jesus is seeing everything we do, say, and think. We have songs about *Just a Closer Walk With Thee,* and we dream of walking where Jesus walked and feeling his presence there with us. Taking this scripture seriously means we would count on Jesus praying for us in our hour of need just as he promised to pray for Peter in the clutches of Satan, as Jesus pointed out at the last supper with his disciples.

Peter wants you to make a leap of faith and believe the Gospel story—it's the gospel truth. He wants you to trust Jesus in his life, his death, his resurrection. He wants you to enter into a relationship with Jesus through your acknowledging that you are a sinner, and that you trust Jesus to forgive your sins through his sacrifice in your place. Peter wants you to let Jesus not only save you from the punishment of your sins, but let him also change your life from the inside out, through prayer, the study of the Bible, through daily walking with him through the Holy Spirit.

What's your spiritual condition? Since his death and resurrection has Jesus come and preached to your spirit in these days? Do you feel the need to publicly take a stand as a believer in the fantastic story of Jesus?

The Present

Psalm 118:24; Matthew 6:25-34

Perhaps you saw the bit of philosophy in a recent Family Circus cartoon. The little girl is telling her brother about time: "Yesterday is the past, tomorrow's the future, but today is a GIFT. That's why it's called the present." She did indeed sum the matter up. For time, the days of our lives, is under the control of God. Each day is a gift to us. We do not know how many more days will be allotted to any of us. Nor can we change those days already past. As R.G. Lee, one of Southern Baptists' greatest orators, once put it, yesterday is the tomb of time; tomorrow is the womb of time. But today is the present; the gift. Like the sands of the hourglass, the hours of the present will slip away into the past, but a new day, at the throne of God, is being wrapped as a present. Someone wisely said, "We have no control over the two dates on our tombstone—but we can influence the dash between the dates!" And that is what I want to talk with you about as we worship today.

This Day: Not Tomorrow or Yesterday

So this day, the present, is the only one within our control; how should we approach today and each day as God unwraps it with the sunrise? The psalmist says, "This is the day that the Lord hath made; we will rejoice, and be glad in it" (Psalm 118:24). Yet many folks—and I preach to myself and to you—have trouble accepting each day as a gift and rejoicing in it.

Focusing too much on the future dampens today. Many people see life, perhaps without knowing it, as a journey, but not in the biblical sense of a pilgrimage of faith. That is, they are always heading toward some goal, some destination—and I do not mean heaven—which will provide the happiness and joy they seek. And in the mad rush toward this mythical destination, too many of us throw aside the present day as of no value. The Bible tells us this day is the day that God has made; this day is the day which holds happiness for us if we are to find it.

So it isn't the burdens of today that kill us; it is the twin thieves of worry about tomorrow, and the regrets about yesterday. Living in the past, living with the mistakes and regrets of the past, can be as deadly as always chasing the rainbow of tomorrow. Some folks, like Coleridge's ancient mariner, wear the past like an albatross around their neck.

Sanctifying the Day

Let me make some biblical and practical suggestions about how you and I can rightly use each day God gives us and rejoice in it. We need to, as the old rabbis said, sanctify every day; regain the biblical perspective that God is in charge of this universe. We forget that God gives the gift of each day. The psalmist bids us rejoice and be glad in this day, but that is possible only if we sanctify each day. By that I mean acknowledge its nature as a gift; as a gift from God; as a good gift designed to bless us and fill our hearts with joy.

The psalmist's joy comes not from anticipation of anything that might happen in this particular day, but from the realization and affirmation that God made this day; therefore it has to be good. If we take each day in the spirit of the hymnwriter, Caroline Sandell-Berg, we will sanctify our days:

> *Trusting in my Father's wise bestowment,*
> *I've no cause for worry or for fear.*
> *He whose heart is kind beyond all measure*
> *Gives unto each day what he deems best—*
> *Lovingly, its part of pain and pleasure,*
> *Mingling toil with peace and rest.*
>
> *Help me, Lord, when toil and trouble meeting,*
> *E'er to take, as from a father's hand,*
> *One by one, the days, the moments fleeting,*
> *Till I reach the promised land.*

We live in a time enthralled by the advance of science, and sometimes we forget who created this world. I marvelled, as I am sure you did, at the spectacular photographs the Hubble Space Telescope made of the obstetric ward of the universe recently. There was a front-page color photo of the gigantic towering clouds, 6 trillion miles long, of cold hydrogen gas with glowing fingertips larger than our solar system. And we are told that in the small, glowing fingertips are brand new stars. All this took place 7,000 light years ago and we are just now seeing it here on earth! It "blew away" the astronomers and us common folk. But remember that our God created all this; he is in control of the world, in control of time, in control of our lives, in control of this very day.

We find it easy to believe God is in control of what we call the big days, the great days—the night of the star which appeared when Jesus was born, the day of the cross, the morning of the resurrection, the day of Pentecost. But to think that this day is anything worth his attention? Yet the psalmist says, "This is the day that the Lord hath made; we will rejoice and be glad in it." Let's begin each day with the realization that this day is a special day; it is God's gift to you and me.

Seek His Guidance

Second, in keeping with this realization that this day is a special gift of God, let us seek his guidance for each day. For with the gift of this day came God's intention, his plan for it in our life. Indeed, it may well be true that every minute spent in prayer early in the morning may change an hour later on in your day.

Do Our Best

Third, having accepted this day as a gift and sought his will in the use of it, let us do our best, all we can do, and leave the rest to God. Let us not procrastinate, let us not put off what we ought to do this day. An illustration even as I was working on this sermon: a visitor to our church inquired about adult softball teams. We called Charles Briggs, who said that just the day before he had reluctantly cancelled the men's team due to lack of interest—but no doubt there would be several church members who would inquire, too late. We procrastinate. Let us do what we should do. And after we have done what we can, let us leave the rest to God.

Reinhold Niebuhr, possibly the greatest theologian of this century, was guest preacher in a church in New England one Sunday in 1934. One of the church members asked him for a copy of his prayer that morning, and Niebuhr gave him the original, thinking he would not need it again. That prayer has gone all over the world, because it speaks to our need to do what we can, and leave the rest to God:

"God, grant me the serenity to accept the things I cannot change; courage to change those things I can; and wisdom to know the difference."

A Day at a Time

A fourth suggestion: let us take our days one at a time. It is possible that more people get sick from trying to handle several days at once than for any other reason. A juggler can keep several balls in the air at one time, but a human being can only deal with one day at a time. We need to remember the Titanic: it sank because the iceberg ripped open the double-hulled, watertight compartments. As long as the compartments were sealed and watertight, the great ship was queen of the seas. Make each day a separate compartment; you can only handle one day at a time.

In the Sermon on the Mount, Jesus pointed out that each day has a sufficient amount of evil and stress in it through our sinful nature; don't add to it by dragging the fears of tomorrow into today. Paul is a good example of one who lived in watertight compartments—he told us how, "forgetting the past, I press on toward the prize of the high calling."

Perhaps the old parrot can teach us something. He had belonged to a rough old sailor, and then to a circus gate-keeper. He had learned to say, as the people entered the circus turnstile, "One at a time, please, one at a time." Well, the parrot got loose one day and flew away. He lit on a hornets' nest, and naturally, the hornets came swarming out. The poor parrot said all he knew to say: "One at a time, please, one at a time." When the days seem to stack up and charge at us in groups, let us remember to say, "One at a time, please, one at a time."

I ran across the following essay on handling today:

Just for today I will try to live through this day only, and not tackle my whole life problem at once.

Just for today, I will be happy.

Just for today I will try to strengthen my mind. I will study. I will learn something useful.

Just for today, I will adjust myself to what is, and not try to fit everything to my own desires.

Just for today, I will exercise my soul in three ways: I will do somebody a good turn, and not get found out. I will do at least two things I don't want to do—just for exercise. I will not show anyone that my feelings are hurt; they may be hurt, but today I will not show it.

Just for today, I will be agreeable. I will look as well as I can, dress becomingly, talk low, act courteously, criticize not one bit, and not try to improve anybody except myself.

Just for today, I will have a program. I may not follow it exactly, but I will have it. I will save myself from two pests: hurry and indecision.

Just for today, I will have a quiet half hour with God. I will try to get a better perspective of my life.

Just for today, I will be unafraid. Especially I will not be afraid to enjoy what is beautiful.

Today is a very special day; it is from God, it is a gift. It brings with it, however, a sense of urgency. There are some things we need to do today. Now is the time, as Paul says, to awake out of our sleep. Now prove me sayeth the Lord, and see if I will not pour out a blessing upon you. Now all things are ready for the marriage feast of the Lamb. Today is often crucified between two thieves: yesterday and tomorrow. Let us not rob this day of its urgency—the Bible never tells a person to believe tomorrow, or yesterday; today, if you will hear his voice, it says. This is the day of salvation. The psalmist bids us rejoice and be glad in this day, and there is no joy and rejoicing like that of the redeemed.

What Jesus Thought of Money

Luke 12:13-21

A mathematical wizard I am not, but if my figures are correct, the 1500 or so family units in our church have given so far in 1989 in tithes and offerings an average of $780.38 to our church. And, assuming we are tithing our financial blessings from the Lord, that means our average income per family unit for these seven months has been about $7,800—for a yearly average income per family unit of about $13,500. You don't buy that, and neither do I!

Statistics can prove anything, they say, and these simply show that First Baptist Church members have the same struggle with our money that everybody else has. Statistics also show that the average American gives only 1% of his income to his local church, while spending 7% on recreation. Why is this? Why do we as Christians have such a problem with our money? Did Jesus have that problem? What did Jesus think about, and do with, His money?

Material Things Meant Nothing

I suggest you spend this afternoon going through the Gospels, underlining what Jesus said and did with and about money. You will be struck with the *realization that money, material things, meant nothing to Jesus.* I do not mean to insinuate that Christians, then, should be financial fools, but hear me out. Look with me at a few scriptures. He had no home. Remember the scribe from Tennessee-he volunteered to follow Jesus-and Jesus' reply (Mt 8:20). He had no home, really. In Capernaum He stayed with Peter, in Bethany with Lazarus and his sisters, in Jerusalem He ate the last supper in a borrowed home.

He had no money. Oh, Judas was the treasurer for the little band, but it surely wasn't much. Any check Jesus would have written would have bounced; He didn't even have a treasure buried in a field. Remember when the authorities asked about his paying the temple tax? (Mt 17:24f). In order to pay it He had to send Peter to catch a fish in whose mouth the coin was found. He had no money. We see Him riding only once, on Palm Sunday, to fulfill a prophecy, and that was a borrowed donkey!

There were those who thought that not only did He have no money; He cared little for the material possessions of other folks! Remember the Gadarene demoniac and the 5000 hogs which stampeded over the cliff? The issue there was not whether hogs have any value, but which is more valuable-hogs or souls. The anger of the locals was due to the fact that they valued hogs over souls. What a striking contrast of values!

We will not be surprised at Jesus' attitude toward material things if we read Phil 2:5-11 carefully. In this key passage we see that He did not come to revel in the materialism of this world. So let us nail this point down: Material things meant nothing to Jesus. And no less revealing is the Biblical truth that conversion ought to change our view of material things, too. I call as witness only two folks; Zaccheus and Barnabas (Lk 19 and Acts 4). Conversion changed their view of material things!

The Terrible Danger Of Money

A second truth you will discover in reading the Gospels and underlining all references to money is this: *material possessions put us in great danger.* Now we need to get some facts clear: it is not a sin to have a lot of money, nor is it a virtue to be poor. Jesus didn't glorify poverty; He included among His disciples and followers several apparently wealthy men-James and John, Matthew, Zaccheus, and Joseph of Arimathea. But Jesus did stress over and over the danger of our material possessions. He speaks of money and possessions as if they have a life of their own; as if they will choke us to death if we are not very careful. Look at Lk 8:14. And turn to Lk 12:20 in a good translation, and see that in the parable of the Rich Fool the judgement upon his materialistic life is couched in these words: ". . .this night they will require your life!" They being his possessions; his bulging, straining, overloaded barns!

We worry so about the pollution of our air; when we read the Gospels it seems as if the power of money is a pollution in the air, poisoning all of us. Do you remember some years ago when Clare Booth Luce was the Ambassador to Italy, she became ill-began losing weight, was lethargic, had headaches, anemia, etc. The doctors ran all sorts of tests and found that the woman was being poisoned! You can imagine the uproar among the security forces and the questioning of the embassy personnel. But the source of the poison remained a mystery, and the Ambassador continued to weaken. Finally the answer was found-in the ceiling paint! The dust from the old lead paint on her bedroom ceiling was slowly and surely poisoning her!

Jesus taught that our possessions will choke us, will poison us, if we are not very careful! Money will destroy the careless person spiritually in at least three ways: by turning our thoughts away from the spiritual nature of this world, away from God; by deadening us to the need of other people; and by leading us into a destructive lifestyle physically. Consider those three statements. Is it not true, in general, that money makes us less interested in God, less concerned about spiritual things, more concerned with houses, cars, boats, brand names, and keeping up with the Jones than with God? Sure, that's why the ascetic tradition arose in Christianity; an effort to subdue the craving of the flesh and materialism. Does not money tend to deaden us to the need of others? Last week vacationing in Colorado, I found myself thinking how nice it would be to own one of those homes in the mountains, next to a golf course, etc. After all, there were hundreds, one more for me wouldn't hurt. Then I saw the price on one of those few vacant lots—the one I'd picked out for my dream house-only $700,000! And with a world starving around us! Let us remember that the sin that sent Dives to hell was clear and simple: he simply was so blinded by materialism that he never saw Lazarus at his gate! And as for money and affluence leading us to a destructive lifestyle physically, just consider: we live in the wealthiest country on earth, and we are destroying ourselves with a lifestyle of moral confusion, drugs, crime.

Master Or Be Mastered

Over and over Jesus kept saying we must either master our money or be mastered by it. In order to master our possessions, we must do two things. First, we must realize that material things have no life, no value in themselves in the sight of God. When I was just a child, I had measles. I yet remember how, imprisoned in my bed for several days, I amused myself by using Coke bottle tops-that was back in the days when you drank Coke from bottles-as money to "purchase" my lunch, a candy bar, etc. I'm sure God looks upon our use of gold just like that. It's just another rock in His sight. The last book in the Bible describes the streets of heaven being paved with gold; in heaven we will walk upon that for which men will kill each other down here! Jesus is saying we'd best learn to walk on it here, too! Second, we must realize that money is a tool to be used to service higher spiritual aims. While we're in this world, money rightly used can be our servant, and can glorify God. We are constantly transferring ourselves into money-as the great British preacher Studdert-Kennedy said, money is just brain, flesh and blood, the ability to get things done. When you have a coin, a piece of money, in your pocket, you have a piece of a man in your pocket. So we are all constantly changing, transferring ourselves into money-but to what purpose in your life? What purpose?

Advice To Materialists

Jesus understood so clearly that our lives revolve around possessions, and often spoke of heavenly things in those same terms. He said the Kingdom of God is like a treasure in a field, like a pearl of great value. He taught lessons of forgiveness in terms of debts owed, and spoke of the joy in heaven in terms of a woman who found a missing coin. So Jesus knew well our craving for "things." He also knew why we have that weakness: it is a symptom of sin, of our desire to be independent from God; an effort to stand on some other foundation than the grace of God.

And so Jesus gave a word of advice to us all in light of our craving for money, for treasure. Lay up your treasure in heaven. Quickly make a survey with me about laying up treasure in heaven. Mt 6:19-21 is the first reference to our laying up of treasure in heaven. Now see Mk 10:17-21 and see two sad men, one of whom has our problem. And turn to Lk 12:21 to see the conclusion of the parable of the Rich Fool. And now a last passage, Lk 16:1-9. It is another of those parables dealing with materialism; a dark parable we seldom probe. What is its point? The children of this world are wiser than the children of light in that they know how to exchange money for relationships! That's what the scoundrel did, and that's why he was commended in the parable. And that is the key to laying up treasure in heaven-by exchanging, by investing your money in people, in souls, in the kind of coinage that you can use in heaven. Not only is it impossible to take our money with us to heaven; if we could take it, we couldn't spend it! It's just not the coinage for that place.

You'll know you have treasure in heaven if, when you go in the pearly gates, somebody comes up to you and says, "I'm so glad to see you; I've been waiting to greet you and thank you! Because, you see, I came to know Jesus through you; through your giving your money that made it possible to have that Vacation Bible School where I learned of

Jesus, to send that missionary who told me of Jesus' love, to hear that sermon on television which led me to Christ. I want to thank you for giving of your money, of your time, of yourself.

And folks, that's why our setting aside next Sunday as a time of catching up on our tithes and offerings is more than meeting a cash flow need in your church; it is an opportunity to lay up treasure in heaven, to change some of the coinage of this world into the coinage of that world. Take advantage of that opportunity.

But one final word. We are so closely tied to our money that Jesus could say that our heart follows our treasure. And what God wants is our heart. When we give Him our heart, our treasure follows the heart! And the heart committed to God enlarges and magnifies our treasure in the right way. Remember the poor woman who had only two pennies, and put them both in the offering plate? Jesus' comment was that she had put in more than anyone else in that church. . .because she gave all she had. She had already given her heart to God, and her earthly treasure naturally followed her heart! Let's do the same.

What Really Is Faith?

Hebrews 11:1-3,6

Several of you have urged me to see the movie *The Apostle*. It is a movie about a Pentecostal preacher who calls himself "The Apostle." The preacher is, as a reviewer put it, "flawed but faithful." I'm not praising all the movie, but it was most interesting. The movie script was written by, directed by, and stars Robert Duvall, and is based upon his visits to churches through the years. Duvall says he spent 13 years trying to get Hollywood to make the movie, and finally put $5 million of his own money into producing it. He seems to have been on target, since he has been nominated for an Oscar for his role in the movie.

"My guy makes mistakes. But he's more good than bad. He hangs on to his faith, because it's real." He sure does, even when a man the Apostle has a brawl with comes back with a bulldozer to tear down the church! The Apostle puts the Bible down on the ground in front of the dozer blade and declares the man will not run over it. The man doesn't, and in a lengthy scene, the man is converted on the spot.

What Really Is Faith?

Duvall's own faith is getting a lot of attention. He's a mix of Methodist and Christian Science. He says he is a believer, and that the key is that he respects the role faith plays in the lives of millions of Pentecostals and Fundamentalists.

So he says faith is the key. Whose brand of faith—the Apostle's bulldozer-fighting brand? Or Duvall's "respect others" kind of faith? Do you have faith? How would you define faith? (Let the congregation, in small groups, define faith, before continuing).

Faith Examples In The Bible

Faith is one of those religious terms folks throw around lightly. But what does it mean? The Gospels have many references to faith. When the Centurion with a sick servant comes to Jesus (Mt 8) and asks Jesus but to speak the word and the servant will be healed, Jesus responds, "I have not found such faith, no, not in all Israel." The beautiful descriptions of the lilies and the birds of the fields in the Sermon on the Mount are followed by Jesus' statement: "O ye of little faith; if God so clothe the grass of the field. . ."

When the storm arises while the disciples are crossing the Sea of Galilee, and Jesus is sleeping on the boat, they wake him. His response then is, "Why are you afraid, O ye of little faith." When the man is let down through the roof (Mk 2) we are told that Jesus, seeing the faith of the friends lowering the man, healed him. When the woman with the issue of blood touches the hem of his garment, Jesus tells her, "Your faith has made you whole." When Peter tries to walk on water and begins to sink, Jesus chides him, "O you of little faith; why do you doubt?" In his teaching Jesus says, "If you have faith the size of a mustard seed, nothing shall be impossible to you." And at the Last Supper, Jesus says to Peter, "Peter, I have prayed for you, that your faith fail not."

In the Book of Acts, Stephen is called a man full of faith and the Holy Spirit. When Paul was at Lystra on his first missionary journey, a crippled man listened to the preaching, and we are told that Paul perceived that he had faith to be healed. Paul tells the church at Rome: "Your faith is spoken of through out the whole world." John declares in I John that faith is the victory that overcomes the world.

The supreme example of the man of faith—in both Old Testament and New—is Abraham. Paul spends an entire chapter (Romans 4) speaking of Abraham's faith. He says: "Abraham staggered not at the promise of God through unbelief, but was strong in faith, giving glory to God." What an image; imagine a man staggering backward in shock at the promise of God to give him a child when he is in his 90's. But Abraham didn't do that, says Paul. He stood tall, and marched into the future in confident faith.

The writer of the book of Hebrews is dealing with Jewish believers whom he believes may be about to turn back from Christ. In battling this situation the writer draws up a list of folks of faith, and says that Christian believers are not in the group that fell back into oblivion through lack of faith—we are among that glorious company who keep their souls through faith. And he defines faith in Hebrews 11:1-3, then proceeds to illustrate it from the lives of the Old Testament saints. Can we, using these passages I have mentioned, and especially this Hebrews passage, define faith for our own lives?

The Person of New Testament Faith
Believes in the Reality of God

A man with religious faith believes in the reality of God (verse 6). But notice: everybody has faith. You had faith, based upon past experience, that the chair you are sitting in, would hold you up when you sat down. To go a step further, a man with religious faith believes that God exists. But that is not what Jesus, Paul, or the writer of Hebrews means when they speak of believing in God. The Christian believes in God, not as we may create him, but as he has revealed himself to us. When Abraham believes in God, he believes in the holiness of God, the trustworthiness of God to keep his promise, the essential goodness of God. When the New Testament speaks of believing in God, it is

What Really Is Faith?

God as he has been revealed to us in the life and death and resurrection of Jesus. Loads of folks run around saying pious and religious things about believing in a supreme being, accepting God; but it is a god of our own making.

The Person of New Testament Faith Is Convinced God Rewards the Seeker

A man with religious faith is convinced that God rewards those who seek him (verse 6). What an interesting statement! The writer is saying that God doesn't appreciate it when he is slandered, when he is mischaracterized. Well, I don't like it when folks characterize me in a fashion that I know is not true! But have you ever thought about God having feelings about the way we describe him? This scripture says that God is pleased when we act on the fact that he is kind; when we realize that he is the source of every good and perfect gift in our lives. What parent would want their children to go around acting like their parents are mean people? If we have faith, we live out our belief that God is good and kind, and rewards us with his presence.

The Person of New Testament Faith Fixes a Vision of God in his Mind

The man with religious faith fixes a vision of God and God's work in his mind, and lives out of it. Consider verses 8-10, in which we see the power of Abraham's vision. David had a vision of the house of God, and it was his guiding light. Paul's vision of the work of the Gospel included calling the Jewish people, and even though he was commissioned as the Apostle to the Gentiles, he dared hope and dream that the very success of the preaching to Gentiles might lead the Jews to embrace the Messiah. John, on Patmos, was granted a vision of Jesus that inspired and guided his writing of Revelation.

Folks, you need a vision of Christ that will support you in hard times; you need a vision of Christ's work and your part in it. I find that people with a vision keep moving forward; that people who do not become fossilized, like Lot's wife. After all, the prophet said, "Without a vision, the people perish." One of my favorite hymns, and one of the oldest Christian hymns, written perhaps as early as 700 A.D., is *"Be Thou My Vision."*

> *Be thou my vision, O Lord of my heart;*
> *Naught be all else to me, save that thou art:*
> *Thou my best thought, by day or by night,*
> *Waking or sleeping, thy presence my light.*

> *High King of heaven, my victory won,*
> *May I reach heaven's joys, O bright heav'n's Sun!*
> *Heart of my own heart, whatever befall,*
> *Still be my vision, O Ruler of all.*

The Person of New Testament Faith
Acts on what his Mind and Heart Believe

And finally, the religious man of faith acts on what his mind and heart hold true. In other words, he sells out to God. Observe Paul, casting aside all the pride of his past to follow Jesus. The difference between Paul and the Rich Young Ruler is that one turned his back on his possessions and his past, and the other didn't. And if, as some scholars have mused, Paul was himself the Rich Young Ruler, then the difference faith makes is all the more striking!

While faith is hard to define, we know it when we see it. When we see a person who lives out of what his mind and heart hold true about the reality of God and the work the Father God has done through the Son, who acts out of the vision of God and God's work in his heart—we credit them with faith. So while we do not have to buy all the life-style of Robert Duvall's The Apostle, we stand silent before his faith in daring the bulldozer to come further!

For the person of faith, his vision of God and what God has done and is doing in this world, is greater than any other circumstances of life. That is faith. I recently read of an oncologist, a cancer doctor who was

What Really Is Faith?

making his hospital rounds. He came into the room of a man to whom he had recently been obliged to give a death sentence as he shared the massive spread of the cancer. As he entered the room the patient looked up from his Bible, turned to the Book of Revelation, and said with a smile, "It's going to be a wonderful place, isn't it!" The realities of his eternal faith were more real than this fading world.

How does the writer of Hebrews put it? Faith is the substance, the weight, of things the world cannot see. Faith gives us a sense of assurance and peace about the invisible kingdom. Faith takes us by the hand and leads us to the Promised Land when sight fails us.

A closing word about saving faith. This kind of faith refers to believing that God was in Christ, bringing us sinners back to Him. Saving faith is faith that acts on the conviction that Jesus died and rose again for us; faith that asks Jesus to dwell in our hearts.

When Satan Is Most Active

Acts 4:32-37

If you were in my place, what would your sermon topic be this morning? On a day when our congregation has stepped forward and sacrificially pledged $2.6 million [the actual total reported at the end of the service was $2.,729,000] to build a new chapel and educational unit; on the morning when we certainly need to celebrate—what text would you choose? The celebration texts from the building of the temple in Chronicles? Perhaps one of the praise psalms? Or maybe a victorious passage from the Book of Revelation?

Under the guidance of the Spirit I have felt led to point us to the Book of Acts, chapter 4. It's a wonderful picture there; a scene of sacrifice and love, commitment and unity. It is a picture churches come back to again and again. But I have an idea that Peter, with his experience of denying Christ, was waving a red flag of danger in the midst of that celebration. For Peter certainly believed in the devil and his rage toward the church. He had firsthand experience with the devil! Do you believe in the devil? I urge you, on this blessed occasion, to take seriously the reality of the devil. Martin Luther liked to quote: "When the Lord builds the church, the Devil builds the chapel." I don't think Luther was against building chapels; he just meant the devil is hard at work, too. These next three years, as we build this new building, as we enter the new building and begin to enjoy the new recreation fields, as we reach out in a stronger way to the community, as we pay off our pledges—this will be a training school in the reality and power of the devil.

See What Satan Did

See what the devil did in the Early Church in the midst of their spiritual victory. In the very next chapter, in the very same time frame, Satan is at work. Ananias lets Satan put deceit in his heart, even with respect to his financial pledge, as Peter points out: "Ananias, why hath Satan filled your heart to lie to the Holy Spirit and keep back part of the price of the land?" The unity and the power of the church even brought the arrest of the apostles. Satan then used jealousy to disrupt the church fellowship: "And in those days . . ." there arose a division in the church over the treatment of some of the widows. One of the men selected to deal with that problem, Stephen, was so filled with the Holy Spirit that he began to preach, and ended being stoned to death.

Proportionate Is The Struggle With Satan

And all these events took place within 5 or 6 years after the great sacrifice I read for you, and perhaps even sooner. Do you believe in the devil? I say to you that he is about to try his best to cripple this church's witness and unity. How can we arm ourselves against his onslaught? Perhaps a start is to realize that in proportion to our commitment, our sharing, our zeal in witnessing will come our buffeting by Satan. Satan doesn't waste a lot of time on folks who are already in his camp; he already has them. But Satan realizes even more than we do the power of the stirred-up church; the church filled with the presence of the Spirit; the church excited about its mission. So the more we get stirred up for good work for Christ, the more attention we will get from Satan.

Consider The Lessons Of Ananias

Consider with me two lessons from our text passage and its immediate aftermath. There is good news and there is bad news. Here the bad news. First, the story of Ananias warns us that Satan's beachhead is usually financial, the material side of life. We see from the Ananias story that (1) giving makes us more open to spiritual possibilities in our lives. Why, even Ananias, who obviously craved attention more than he loved God, became more open to the spiritual realm when he saw Barnabas and others making sacrificial gifts to the church. But he let the devil guide his spiritual openness. (2) When it comes to our giving to the church, Satan will tell you that since you pledged so much from so little, you have a right to run the church. I think it says a great deal about Barnabas' spiritual depth that he gave so much to the church, but is never in the limelight. So let us remember that the church still belongs to God. (3) Satan will constantly be by your side telling you that you shouldn't have pledged so much, and that you simply cannot pay that pledge without cutting back on your regular giving. In these days you need to tell Satan to get behind you!

Consider The Blessings Of The Time

There is a second great lesson in this text for our church, however. Now hear the good news. Notice the blessings poured out on the church in that time of giving and commitment and unity. (1) There was more zeal, more evangelism, more outreach than ever before. The Ananias incident resulted in new growth (Acts 5:13-14). After the deacons were chosen to deal with the problem of the widows, there was a great ingathering (Acts 6:7).

And (2) there was a much wider vision about what God wants to do in his church and how He wants to use us. Stephen would not be content to serve tables, but started preaching. Philip begins to preach in Samaria, Paul is converted, and even Simon Peter begins to have visions about how God accepts everyone.

So we stand here today having, by the grace of God, done what sensible folks didn't think could be done. We have raised, in gifts and

When Satan Is Most Active 267

pledges, $2.6 to carry out the expansion of the kingdom in our midst. We can count on the opposition of Satan to begin. I challenge you now to go beyond the giving of your gifts and give yourselves to God in a deeper fashion than ever before.

A pastor who is a former Marine says the Marines have a couple of mottoes, one being: Die facing the enemy. He says whenever the battleground is recaptured and the dead surveyed, Marines always check to see how their dead faced when they died. When you die, let someone say you were right in there at Trinity Church doing your part against the devil! There is another Marine saying: If you take a hit, fall forward. That is so you don't clog up the advance for those Marines behind you. I urge you to consider these days a time of spiritual warfare against the devil.

Claiming The Blessings Of This Time

Let me lay before you some of the ways you can be a part of the enthusiasm, the growth, the vision, the spiritual warfare of these days. First, looking at the biblical model, we need, all of us, to pray for each other and for the work of the church in general as we have never done before. I urge the Finance and Building Committees to keep our congregation fully informed, so that we can pray about the progress of what we are doing. Pray for teachers, evangelists to be raised up among us.

Second, pray for and be involved in bringing about a great outreach thrust by our church. Folks, this is a burden I have. I have not been able to give the needed attention to encouraging our Bible Study teachers, having regular training meetings, and devoting the time necessary to promoting visitation and outreach through our Sunday School. That is what a Minister of Education does, but we do not have that staff member and will not have one for some time. I ask you to pray that God will raise up from among us a person or a couple who will work with me to strengthen what we are already doing in outreach and evangelism. Some of you are doing such a wonderful job of helping or teaching in Sunday School need to inquire of the Lord whether he wants you to step up to an even more demanding, but fruitful work for Him.

While we are already doing many innovative things in outreach, it is my desire to have as our theme for the fall a greater outreach by our church. Find your niche in our outreach program. I read of a dude ranch in west Texas with a sign that boasts:

Horses for Everyone.

In small print it reads:

For skinny people, we have skinny horses.

For fat people, we have fat horses.

For tall people, we have tall horses.

For short people, we have short horses.

For people who have never ridden horses, we have horses

that have never been ridden.

Even if you've never done much in outreach and evangelism, I urge you to begin to think in terms of growth for your class or department, and begin to pray about it, and begin to have a divine dissatisfaction about our present growth rate. There's a horse for you!

In conclusion, let us be steadfast in our commitment, knowing our enemy the devil, is like a stalking lion. Let us remember that the devil, not our fellow members, is the enemy. Let us recommit ourselves to the work of the kingdom through this church, saying only the encouraging and positive word to fellow members, and remembering to say a winsome word of testimony about the Lord Jesus and this church as we go about our daily work. And God will bless us.

Christmas and Common Things

Luke 2:8-20

Christmas is a wonderful time, but one filled with paradoxes, opposites put together. Department stores lull stressed out shoppers with Christmas music telling of the Saviour's birth, but the music is handmaid to the merchandising goal—perhaps half the store's profits will come in during December! It is the Saviour's birth, but liquor flows more freely in December than at any other time of the year. But the greatest paradox of Christmas is not of our making, but God's. And we echo this paradox when we take the common things of life and decorate them and dress them up and give them magic at Christmas time. For instance, Pegeen and Co. spent the last two days taking our ordinary house and turning it into a Christmas scene. And I put 3000 lights on the shrubs and trees at our home— transforming the ordinary bushes which will be the bane of my existence next spring and summer! Almost every family here will take an ordinary tree—cedar, fir, etc.—with its misshapen limbs and tangles and turn it into magic with beautiful decorations.

A Gospel With A Common Touch

All our decorations of ordinary things at Christmas are an echo and a reminder of God's Christmas paradox when he brought the wonder and the magic of the Christmas event into the common, ordinary aspects of life. God rooted Christmas in common soil. For instance, if you had been in charge of announcing the birth of Jesus, to whom would you have sent the angel choir? To a bunch of shepherds? Not likely. This kind of news needs to go right to the top, we say. Go announce the coming of the Messiah to the head hauncho, Herod! In fact, if we had been staging the appearance of the long-awaited Messiah, would we schedule the birth of a baby, or a victory parade of the adult conqueror with open convertibles and ticker tape and all the rest?

But God chose to set the redemption of mankind in motion in the midst of everyday, ordinary people and everyday, ordinary events. He chose folks like Joseph, a carpenter with apparently neither the price nor the power to get a night's lodging in his pocket to wrestle with this premarital predicament; he chose a young, unmarried, sexually pure teenage girl named Mary to be the mother of the Christ child; he sent the herald angel to a handful of shepherds with nothing to commend them—I rather like Rembrandt's etching of the shepherds as very average and very scared men; and God honored an old man named Simeon who hung around the temple by letting him be the first to bless the baby. To top it off, God scheduled Jesus to be born in a stable and then be placed in the feeding trough of the animals! Christmas has such a common touch to it! Why such common roots for this glorious tree of redemption?

God Loves Common People

It is because God loves all people, the common and the uncommon. God is interested in all people, he seeks to redeem all people, and seems to have a special place in his heart for the poor, the needy, the downcast, the outcast and the very common and ordinary folks. Someone said that God must love common people; he made so many of them! Paul looked around at the church of his day and said, "God

Christmas and Common Things

hath chosen the foolish things of the world to confound the wise; and God hath chosen the weak things of the world to confound the things that are mighty" (1 Corinthians 1:27).

When God gets ready to give a revelation, he does not often give it to the powerful or to those in charge, but rather to folks who like Moses who are at working tending the sheep and turn aside to see an odd tree; to men like Gideon who are at work at the threshing floor; to men like Elisha who are following the plow; to men like Matthew in the tax assessor's office; to men like Peter and Andrew and James and John who are mending their nets after a night's work. Ordinary, common men carrying out the ordinary, common pursuits of life.

And so it happened that in the fullness of time God chose to unveil the greatest revelation by sending the baby to a stable and the angels to the shepherds on the fields keeping their flocks by night, and the shepherds to the young couple in the stable.

Have you ever stopped to reflect that to Mary and Joseph there was nothing exceptional about the night of Jesus' birth until the shepherds turned up with their strange tale of an angel choir! The couple had been too busy with the tasks of childbirth to seek or see anything unusual that night! God planted Christmas in the soil of the common life!

And I think there is more gospel than we realize in stories such as "The Littlest Angel" and "The Little Drummer Boy"; stories of the weak and small who bring their best to Jesus. For our God is a God of the ordinary people and the ordinary things and ordinary days of life. Now we forget that every now and then, and rush next door to Matthew's Gospel and borrow the kings and the touch of royalty they bring to the birth story. Which is exactly what Peter Paul Reubens did when he came to paint the Christmas story! I think Rembrandt and Breughel—with his ordinariness of the scene of the census at Bethlehem—caught the biblical flavor better. The kings came later.

So let me underline for you that God is interested in each of us; that God loves the homeless, the prostitute, the addict as much as he loves the church member, or the wealthy or the mighty. For that reason Jesus came into this world amidst lowliness and poverty and rejection.

God Forgives Common Sins

God planted Christmas in the common soil of everyday life not only because God loves common people, but also because God forgives common sins as well as the huge and awful sins. Christmas is for sinful people, and the power of the Saviour transforms all kinds of people. The Messiah, the stable child, was born to transform the life of the Adulteress as well as the life of Zaccheus; the life of blind Bartimaeus as well as the life of Joseph of Arimathea. I came to seek and to save the lost, Jesus said, and he was accused of hobnobbing with the poor and lowly, sinners and outcasts.

You may remember that last Sunday in our children's time with the pastor I asked the children what gifts the three kings brought to Jesus. One little fellow replied, "Gold, Frankenstein, and myrrh." Having experienced that, you can identify with the father of five children who agreed, one evening just before Christmas, to keep the older four while the wife took the youngest to the doctor for his checkup. Babysitting to this father meant barricading yourself in the study while the children tore up the rest of the house! But just as he settled in with his newspaper, a tiny voice at the study door announced, "Daddy, we've got a play for you. Do you want to see it?"

Really, he didn't, but how can you tell your kids that? So off he trooped to the den. There he beheld, next to the piano bench, a flashlight—turned on—wrapped in tissue paper and laid in a shoe box. So the stage was set. the first actor appears, the 6-year-old son, in a bathrobe and carrying a mop handle. He gravely took his seat on the piano bench. then came in the 10-year-old daughter, who stood immediately behind "Joseph." She remarked to the audience, "Usually Mary is seated and Joseph stands behind her, but in our case Mary seated is still taller than Joseph, so we thought it would be better for Joseph to sit down." Suddenly the 4-year-old daughter came running into the room, wearing pillowcases on her arms, waving and fluttering around. Obviously the angel had arrived. Then came the 8-year-old daughter, clearly riding a camel; or perhaps it just seemed that way since she was teetering on her mother's high heels. She carried a pillow upon which lay 3 objects, obviously the gifts of the kings: gold, frankincense, and myrrh. Approaching the shoebox, she announced, "I am all three kings; I bring gold, circumstance, and mud!" That is exactly what God did—Jesus was born in a stable to tell us that he came right into our circumstances and the mud of our lives. God came to deal with sinners; to redeem sinners, and the only way to do that was to start where we are.

The shepherds give the baby three titles: Saviour, Messiah, and Lord. The title Lord affirms his divinity; the title Messiah affirms his place among the anointed, the rulers of the world; and the title Saviour affirms his purpose in coming to this world.

It is interesting to note that while the shepherds tell Mary and Joseph the message of the angel, including the titles of Jesus, when Mary names the child in the temple eight days later, she calls him Jesus, for as the angel had earlier said to Joseph: he shall save his people from their sins. The most common trait of mankind is that we are all sinners and need a Saviour.

Above all else, Christmas means salvation. Salvation not just from the big sins like murder or bank robbing or adultery; salvation from the common sins of our lives, from the common fears of our lives. The writer of Hebrews says that Jesus took on flesh and blood that through death he might destroy him that had the power of death, that is, the devil; and deliver them who through fear of death were all their lifetime subject to bondage (Hebrews 2:14-15). There is no sin too great, no sin too disgraceful, no sin too distasteful for Christ to set you free. For this he was born in a stable and died on a cross.

An Uncommon Saviour

It is a gospel with a common touch because God loves common people, and we all have a common need for forgiveness. God forgives common sins by sending an uncommon Saviour. Not that it was apparent to many folks—I have always marveled at the apparent faith of the shepherds when they followed the angel's directions and came to the stable and the manger. Would I —or you—be impressed at that scene? Would we be able to glorify and praise God for what we had heard and seen? They realized that the manger was just the beginning, and they went out and told everybody they met that the Saviour, the Messiah was born!

There was a second group who reacted to the Christmas news—those people to whom the shepherd related their story. We are told in verse 18 that all those people wondered—marveled; were amazed—at what they heard. And then there was Mary's reaction (verse 19) as she pondered all these things. She knew her son was no ordinary baby, would be no ordinary boy or ordinary man, although she did not understand all God was going to do.

I can imagine a sleepy Joseph making his way the next morning to the office of the census taker. "Name?" Joseph. "Occupation?" Carpenter. "Present residence?" Nazareth in Galilee. "Married?" Yes. "Children?" And here Joseph came alive with a broad smile—A son; born last night. But the census taker had already dismissed this man and his child. After all, just another Jewish boy.

What is your reaction to the Gospel of Christmas? Christmas is the beginning of the glory of redemption—the people that walked in darkness have seen a great light.

Christmas and the Cradle

Luke 2:10-12,15-16; John 1:10-14

If, on your way to the mall during these final hectic days before Christmas you meet a little green man from Mars who asks you what all this is about, what will you say? Some folks will give the standard secular answer that we celebrate the hope of peace for mankind. That's about as close to the real meaning of Christmas as kissing your sister is to kissing your boyfriend or your girlfriend. We are the buckle on the Bible belt and surely many folks would reply that we are celebrating the birth of a baby born 2000 years ago. And our little green man would no doubt reply that this seems harmless. But I would hope that the members of Trinity Church would reply without hesitation that we are celebrating God's decision to become one of us. The cradle of Christmas holds the mystery of the incarnation.

And the question of the ages is simple: *Why would God send his son to be born*—in a stable *or* in a palace? Why would God become a human baby? Why would he do that? What do you suppose was going on in the minds of the people who gathered around that manger—Mary, Joseph, the shepherds? Who did old Simeon think he was holding there in the temple, eight days after Jesus was born? What did the Magi think as they gazed upon this child and presented their presents? Let us ponder Christmas and the cradle; the meaning of the incarnation. I would have us consider the wonder of his coming to the cradle; the how of his coming to the cradle; and the why of his coming to the cradle.

The Wonder of the Cradle

The idea of God becoming a human being, truly one of us, has astonished men for two thousand years! Consider what it meant for God in Jesus Christ to become part of his creation. Turn to John, chapter one, with me. We see in verses 1-2 that the babe in the manger is God, and was with the Father from the very beginning. Not only was he present at the start of this universe, but he is the architect and builder, the creator of all this universe, seen and unseen. If it isn't clear enough here, turn to Colossians 1:16-17, where we read, For by him were all things created, that are in heaven, and that are in earth, visible and invisible, whether they be thrones, or dominions, or principalities, or powers: all things were created by him, and for him: And he is before all things, and by him all things consist.

With this background of eternal existence and being the creator of the universe, we then read (verse 14) that the Word (Jesus) became flesh and dwelt among us. Look at Philippians 2:5-11. ". . .Being in the form of God, he did not think his equality with God something to hang on to. . ." He laid aside his glory, left the heavenly home to submit to this darksome house of clay. As Chesterton puts it, he was homeless where we are at home; he left behind all the trappings of divinity.

In 1947 crowds lined the streets of old London and kings and queens came from all over the earth to attend the wedding of Princess Elizabeth and the Duke of Edinborough. As the carriages of royalty and the splendid horses pulling them came through the crowded streets, a 12-year-old boy ducked under the rope barriers in order to get a better

Christmas and the Cradle

look at the horses—12-year-old boys care little for princesses! The bobby spoke rather roughly to the boy and herded him back to the curb. The next morning a British newspaper, *The Scotsman*, reported on the incident and apologized for the policeman's actions. You see, it wasn't just any 12-year-old; it was King Feisal II of Iraq who had ducked under the rope! The newspaper went on to say, however, that the incident would never have happened if the king had been wearing a crown! In the same way Jesus came to earth without his crown, leaving his equality with God behind.

Have you ever pondered the meaning of the incarnation— perhaps you have a favorite cat or dog. A nice cat or dog, mind you. Clean, no fleas, adorable in every way. Can you conceive of becoming a dog or a cat, even as nice a one as your pet? I do not think I stretch the truth to say the incarnation crossed an even greater gap!

God crammed into human form! Turn to John 14:9 "Jesus saith unto him, Have I been so long time with you, and yet hast thou not known me, Philip? He that hath seen me hath seen the Father. . ." This has been called the most staggering statement in human literature. I put it alongside John 1:14: "The Word was made flesh, and dwelt among us." Christianity is the religion of the incarnation—the enfleshing of the divine God. Other religions speak of your re-incarnation, as a mosquito or water buffalo or worse; but the Bible speaks of Almighty God himself becoming one of us!

The How of the Cradle

Now think a moment about the how of God coming to this earth in flesh, as one of us. Let us turn to Luke 1:30-35. It is rather humorous that some folks choke on the biblical teaching of the virgin birth, which is simply the method, the way chosen, to accomplish the far more astonishing fact of the incarnation! The virgin birth is a fact; accept it. If you need to choke on some biblical doctrine, choke on the very idea of the incarnation; God becoming one of us—the virgin birth is the method by which God accomplished the larger miracle!

The virgin birth underscores the double nature of Jesus. Look at verse 35 carefully. See the therefore? The power of the Holy Spirit is responsible for the pregnancy of Mary. The Holy Spirit's involvement in this birth speaks of the divinity of Jesus; while the human mother speaks of the humanity of Jesus. The New Testament gives us three facts about Jesus' nature, not two. He was God; he was man; he was both at the same time.

So God became a man, a child, a baby who caused his mother pain and fear and confusion; a baby wrapped in coarse wrappings to keep his body straight, then laid in the feeding trough, in which he probably cried off and on that entire night. Does such a description make you a bit uneasy deep down? The church has always had to work hard to keep the incarnation before us. A century had not passed before there were those Christians called Ebionites, "Poor," who could not believe that Almighty God really became one of us—they said that the man Jesus was adopted by God and given an extreme measure of the Spirit during his life. They were really Jews in the church.

But it is Docetism, or "Seemism," that has continued to be a problem for the church. The Docetics declared that Jesus only "seemed" to be human, to have a human body. Cerinthus, a Gnostic, taught that Christ came into Jesus at his baptism and left before his crucifixion. In fact, the heretical writing, Acts of John, relates a conversation supposed to have taken place between Jesus and John on a hillside at the same time the crucifixion was taking place, in which Jesus speaks of how those below think they are crucifying him. This was—and still is—a dangerous heresy, because it comes from a misguided reverence for Jesus; a reverence that shrinks from involving God in our human life. It makes us more spiritual than God, for the Bible says God truly became a man!

The Why of the Cradle

Now let us look at the why of the cradle. There are two major reasons God would do such a dramatic, unexpected thing like the incarnation.

Christmas and the Cradle

First, the cradle, the incarnation, gives us a picture of God, an understanding of his intention and character that will sustain us through all that our life may bring. There are many strange ideas about God, and none of us fully understands God. But clearly Jesus was born in a manger, grew up and walked and taught among us that we might have a more adequate understanding of God. It has been said that Jesus is what God means by man, and Jesus is what man means by God.

Jesus came to tell us of God—someone said that the incarnation is the translation of God into monosyllables for our understanding of him. I read of a mountain girl who was adopted by a wealthy family in the city, on the condition that she not go back to the mountains even to visit until she was grown. The years went by, and finally the girl, now a grown woman of wealth and culture, determined to go back and visit her father and mother. She took the train to the closest big city, where she bought common mountain clothes. Then, laying aside the jewels and expensive clothes, she dressed as a mountain woman and made her way to the home she had known as a girl. When she was admitted to the simple home, the old man and old woman burst into tears and hugs. "We were afraid you would not want to claim us now," they said. And then, "But why are you wearing simple mountain clothes?" "Because I wanted nothing to come between us," she said. That is what the incarnation is about.

And what does the incarnation teach us about the character and intent of Almighty God? It tells us that the Old Testament is to be interpreted by the New; that the New Testament is to be interpreted by the Four Gospels; that the Four Gospels are to be interpreted by the portrait of Jesus we find there. For Jesus is the final word about the nature of God. "He who hath seen me hath seen the Father. The Father and I are one."

But the cradle also shows us that God takes sin seriously. The Bible says God has created us for fellowship with him, and he created a wonderful world for us. But Adam and Eve and you and me chose to turn away from God and become his enemy. It is in our nature.

The righteousness of God demands punishment, while the love of God cannot give us up. The only answer was for God himself to satisfy the demands of both justice and love, and that he has done by coming to earth as one of us and suffering the penalty of sin for all of us.

This is what is behind Paul's description of Jesus laying aside his equality with God, emptying himself from his glorious nature and taking upon himself our nature, yet without sin. Only by the descent into humanity, into servanthood, into unjust accusation and crucifixion could he take all our sins upon himself, even as it is described for us in Isaiah 53:3-7.

Only by becoming one of us could God take upon himself our sins, our punishment, and destroy all that would separate us from him. Only by becoming one of us could God destroy the one who most hates us and seeks to destroy us. Turn to Hebrews 2:14-15, one of the most passages in the New Testament and one of my favorite scriptures: "Forasmuch then as the children are partakers of flesh and blood, he also himself likewise took part of the same; that through death he mighty destroy him that had the power of death, that is, the devil; and deliver them who through fear of death were all their lifetime subject to bondage."

 Jesus came to show us God, to walk in our shoes, to take upon himself our punishment for sin, to destroy our old enemy the devil. As Paul puts it in 2 Corinthians 8:9, Jesus, who was rich beyond our imagining, became poor that we might become rich. He came to earth that we might go to heaven. The Word became flesh and dwelt among us; that is, the babe in the manger grew up and went to the cross. For you and me.

Christmas and the Crown

Matthew 2:1-2; Revelation 11:15

The amazing thing to me about the Wise Men, or the Kings, or the Magi, is not the wondrous star they followed over moor and mountain, field and fountain. The amazing thing is that they should come all that distance looking for a king, kneel down before a peasant girl's child and present him gifts fit for a king in a stable behind the hotel!

This marvel is beautifully expressed in a painting by Giovanni Tiepolo in the Alte Pinakothek museum in Munich. As the Magi present their gifts, we see that one of the kings has carelessly flung his crown down on the steps before the babe. I think the pilgrimage of these Magi, or kings, can be explained by the influence of the Exile, when these royal advisors would have heard of the prophecy of Balaam: "I shall see him, but not now: I shall behold him, but not nigh: there shall come a Star out of Jacob, and a Sceptre shall rise out of Israel" (Numbers 24:17). Did they get the right baby? Is this child a king? If so, what kind of king? What kind of kingdom?

Prophecies of a King

Let us turn to the prophecies. The time was right; people everywhere were looking for a great deliverer, a great peacemaker. "The world in solemn stillness lay . . ."

The Jews were looking for the Messiah, prophesied not only by Balaam but by other prophets as well: Isaiah spoke of the Messiah, the anointed one, as the Wonderful Counselor, the Mighty God, the Everlasting Father, the Prince of Peace and of his everlasting kingdom as he inherited the crown of his father David (9:6-7); Micah reported God's promise to little Bethlehem, that out of this village would come a ruler in Israel whose goings forth have been from everlasting (5:2). And so the finger of prophecy underlined the hope as the Magi came looking for a king, and Mary hid all these things in her heart.

Are You a King?

The question of kingship dogged Jesus throughout his days in the flesh. After the feeding of the 5000 we read that Jesus had to go away by himself to keep the crowds from crowning him king (6:15). When Jesus was finally arrested, the charge against him was that he said he was a king (23:1-2). Pilate asked him bluntly if he were a king (23:3), and when Pilate tried to set Jesus free the people screamed, "If you let this man go, you are not Caesar's friend: whoever makes himself a king speaks against Caesar" (John 19:12). Pilate picked up on the theme of kingship and announced to the Jews: "Behold your king! Shall I crucify your king?" The people replied, "We have no king but Caesar!"

And it did not rest there. Pilate wrote an inscription to be posted above Jesus' head reading in three languages: Jesus of Nazareth the king of the Jews. And even then the priests objected that it should read he said he was king of the Jews. But Pilate replied with the boldest statement of his weak career: "What I have written I have written!' And so the Magi seem to keep marching through the gospels declaring this man to be the king.

Jesus Said He Was a King

What did Jesus say about the question of his kingship? He said he was a king. He clearly took upon himself the designation of Messiah and the fulfillment of the Old Testament prophecies. In his first sermon he read from Isaiah's prophecies of the Messiah's work (Luke 4:18). When he came into Jerusalem on Palm Sunday he deliberately fulfilled the prophecy that the messianic King would come into the city riding on a donkey (Matthew 21:5). In his parables Jesus refers to himself as a king (the Sheep and the Goats in Matthew 25). At the last supper Jesus spoke of possessing a kingdom and giving one to his followers (Luke 22:29-30), and before Pilate he did not deny that he was a king.

The Church Preached King Jesus

Within weeks of his death and resurrection Jesus was preached at Pentecost as Messiah and Lord (Acts 2:36-39), and the early Christians were convinced that the holy child Jesus was the anointed king to come (Acts 4:26-27).

The prophets, the gospels, Jesus himself, and the early church testify that this child in the manger is King Jesus. Some of the finest Christmas theology of his kingship is found in the traditional Christmas carols:

> *Nowell, Nowell, Born is the King of Israel.*
>
> *Joy to the World! The Lord is come; Let earth receive her king; let every heart prepare him room.*
>
> *Hark the herald angels sing, "Glory to the newborn king!"*
>
> *O come all ye faithful, O come ye to Bethlehem! Come and behold him, born the king of angels.*
>
> *Silent night, holy night; with the angels let us sing Alleluia to our king.*

*The sky was bright with a holy light,
'Twas the birthday of a king.*

*Born a king on Bethlehem's plain: Gold I bring to
crown him again, King forever, ceasing never
over us all to reign.*

*What child is this, laid to rest on Mary's lap, is sleeping?
This, this is Christ the King whom shepherds guard
and angels sing.*

What Kind of King?

A king, but what kind of king? And what kind of kingdom do we celebrate here at Christmas? Surely no ordinary king or kingdom! Born a king on Bethlehem's plain; King forever, ceasing never, over us all to reign. Consider what it means to call this one born in the manger king.

He is the king who emptied himself of royalty. Last week we talked about the paradox of the eternal Son of God, the creator of all things, laying aside his glory and putting on human flesh and being born as a human being. This king will always be a paradox to us, beginning with the paradox of his being born in a manger and visited by the kings of the earth.

He is the king who wore a crown to the cross. In a horrible devil's joke, a crown of thorns was shoved down on Jesus' head, and the soldiers put an old royal robe on him and put a stick in his hand and bowed before him, calling him "King Jesus!" He wore that crown to the cross, where he became not only King of Life but also the victor over death. He was a king destined for the cross, and Holman Hunt has pictured for us the meaning of the verse in Luke's birth story which tells us that Mary hid all these things in her heart and pondered them. Hunt's painting shows the inside of the carpenter's shop at the end of a day's work. The young man Jesus is stretching tired muscles, and his shadow falls on the wall in the form of a great cross. In the forefront of the picture we see Mary kneeling before an open trunk in which are the gifts of the Wise Men, pondering them. And suddenly

Christmas and the Crown 285

turning, she catches sight of the cross looming against the wall. Yes, Simeon had said a sword would pierce her heart for this is a king who will wear a crown to the cross.

There is a musical program, I believe, called "The Day He Wore My Crown." It puts it correctly; the crown of thorns he wore on the cross belongs not to him, but to you and me. It belongs to the punishment—the death and eternal separation from God—that is due us. This king came to die for us.

He is the king of a kingdom not of this world. Jesus told Pilate that his kingdom was not of this world; it is an invisible, silently growing kingdom. It operates differently than the kingdoms of this world. His kingdom is the hearts of men and women who are committed to him. And all who trust their life to his guidance enter his kingdom; an everlasting kingdom of peace and joy.

He is the once and future king. Not only was he proclaimed king by the Wise Men; not only did he die wearing his crown; not only has he been proclaimed as King forever by the church for these twenty centuries—he is the king who is coming again. In his parables Jesus speaks of the Son of Man coming in his glory and all the holy angels with him; he spoke in clear terms of his return in power and glory (Matthew 24:30-31). Paul speaks of the return of King Jesus in 1 Thessalonians 4:16-18. In the book of Revelation we find the most vivid picture of the coming again of King Jesus, the King of Kings in Rev. 19:11-16.

King of Kings! King above King James whose name is synonymous with the greatest translation of the Bible; King above King Richard the Lion-Hearted who fought the crusades; King above King Arthur in all his legend; King above all kings and emperors and czars and rulers and conquerors. King above Napoleon and Alexander the Great and Julius Caesar. King of Kings, this babe born in Bethlehem!

Jesus is king, and the King is coming again to judge this world and rule supreme. Last Sunday we saw in Philippians 2:5-11 the descent, round by round, of Jesus as he laid his glory aside. But note that the passage ends with the exaltation of Jesus; a sweeping up to glory: "Therefore

God hath highly exalted him, and given him the name which is above every name: that at the name of Jesus every knee should bow, of things in heaven, and things in earth, and things under the earth." He is the king who is coming back to earth.

But finally, let us note that he is the king who stands at your heart's door. Again, artist Holman Hunt has dramatically illustrated this scene from Revelation 3, in the familiar painting in which the crowned Jesus stands at our heart's door knocking: "Behold, I stand at the door and knock; if any person will open the door, I will come in . . ." The throne of King Jesus is first of all in your heart. Is he the king of your life? Tennyson raises a profound question in Idylls of the King when he writes: Live pure, speak true, right wrong, follow the King—else, wherefore born? Are you following the King of Kings?

A verse of the hymn, Saviour of the World, says
I cannot tell how all the lands shall worship,
  When, at his bidding, every storm is stilled,
Or who can say how great the jubilation
  When all the hearts of men with love are filled.
But this I know, the skies will thrill with rapture,
  And myriad, myriad human voices sing,
And earth to heaven, and heaven to earth, will answer
  At last the saviour, Saviour of the world, is King!

Is he king of your life? Remember the beautiful carol:

Thou didst leave thy throne and thy kingly crown,
When thou camest to earth for me;
But in Bethlehem's home was there found no room
For thy holy nativity.
O come to my heart, Lord Jesus,
There is room in my heart for thee.

Christmas and the Curse

Galatians 3:10-14; Genesis 3:12-19

Christmas is God's own answer to the curse. We use the word curse so lightly—we speak of "cussin' somebody out," and so we change the idea of curse to profanity, bad enough—but not like a curse. The idea of a curse, whether it is pronounced by the tribal shaman or by the witch doctor or by the Pope as he declares someone anathema or by God, is that in the very speaking of the curse the punishment is brought into motion. Do you think you are under a curse?

In this passage before us Paul says that all those who are under the Jewish law are under a curse, and he quotes Deuteronomy 27:26 as proof. That verse says if a person does not keep all the Law he is cursed. And Paul says no one can keep the Law—he ought to know—therefore all are cursed. A vivid description of the curse on Israel is given by Jesus as he curses a fig tree on the outskirts of Jerusalem during that last week and declares it will never bear fruit again (Matthew 21:18-20). It was an acting out of the curse, the removal of Israel, from the salvation plan of God for three reasons: they sought salvation by works of their hands; they had refused to be God's servant people; they had rejected the Messiah.

But Who Is Under A Curse?

But does a curse upon those who are trusting in the Law for salvation, those who are trusting in works, mean that there is also a curse upon the Gentile—upon you and me? Yes, because the scriptures plainly tell us that all are sinners, and all are under the wrath and judgement of God. Romans 1 tells us that the moral law of God is written by the finger of God upon every heart and conscience. The Bible also tells us that we are all sinners, falling short of what God demands; that we are children of wrath, deserving the curse and its punishment. So all of us who lean on their own righteousness, who trust in good works, who ignore the plan of God for salvation, are under the curse.

The Curse And The Garden

But this curse of the Law, a curse upon self-made salvation, in Galatians 3, is tied to the Garden of Eden and the curses pronounced there. Reflect upon the words of the third verse of Isaac Watts great Christmas carol, Joy To The World!

> *No more let sins and sorrows grow,*
> *Nor thorns infest the ground;*
> *He comes to make his blessings flow*
> *Far as the curse is found.*

Turn with me to Genesis 3:12-19. I call to your attention in this passage dealing with the discovery of the fall of Adam and Eve, the cursing of the serpent (vv. 14-15). And ever since the cursing of the serpent, there has been a natural fear and horror of snakes. But the curse is not so much upon actual serpents as long as the world stands—yet hear Isaiah 65:25—as it is upon Satan. The snake is a symbol of Satan. The curse that fell on snakes that day is a symbol of the doom of Satan.

Cursing Of Serpent And Soil

Notice what the scripture says about the actual curse on the snake: (1) he will go on his belly all his days—a mark of degradation; (2) he will eat dust—perhaps not as food, but as a result of crawling in the dirt; (3) he will be an object of fear and horror; (4) there will be conflict between mankind and the snake forever (v. 15)—the statement about the head and the heel. Yet the victory is to the seed of the woman. Not only is the serpent cursed; the ground is also cursed (verses 17-19); cursed on account of the sin of Adam and Eve. The result of this curse on the ground is not that man must work; earn his living by the sweat of his brow—but that the work will be hard and unfruitful due to the barren earth.

Pronouncement Upon The Pair

Tied in with the curse upon the serpent and the curse upon the soil are the pronouncements God made upon Adam and Eve. For Eve there will be the pain of childbirth, due to the twisting of all creation through their sin, and subjection to Adam. For Adam there is the result of the curse on the soil, and the removal of the Tree of Life, accomplished by the banishment of the couple from Eden. So death now enters into human existence.

So due to the transgression of the first guilty pair, the ground is cursed, the serpent is cursed, and all mankind is under the curse of the Law, the impossibility of saving ourselves and mending the lost relationship with our Creator. The bottom line is that you, me, every human being is under the curse of the Law; under the judgement of God which comes upon all who seek salvation by our own merits and works. This is what Paul is talking about in Galatians 3. And none of us can lift the curse pronounced on all those who come short of keeping God's commandments, short of doing God's will.

Jesus The Curse

The Bible says that Jesus became a curse for us. How did that happen? Why did that happen? At the very heart of the Gospel is the matter of substitution—the just taking the place and the punishment of the unjust; the pure dying for the impure; the good suffering for the bad; the holy for the unholy. It is stated succinctly in Romans 5:6-8. Paul says Jesus took our place; our place under the curse, by becoming cursed himself, and thereby allowing the mercy of God to take effect in the lives of those who will believe in him.

A Curse In Two Ways: Hanged

How did Christ become a curse? In Galatians 3:13 we see that those who were under a curse of God were, after their execution, then fastened on walls or posts for public humiliation as a final sign of God's curse. Those whose bodies were hanged between heaven and earth were assumed to be abandoned by both God and man, of no value or concern to either.

So Jesus' death on the cross was more than just an execution; it was the death of one who was cursed of God. Those who were hanged after their executions were always taken down before the sun set lest the sight be an affront to God. So it was that the sword was thrust into Jesus' side and the legs of the thieves on the crosses were broken—that death might be hastened and the bodies removed before sunset. So Jesus became a curse in the way he died. This is what Paul is referring to in Galatians 3 to underline Christ's death for us—Jesus in his manner of death was under an Old Testament curse.

A Curse In Two Ways: Our Curse

Such an end is the just due of all of us, for we are under the curse of the Law, unable to remove the curse by fulfilling all the requirements and commandments of God. Secondly, Jesus became a curse for us he took our place under the curse of the Law. He became a curse by having all our sins laid on him: ". . .And God hath laid on him the iniquity of us all." Our sins are lifted off us and counted as his; they are looked upon by God as if Jesus had done them, not us.

It is this weight of our sins and the destruction of the relationship with the Father that brought the sweat of blood in the garden; Jesus felt and saw God treating him as a sinner—he who never had an evil thought, never knew a glance of malice, returned good for evil. It was an anguish we cannot measure or comprehend. In the old Greek liturgy there is a reference to "thine unknown sufferings," an admission that we cannot fathom the depth of the curse laid on Christ.

Christmas And The Curse

The Bible teaches us that Christmas is all about the coming of the Son of God into this world to be rejected of men and hanged on a cross, to come under the curse so the curse could be lifted from you and me. Now go back with me to Genesis 3:15 and see why this verse has been called the *Proto-evangelium*, the earliest Gospel. In the battle between the heel of man and the head of the serpent, the Bible says the seed of the woman shall bruise, crush the head of the serpent. Now Eve apparently thought the struggle would be brief, for when she gives birth to a son, she says, "I have gotten a man from the Lord!"— But his name was Cain and he was a murderer. A bit later Lamech says of his son Noah, "This one shall give us rest from the toil of the ground which the Lord cursed." But he didn't.

Through the ages the struggle goes on between the man, made of dust and the breath of God, and the serpent, Satan. Many folks look at this passage in Genesis of the battle of the heel and the head and call mankind to a mighty struggle of moral warfare against the devil, pointing to this promise of victory. But the victory will not come through us, no matter how hard we try to be moral and upright. That kind of thinking leads to death under the Law!

The Seed Of The Woman

When Paul in Romans 16:20 pronounces a benediction upon his friends, "The God of peace will soon crush Satan under your feet," he knows God will bring that victory to pass not through the seed of Adam and Eve, but through the seed of the woman. The victory is promised to the seed of the woman, not the man. Through the woman Satan made a beachhead into the human race, and through the seed of the woman without a human father, the victory will be won. It is a reference to Jesus, through whom alone we can win the victory over the serpent.

What are the consequences of Christ being made a curse for us? (1) He has redeemed us from the curse of the Law; from the futile effort to make ourselves acceptable to God through our morality or good works or wealth. (2) After dying for us, Jesus rose from the grave to bring into our lives a supernatural hope and peace and joy.

Our choice is clear: we must either be cursed of God eternally, or we must allow Christ to bear our curse.

Can Santa Come to the Manger?

I Corinthians 1:18-25

I think it was Gene Autry who most guided my ideas about Santa Claus. When I was a child a vital part of Christmas was hearing Gene Autry sing *"Here Comes Santa Claus, right down Santa Claus lane..."* And with him came *"Rudolph the Red-Nosed Reindeer."* About two weeks before Christmas, we began to watch the Brothers' home. That family had a big two-story home with a large front porch. On that front porch roof Santa would appear, and every day as we went by we saw that Santa had moved a few feet closer to a window on the second floor. By Christmas Eve, only his legs were sticking out the window. Now, we knew this guy was just a helper of Santa, but even so, it was exciting to mark the march of Santa toward Christmas.

You know, as I think about it, at Christmas time I have seen Santa Clause just about everywhere! In clothing stores, on rooftops, on billboards, in magazines, on TV... just about the only place I have not seen Santa is at a manger scene!

And that leads me to ask: What does Christmas mean to you? What connection is there between the frantic shopping and the biblical story of the manger; between Santa's coming and the Wise Men's coming; between their giving and his giving; between our giving and God's giving?

Some of us say the holiday celebration points directly to the birth of Jesus, and is properly reflected in such decorations as the manger scene at the fire station, and on church lawns. Others say just the opposite, that Christmas is a secular holiday—a view reflected in the judge's ruling in Jackson, Mississippi, that a state office building's lights could not be left on to form a cross on the side of the building. Still others would make Christmas a multi-religious holiday, as reflected in the decorations along Poplar Avenue, put up by the city. While there is no clear Christian Christmas symbol included, there is a distinctively Jewish symbol! It poses a probing question: Is Christ in our Christmas? Or just Santa?

Sometimes we see Christmas written as "Xmas." In itself, the "Xmas" is not bad. The "X" has been a symbol for Christ for many centuries, referring not to the English letter X, but to the first letter in the Greek word "Christ"—Chi, written as a large "X." Many greek manuscripts of the New Testament abbreviate Christ as Chi, or X. But for many people today, Christmas is spelled as Xmas, with the X standing for an unknown quality.

Murder and violence increase during the Christmas time; more people enter psychiatric hospitals, and suicides are higher at this time of year. Many people don't look forward to Christmas, because for them Christmas is a time of fear, depression, suicide, violence, hopelessness and despair. For them, Christmas is "Xmas."

What will it take for Christmas to be what the words Christ and mass truly mean —a religious service commemorating the birth of Christ? Put in other words, what will it take for our secular society to understand Christmas? For Santa to come to the manger?

Can Santa Come to the Manger?

First of all, Santa, and we, must come to terms with who we are before we can, or will, come to the manger. Our society has turned Santa into a lackey boy of the world of materialism; a delivery boy for department stores. As an article in yesterday's newspaper pointed out, Santa doesn't come to the poor! But Santa's real name is Saint Nicholas, and he is a bishop of the Early Church. There's a lot more to his past, and maybe Santa will tell our children about himself tonight at our First Family Christmas party. It seems natural that this one, a saint and a bishop of the church, would be seen at the manger. But we have made him to reflect our culture, and he will not come to the manger until he remembers who he is.

Just so, we will never kneel before the manger rather than reel before the punch bowl, until we remember who we are. We are sinful human beings who crave a sense of being loved, a sense of meaning and accomplishment in our lives, a relationship with God. We'll not get that in the swirl of holiday parties, but in the quietness as we kneel at the manger.

What's Santa bringing you this year? A recent newspaper article listed some of the gifts you may get or give this year. They include a sable coat for your little Rolls-Royce hood ornament at only $495; an Egyptian temple model doghouse for Fido at $1.1 million; a four-hour miniseries of your life done by Hollywood professionals for just $5 million; or a million dollar custom designed personal fireworks display including your own portrait towed by a helicopter. I say, what's the jolly old man bringing you this Christmas?

Neither we nor Santa can come to the manger until we realize that his sleigh is full of gifts as a reflection of God's great gift to us. The coming of Jesus is a gift; God's greatest gift. The birth of Jesus, surrounded as it was by such common people as shepherds, happening as it did in such an ordinary place as a stable, yet was the fulfillment of God's promise to Abraham to bless all people. One of the most beautiful expressions of the true meaning of Christmas is seen in the words of the old man in the temple, Simeon, who held the baby Jesus in his arms and said:

> *Lord, now lettest thou thy servant*
> *depart in peace, according to thy word;*
> *for mine eyes have seen thy salvation*
> *which thou hast prepared in the presence*
> *of all peoples, a light for revelation*
> *to the Gentiles, and for glory to thy*
> *people Israel.   (Luke 2:29-32).*

To celebrate Christmas rightly is to join with angels in praising God for the beginning of the plan of salvation, knowing how it travels to the cross, the grave, the garden, and through the centuries bringing salvation to all who believe. Each gift we give ought to be a reminder of the great gift of God—our salvation through Jesus. If every gift we gave reminded us of God's gift, wouldn't Christmas be wonderful?

Before Santa, or we ourselves, can come to the manger, we must not only realize that Christmas gifts are a symbol of God's great gift to us; Santa must also make sure that his sleighload of gifts includes a gift for the Christ child, which he will bring as he kneels at the manger. In all the flurry of gift getting and giving, did you remember to give a gift to Jesus? Christmas is really a birthday celebration for the Christ child. When you compare the cost of the gifts you gave others, how do you feel about the gift you gave to Jesus?

Gift-giving at this season is much more beautifully represented by the Magi of the Bible than by our secular Santa. After following "yonder star over field and fountain, moor and mountain," the Gospel simply puts it like this: "Then, opening their treasures, they offered him gifts, gold and frankincense and myrrh." Gifts for a prophet, priest, and king. What view of Christ does your gift show?

Long ago, in a rural community, every Christmas there was a Christmas tree and party in the old schoolhouse. The children always exchanged presents. A handicapped, retarded boy always attended, but never received a present. He would wait and watch as the gifts were handed out, but his name was never called. Then one Christmas, his name was called for the biggest present under the tree! He couldn't believe his ears, but it was true. The most beautiful package under the tree was his! As he carefully unwrapped the box, everyone gasped. —The box was empty! Someone had played a cruel joke. Is it possible that all some of us give the Lord in this season is an empty box?

Finally, Santa cannot come to the manger until he realizes that the best of this world's gifts are futile, fleeting, fragile toys. Most of them are soon torn up; their batteries run down; we sooner or later outgrow them. They have not the power to give us true happiness. And what is true of a five-year-old child's toys is also true of a fifty-year-old man's toys! The gift that remains through this life and beyond is not what we give, but what God gives—a wonderful gift of salvation.

And that is the way Jesus' coming is described...as a gift. A gift of great joy: "Fear not: for behold, I bring you good tidings of great joy, which shall be to all people. For unto you is born this day in the city of David a Saviour, which is Christ the Lord." A gift of peace to Simeon, in the temple. A gift rejected: "He came unto his own, and his own received him not." A gift of redeeming power: "But as many as received him, to them gave he the power to become the children of God." *"How silently, how silently the wondrous gift is giv'n! So God imparts to human hearts the blessings of his heav'n."*

I have noticed that each time I go by a church in our city which has a live manger scene, there is a crowd standing there watching the scene. What a parable of our lives. Every Christmas, with every gift and every church service, with every chime that rings out and every manger scene we see—we become a part of that crowd who came to his stable that night, one of those for whom the gift is meant.

God's Will and Christmas

Matthew 1:18-25; Luke 1:26-38

Billboards, ads on radio and TV, crooners of Christmas songs, makers of public proclamations and even the gambling joints at Tunica all say with one voice that this is the season of brotherhood, merriment and family reunion. All this is good and true; but is there a deeper meaning in Christmas? The deeper meaning of Christmas is found in the fact that Christmas is a statement of God's will.

Christmas shows us how determined God is that Satan shall not conquer, shall not destroy this creation—that the serpents in the garden of each heart will not forever beguile us, that the pharaohs of this world will not always prevail, that promises under a starry sky to Abraham will be kept, that the root of Jesse will yet sprout and the throne of David be occupied in splendor.

Three Christmas Truths

Christmas embodies three truths about God's will: (1) *God is carrying out a plan of redemption in history*, a plan that crested in the first Christmas and has spread over all the earth; (2) *Christmas says*

God's Will and Christmas

that God is determined that His plan to redeem this world shall succeed using ordinary people. On that first Christmas, surrounding this stable-born babe, the Godhead veiled in flesh, is an ordinary carpenter without even enough political pull to get a hotel room on a homecoming weekend; a village virgin scarce in her teens for a mother; a few shepherds with little to commend them to anybody; and a pair of senior adults who hang around the temple looking for something not quite clear even to them. Into this circle is born the one called Jesus because, as Matthew says, he shall save his people from their sins; because, as Luke tells us, this one is destined to rule on the throne of David. The third truth of God's will intertwined with Christmas is that *God's use of our life in the service of His redemptive plan varies both with the seasons of life and in terms of whether our response at the time ought to be active or passive.*

Responses to God's Will: Active and Passive

We all wish we had a better idea of what God wants of us; wish it were just written in giant letters on the wall; wish we could, like Paul, at least get a clear, concise answer when we ask, "Lord, what wilt thou have me to do?" We are accustomed to that approach because we emphasize the dramatic stories of the Bible in which God wanted that kind of response from folks. But there are two ways of responding to God's call, God's will in our life, and both are equally valid and both call for equal commitment.

Today I want us to think about these two sides of responding to God's will—the active, doing, on-the-move idea of responding to what God tells you; and the passive, accepting, believing, trusting and waiting side. Look at the Christmas story with me and see that both the active and passive response to God's will is found at the very heart of the gospel. Consider first, in the life of Joseph, the active response to God's will.

This Man Joseph

Matthew's Gospel begins with the genealogy of Joseph, the husband of Mary, then rather bluntly says that the birth of Jesus "was like this":

while Mary and Joseph were engaged (and engagement or betrothal was as legally binding as marriage in Jewish custom; if an engaged girl's fiancee died she was considered afterwards a widow) Mary was found to be pregnant. Verse 19 relates Joseph's reaction: he was a righteous man and decided to privately give her a statement of divorce and each would go their separate ways.

We can interpret Joseph's actions in three ways: (1) It is stressed that he was a righteous, just man—meaning that he kept the Jewish law. If he publicly denounced her, it would be in keeping with a zealous attitude toward the law. But he "was not willing to make her a public example," the point being that his love for Mary was greater than his zeal for the law, which had severe penalties for immorality, and that in spite of his zeal he refused to openly denounce her for, as he must assume, going astray. (2) Another possibility is that because he was a just, righteous man, he had mercy and pity on this poor girl whom he could only assume had gone astray.

But there is a third possibility: (3) that when Mary told Joseph her condition and its circumstances, he believed her, and as a righteous man, he desired to step aside through a pious hesitation to intrude, rather than suspicion of unfaithfulness. He wished to secretly divorce her that he might silently step aside and see what God was doing. So, in deference to the Holy Spirit, Joseph decided to divorce Mary; in consideration of Mary, he would give her the divorce paper in private, without witnesses. So much is background, and in the perplexity of Joseph we see that it is not easy either to know or accept God's will.

Joseph no doubt agonized over that decision—worrisome days in the carpenter shop when Mary no longer came by to see him, this wedge driven between them; sleepless nights when he wrestled with this approach and that approach to the problem—and then one night guidance came in a fragment of a dream in the midst of restless sleep. The angel of the Lord appeared in a dream and spoke to Joseph: (1) Mary has not been unfaithful; this is the work of the Holy Spirit; (2) don't hesitate to go through with the marriage; and (3) who this child really is. And so Joseph accepted God's will in the situation. He would not be the father of his wife's first child; but neither would he be a "fake father," as the schoolchild replied when asked who Joseph was: "He's Jesus' fake father!" No, Joseph resolved to pour his life into fulfilling God's will as best he could see it, even to filling the role of father to Jesus.

Joseph and God's Active Will

And now we see the active side of responding to God's will as Joseph rises from sleep—apparently getting up in the middle of the night. I can imagine he paced excitedly back and forth until the dawn to go and tell Mary. His part in God's plan was, in this season of his life, an active one. Here in 1:24, he rises to go through with the marriage, confident that it is God's will. In the next chapter, verses 13-14, we find an angel again appearing to Joseph in a dream, telling him to rise and take the mother and child to Egypt, fleeing Herod's wrath. And in 2:21, an angel appears for a third time in a dream to Joseph, telling him to take his family out of Egypt back to Israel.

Most of us think God's will should result in our activity, our doing something—like Joseph. We can identify with Joseph in a painting by the mid-nineteenth century pre-Raphaelite painter Holman Hunt entitled "The Triumph of the Innocents." It is a night scene, picturing the flight to Egypt. Mary is on the donkey and holds the child Jesus who is gesturing to groups of cherub friends who are half-walking, half-floating alongside, unseen by Mary. These are the little children killed at Bethlehem by Herod's soldiers. One group goes ahead of the holy family with palm branches and flowers and incense. A second group, more recently slain, walk alongside the donkey, bringing up its colt. One of these cherubs is busily examining a tear in his tiny robe, amazed that he bears no wound from the sword that made the tear. And the third group of cherubs behind the holy family are the most recently slaughtered of the Bethlehem babes; some rub their eyes, still in sleep. Halos are descending upon these cherubs.

But this is a scene of action; the family is fleeing the soldiers. Joseph is leading the donkey, but he is constantly looking back to the watch-fires of Herod's men as he hurries on; his footsteps splashing in the stream of the river of life. And everywhere he steps, bubbles arise from the stream showing within them the beautiful scenes of heaven. Yes, that is how we picture Joseph and that is the way we prefer to know and do God's will—action oriented. But that action is but for a certain season of Joseph's life. The time of passive acceptance of God's will came as he worked year after year in the carpenter's shop. Did Joseph ever wonder if he misunderstood after all? Did he die before seeing the ministry of Jesus even begin?

Mary and God's Passive Will

Leave Joseph and turn to the other side of our knowing and understanding and responding to God's will. Mary symbolizes passive acceptance of God's will. So often God wants us not to rush out and do something, but merely to be a channel of His will. To accept what He wishes to do through us. And to accept what is against the grain of common sense and man's wisdom can be as frustrating as not knowing God's will! Consider Mary in Luke 1:26-30.

An angel is sent to Nazareth; that's about as insignificant a village as you can get—"Can any good thing come out of Nazareth?" asks Nathanael. And this angel is sent to a girl named Mary. She is ordinary, young, apparently poor and has no merit of herself. Yet the angel, coming inside the house, greets her in terms you might apply to the Hebrew judges and heroes long ago—". . . highly favored; the Lord is with thee; blessed art thou. . ." And Mary is troubled, perplexed. She accepts the angel without a blink, for this angelic being apparently appeared to her as an ordinary person; her troubled feelings come from the message of the angel. Even as the angel speaks, she seeks in her own mind for a reason for what she is hearing . . . "How can this be?"

But go on to verses 30-34. This stranger is telling Mary that (1) she is going to have a baby; (2) she is to name the child Jesus; and (3) this child will rule on David's throne. She could have asked, How can this be, seeing that the Romans rule over us? She could have asked,

How can this be, since I am merely a child—have you checked with my parents? Have you checked with my fiancee, Joseph? But being a moral, pure girl, Mary replies to the angel, How can this be, seeing I have not been to bed with any man?

The angel replies that (1) nothing is impossible with God; and (2) the Holy Spirit will put this seed in your womb. It is Mary's response in verse 38 which I would underline for you: Behold the handmaiden of the Lord: be it unto me according to thy word. Here we see that the doing of God's will in her case meant simply accepting the will of God. This does not mean that Mary understood all God was doing in her life. After the baby is born and the shepherds come and go, we are told that Mary kept all these things in her heart and pondered them.

Now let me describe for you the second painting by Holman Hunt, a painting which portrays beautifully this receiving, passive side of responding to God's will. Hunt painted a scene in the carpenter shop at Nazareth; Joseph is dead, Jesus is in his 20's. It is the end of a hard day, and Jesus has just laid aside his tools and is stretching cramped muscles. Mary is shown at the side of the picture, having laid aside the cares of the day for a moment of reverie as she opens a chest and gazes at the treasures she has kept through the years—the gifts of the Wise Men. But she looks up, and there on the wall behind Jesus she sees his shadow; the shadow of the cross looming behind him. It is a poignant picture, emphasizing as it does the surrender of Mary to the will of God through the years, surrendering to God's will even if it means the sword in her heart.

Christmas and God's Will for You

We have come once again to Christmas. Let us be reminded (1) that God is carrying out a plan through the ages; (2) that God uses ordinary people to carry out His redemptive plan; and (3) that God's will in our lives varies through the years and through the seasons of life. Joseph shows us in his actions the active side of doing God's will; Mary shows us the passive side of receiving and accepting God's will. Joseph says, "I'll go where you want me to go, dear Lord; I'll be . . . I'll do . . . whatever you wish." And Mary says down through the ages, "Let it be to me as you say." If we cannot echo their commitment to God, we cannot fully understand Christmas.

Going Home Another Way

Matthew 2:1-12

A man came to me after the Thursday Bible Luncheon this past week to share an exciting insight he had just gained reading Matthew's account of the birth of Christ. As he read of the divine warning and guidance given to the Wise Men that they should not return to Herod to rather go home another way, my friend said it dawned upon him: Of course the Wise Men went home another way; no one ever comes to the manger and kneels there and goes home the same way they came!

He found it more than coincidence that I was preaching on this very theme this Sunday! True, this passage is talking about how the Wise Men went back home a different way geographically; but it is also true that their hearts and lives were changed and they went back different men from the men who came. The thought keeps ringing around in my mind that it would be a wonderful thing if all of us went back after Christmas to our daily walks changed—back to our stores, our offices, our classrooms, our dishpans, back to the weariness of winter as changed persons! Happier folks, more at peace with God and ourselves, more filled with faith and trust and cooperation. What a wonderful Christmas that would be!

The key to going back another way after Christmas is seen in the text story—they came to see Jesus, and the seeing of the Christ child and the realization of what he meant, sent them away different. So I want to make some suggestions which, if you and I will follow them, just may by the grace of God enable us to go back a different way this next year.

Meditate on Meaning of Christmas

First, let us follow in the steps of the Wise Men and meditate on the true meaning of Christmas. As we look at the text, obviously the story of the Wise Men begins much earlier. Surely they had spent some time before the journey in meditation and thought and discussion of the meaning of the star. During the journey they must have meditated on this thing, and then at the house where they found the Christ child they surely prayed and meditated, and then they reflected on this event as they went back home. But much of our modern society does not know the true meaning of Christmas. And in some cases our civic leaders seem determined to hide the meaning of Christmas—I read a few days ago of a city in which the town fathers outlawed all Christmas decorations, religious or otherwise, lest someone be offended! And a few years ago I read of an incident—perhaps it happened here in Memphis—in which a priest went out to purchase a nativity scene. In talking with the shopkeeper he casually mentioned that "This is what Christmas is all about." "All about what?" Said the storekeeper. And the priest replied, "All about the birth of this baby." "You're putting me on," said the merchant. The priest didn't quite know just who was putting who on! Further conversation revealed that the merchant really didn't connect Christmas with the birth of Christ.

We cannot understand the deepest meaning of Christmas if we leave Christ out of it. I once heard a radio announcer say the essence of

Christmas is captured as much by street lamp singers as by the Wise Men. That is sheer foolishness. Our secular society's attitude toward Christmas reminds me of that Christmas over two decades ago when I had a little preschool girl who just loved to see "the baby Jesus" in Christmas mangers. Well, in the city where I was pastor at the time, the Methodist Church had a beautiful nativity scene out in front of the church. So one night in passing by, we simply had to park our car and walk across the church lawn and see the baby in the manger. It was a shock to this little girl to find that there was no baby in the manger! And that's just what our society has done to Christmas! We have taken the baby out of the manger, and the manger out of Christmas! I listened in disbelief one night this past week as a television commercial played the music of "God Rest You Merry, Gentlemen" emphasizing the phrase "comfort and joy" to sell underwear!

Lloyd Douglas, in his book **Time To Remember**, tells about a friend of his brother Clyde. This boyhood pal wrote Clyde a letter which went like this: *Dear Clyde, How are you? Well, I hope. We are alright here. Do you still have the white rat? Mind that pair of rabbits I had? I have sold lots of rabbits. School has took up again. I hate school. Your friend, Sam Logan. P. S. Pap died last night.* That's our society—we put into the letter, we push to the front those minor and minute things that really don't matter, and we relegate to a footnote the things that are earth-shaking!

I urge you to take time in these next few days to sit down and read the Christmas story. Begin with the prophecies in Isaiah 7 and 9 and 11. Think about what it means to say that those who walked in darkness have seen a great light; that the light has shined upon those who dwelt in the land of the shadow of death. Think about the prophet saying the name of the Messiah is Wonderful Counselor, Mighty God, Everlasting Father, Prince of Peace. Think about what it means that a virgin conceived and brought forth a son whose name is Immanuel: God with us; whose name is Jesus: for he shall save his people from their sin. Ask yourself the question—and answer it to yourself: What is the deepest meaning of Christmas for me?

Roy Angell, beloved Baptist preacher of a generation ago, summed it up well in a story about his student days at the University of Richmond. Along with a dozen or so other boys, he was called up to the blackboard to work a math problem. It was a complicated problem and most of the blackboard was filled before the boys finished. Then the professor began to check the work, in front of the entire class. The professor got to Angell's work and pronounced it incorrect, then started at the end and began to work backward. Back and back the professor went until he was nearly back to the initial statement of the problem before he found the fault—but there it was, right at the start. The professor, knowing that Angell was a ministerial student, turned to the class and asked how many were in training for the ministry. A goodly number raised their hands, and the professor said, "Now here's a sermon for you preacher boys! If there is a mistake, if there is something wrong at the very start, there is no way in mathematics or in life that you can come out correct at the end!" And the professor proceeded to preach a sermon, declaring that there is something wrong from the start in every life. Then he said he had a second sermon—and here he took his eraser and erased the whole problem except for the statement of it. Then he worked the first part, correcting the mistake the preacher boy had made, and then he handed the chalk over to Angell, saying "Now, try again!" Turning to the class, the professor said, "That's what the Gospel is all about; a second chance!" Folks, that's what Christmas is all about. It's about the Mighty Creator of this universe saying to broken and sinful people—"I'm giving you a second chance, and a third and a fourth chance with your life!" Our God is the God of the Second Chance . . . The Wonderful Counselor, the Mighty God, the Everlasting Father and the Prince of Peace. Meditate on the depth of Christmas.

Act on the Meaning of Christmas

A second suggestion to help us go home another way after Christmas: Apply the truth of Christmas to your life. Let the glory of the Gospel shine on you; believe and act on the truth that Christmas is all about a second chance for folks like you and me who aren't perfect.

Hear a very homely little story, but one that tells how God uses the beautiful Christmas story to heal, to touch, to change. It happened in a rural area, to a family named Anderson. Bill Anderson was a farmer, and on this winter night he is relaxing after a long day's work. As he sat reading the paper, his son Bruce, 14, came down the stairs. As soon as his sister saw Bruce coming down the stairs, she began to giggle. Bill turned to look at his son Bruce and sure enough, Bruce apparently was wearing an old sheet and a cockeyed pasteboard yellow crown on his head, and he carried an old-fashioned smoke-pot in his hand, wrapped in gold foil. On his feet were sandals. And then Bill remembered. Oh, my stars, he had agreed to take Bruce down to the high school auditorium for the little Christmas play.

Now this story takes place during the depression years. So Bill bundles up and goes out and strains and heaves to crank the old car. It doesn't want to go; the grease is frozen, everything is cold, it's a bitter night. No moon is shining, but the sky is full of stars. The old car groans and chugs, and finally starts. They ramble and rumble on down the road around the barn, heading out toward the highway some two miles away. Just past the barn the old car wheezes and hiccups and coughs and stops. Dad gets out and heaves and puffs and still can't get it to go. He turns around to say something to his son and he realizes that the boy's praying. He's got to get to the school house. And the father who has just decided to say, "Look, there's no point in worrying about it. Let's go back home," realizes he can't say that, he's got to keep trying. So he wrestles with that old crank. The next time he looks back the boy's gone. Down the road he sees him, shuffling along in those old sandals,, freezing to death with that crazy lopsided crown and that smoke-pot swinging. He starts to call but he realizes maybe out at the road he can hitch a ride, and if I can get this thing started, maybe I'll overtake him. He keeps on and finally after what seems to be an eternity it cranks.

He goes into town, but doesn't see the boy on the way. But right there at the edge of town, just where it begins to be divided into streets, there at 5th Avenue he meets his son, grinning sort of crookedly in the cold night air. He gets in the car and he says, "Aren't you about frozen?" "No dad, it really wasn't bad at all. I lit some twigs in my fire pot and I stayed pretty warm." They went on to the program that night, and a s they started out of town to go back home, the son said, "There's where I came out. I took a shortcut." His Dad said, "Yes, that's where the Thompson's live." "Yes, I remember. Their boy burned to death in the fire last year, didn't he?" "Yes, he did, son." As they went on home, the boy said, "Here's where I cut across the fields at Wadsworth's farm." He said, "I picked a star and followed it, and that's why I was able to get on into town." The father noticed all the lights were on at the Wadsworth home, but as far as he was concerned, that was the end of it. That was Tuesday.

About a week later on Christmas Eve God used that simple little incident. The village gossip had come by to bring some Christmas goodies. And so Bill's wife was talking with her in the kitchen. A few minutes later she came in and said, "Bill, you need to come hear this." So Bill went to the kitchen. The gossip fastened her eyes on him and said, "I know, you're not going to believe this, but it really happened." "What happened?" "Well, first it was the Wadsworths. You know that Granny Wadsworth lost her son in the last War, and since then she's sort of withered up. She won't go anywhere and they just sort of close up at night. And then it struck Bill. "I remember we came by there the other night their lights were all on." And she said "Well, here's what happened. Granny Wadsworth thought she heard the dogs barking and a noise behind the barn. She looked out the window and there she said she saw it, just as clear as day—one of those Wise Men out of the New Testament—going along the ridge with his crown and his robe, swinging a firepot and all." And she said, "Oh, I know you don't believe it. But that ain't the only one. The Thompsons saw it too." "It was the bleakest Christmas because it was the first one when their boy was gone. And there they were, all praying in the darkness of this

Christmas. And the kidsv set up such a fuss and a howl because they saw walking down the lane, right by their house, a Wise Man from the New Testament. Swinging his firepot and his crown on his head, and his robe and everything. And they called for their parents and they came running in. But he was gone just like that," said the gossip. "He disappeared. And they went out and they looked all around, but they couldn't find no sign of him. You may not believe it, but it really happened!"

Of course it happened, and it will happen to some folks this Christmas season—the God of second chances will use some of the most unusual ways to reach those who sit in darkness! Be aware in this Christmas season of your own spiritual needs, and look for ways God is speaking to you, to your need, through unusual circumstances.

The Wise Men went home another way because (1) they had meditated on the meaning of the star; (2) they were willing to apply the meaning of this child's birth to their own life.

They were willing to follow the star to a distant land, they were willing to risk the disapproval of men in not returning to King Herod; they were happy to bow before the Christ child and put costly gifts at his feet and walk away and leave them. Some of us need to put gold and silver at his feet, some of us need to put a mean spirit, a bagful of grudges, a worldly spirit down in the hay as the symbol of our depth of commitment to him. Some of us need to put our repentant heart before the manger. Let's make sure we go home another way, a better way, after this Christmas.

Hidden Truths of Christmas

Hebrews 2:9—3:1

According to a recent Gallop poll, only 33% of the American public finds the importance of Christmas in the birth of Jesus. We have become a nation ignorant of the meaning of Christmas! This would have been unthinkable only a couple of generations ago. But it is also disturbing that, even when we connect Christmas with the birth of Christ, there is still the tendency at Christmastime to focus on the Christmas card aspects of Christmas—to marvel at the stooping of God to come into this world in a stable, to wonder at the wondrous star, to shudder at the evil king trying to kill the King of kings, to rejoice with the shepherds on the hillside and to ponder the choice of Mary as the mother of the Messiah. And then it is time to pack up the decorations for another year and get out the black-eyed peas and hog jowls and celebrate New Year's Day.

But today I want us to go deeper into the meaning of Christmas. Let us examine the Christmas story in the epistle to the Hebrews.

God Has Spoken

This beautiful general epistle to the Hebrews begins by telling us that God is not silent in this world. He has spoken through the prophets in times gone by, and in these last days he has spoken to us through his son.

And what the son, Jesus, says is more important than even the precious Jewish law, given to men at the hand of angels according to tradition. The writer stresses the peril of neglecting the revelation of God brought to us by his son saying, "How shall we escape if we neglect so great salvation . . .?" And then in chapter two we have the Christmas story from the perspective of the writer of Hebrews, told to those who believe the Gospel—who at least say they believe— those who are in danger of losing their grip on the Gospel. They sound quite modern to me.

We See Jesus

We pick up these hidden truths of Christmas beginning in verse 9: "But we see Jesus . . ." Like the writer here, we too need at Christmas time to turn our eyes upon Jesus—Jesus not just in the manger, but grown up; Jesus carrying the cross, Jesus lifted up, Jesus dying for us. Let us turn our eyes upon Jesus—Jesus with a greater message than the angels, made a little lower than the angels with his birth in a stable. Turn our eyes upon Jesus, tasting of death for every one of us, yet crowned with glory and honor. Let us turn our eyes upon Jesus— Jesus in his humanity, referred to here not as the Messiah, nor as Jesus Christ, but here simply by the name that all the boys playing in the streets of Nazareth with him knew; the name by which Mary called him to supper; the name of the carpenter who made tables and chairs; the name often on the lips of his companions during those three years of ministry; the name the angel in the tomb used as he told the women, "You seek Jesus who was crucified; he is not here, he is risen."

But even as we turn our eyes upon Jesus, we have to ask, Why this unthinkable, this unbelievable, this unrealistic—from a human, commonsense, worldly perspective—drama? What is behind the stable story? Consider the hidden truths of Christmas in these verses.

The Father Felt It Appropriate

First, in verse 10 we realize that Christmas happened because God thought it appropriate and even necessary that He who brings us to glory as sons and daughters of God should himself be made perfect and complete for his task of redemption through full humanity, including the discipline of suffering. One of the deepest and most striking hidden truths of Christmas is that in order for we who believe to finally stand before the throne of God immortal and sinless, the one who stood before the throne in perfection through the ages must lay aside all that glory and become one of us. He must drink fully of the cup of humanity. I take that to mean that in his humanity Jesus must become all that God intended Adam to be, if he is to set us free from sin and death.

The Son Gladly Put On Humanity

Second, in verses 11 and 12 we see that this great Christmas truth of the necessity of full humanity, extending to the birth in the stable, is not forced upon God as we know him as Jesus, but rather Jesus gladly took upon himself our humanity, saying he was not ashamed to call us brethren. This is one of the most humbling statements in Scripture; Jesus is not ashamed to call folks like you and me, with all our sins, his brothers and sisters. We applauded when JFK made his speech in Berlin at the height of the cold war, and proclaimed, "Ich bin ein Berliner!" We thought it touching when President Jimmy Carter acknowledged Billy Carter as his brother, regardless of his shenanigans; but those instances of shared identity are nothing compared to the proclamation by the maker of heaven and earth that he is our brother. That is the greatest example of identity with another that this world affords.

Verse 14 carries this identification still further, saying that just as blood brothers and sisters have the same flesh and blood, so Jesus also partook of our flesh and blood and became completely human. The glory of the humanity of Jesus is summed up by this writer—"like us, yet without sin."

What Putting On Humanity Led To

Now see what Jesus' experience as one of us leads to. It leads to the realization that human beings are enslaved all through life by the fear of death (14 and 15). Since Eden, mankind has been enslaved by the fear of death—literally, a phobia. You have only to walk through an old cemetery in England and read the verses on tombstones of two or three centuries ago to feel the depressing weight of death upon the living—for it was the then living who carved the macabre sayings and warnings upon the tombstones. For instance, a common verse ran like this:

> *Stranger, stop and cast an eye,*
>
> *As you are now, so once was I.*
>
> *As I am now, so you will be,*
>
> *Prepare for death and follow me.*

But, you say, there is no such fear of death in our society. Why, far from occupying our minds, we try not to mention it. True, we have an overwhelming denial of death; everything about our way of death tries to say it hasn't happened, won't happen, cannot happen—but it does. The death rate always has been, and still is, one per person.

This scripture tells us that Jesus in his humanity was fully aware of the fear of death hanging over humanity. And verses 14 and 15 tells us that he not only realized this fear, but that he resolved to set us slaves free by breaking the grip of the devil upon us—the devil, who has the power of death. Think about that; our fear of death can be traced back to the devil. It is he who is the author of death and holds the power of death over us.

Verse 17 tells us that Jesus, in his humanity, not only realized our enslavement and resolved to set us free, but he intended through his sojourn among us as one of us, to reconcile us to God as he fills the function of both High Priest and sacrifice.

The themes of the High Priest and the sacrifice are central to this letter to the Hebrews. Once a year the High Priest entered the Holy of Holies and sprinkled blood on the "meeting place" the top of the Ark of the Covenant, pleading for God's forgiveness of his sins and those of the people, and asking God to abide with them. It was a drama played out for hundreds of years, over and over. Over and over because there was no perfect sacrifice worthy to take away their sins, nor was there a High Priest worthy to approach God on their behalf. Jesus is both the perfect sacrifice and the perfect High Priest. Through his humanity he offers the ultimate sacrifice as he becomes the unblemished Lamb of God. Through his closeness to the Heavenly Father he is able to live a sinless, perfect life and thus become our perfect High Priest.

And all of this is behind the beautiful Christmas card scenes—the cattle lowing, the angels singing, the soft lamplight, the tenderly smiling Mary and the protective Joseph, the admiring shepherds. It is indeed a night to shake the universe, when the Creator becomes a weak, vulnerable creature in the midst of his creation gone astray and under the domination of the devil. But that is what Christmas is all about.

Christmas is about family and faith and love, yes. But it is about the family of God, and how our older brother, Jesus, came to earth and took upon him all it means to be human, so we can put on all it means to live eternally in the presence of God. It is about God loving us enough to send his son Jesus, who loves us enough to call us brothers and sisters and even to die on the cross to set us free from sin and death. Christmas is about the beginning of the experience of Jesus as one of us, about his victory over temptation and sin and the devil.

Christmas Is Hope

And the writer of this epistle is doing more than talking heavy theology. He is speaking a word of hope to folks who have almost given up on their faith. And verse 18 is very important. It has something personal to say to you. Jesus has been where you are; he has walked in your shoes, he has tasted of the depth of what it means to be human. He knows broken dreams, fearful nights, confused hearts. "For in that he himself has been tempted, he is able to comfort and strengthen those who are tempted." And that word of hope is still valid and true; just as true as Christmas.

The Joy That Belongs to Christmas

Matthew 2:10; Luke 2:10

In The Midst of Herod's wickedness; in the midst of the rejection of Joseph and Mary at the inn; in the midst of the tiredness of the Magi; in the midst of the poverty of the shepherds; in the midst of this puzzling crisis for Mary and Joseph, we read in the Christmas story of joy! "When they saw the star, they rejoiced with exceeding great joy." "Behold, I bring you good tidings of great joy." Did these Wise Men and angels see something we don't see in this story? Did they know something we don't know about the circumstances? What is this Christmas joy of which we read?

Christmas Joy?

The theme of joy, like peace, is another of those themes in secular Christmas cards that make the thoughtful person ponder. What do you think the makers of Christmas cards mean by the phrase, the Joy of the Season? Are they speaking of the parties, the expansive feeling gained from free flowing liquor, the happiness of seeing family and friends, the chestnuts roasting kind of image? Does that pair of 2:10s from Matthew and Luke have a deeper meaning than that? None of our modern secular joy and festivity of the Christmas season surrounded that stable in Bethlehem on the first Christmas.

Biblical Emphasis On Joy

Joy of Creation, Incarnation, Resurrection

There is an emphasis on joy throughout the Bible. There is the joy expressed at creation: ". . . When the morning stars sang together, and all the sons of God shouted for joy" (Job 38:7). There is the joy at Christmas, the joy of the incarnation: "When they saw the star, they rejoiced with exceeding great joy" (Matt 2:10), ". . . I bring you good tidings of great joy" (Luke 2:10). There is the joy of the resurrection: "And they departed quickly from the sepulchre with fear and great joy" (Matt 28:8), "And while they yet believed not for joy, and wondered, he said unto them, Have ye here any food?" (Luke 24:41).

Joy That Belongs To Salvation

There is the joy which accompanies salvation: "With joy shall ye draw water out of the wells of salvation" (Isa 12:3). A joy that pervades and enriches all our days after we experience that grace, and a joy of salvation that resounds even into heaven: "I say unto you, that likewise joy shall be in heaven over one sinner that repenteth, more than over ninety and nine just persons" (Luke 15:7).

Joy That Belongs To Heaven

There is the joy which belongs to heaven: "I say unto you, ye shall be sorrowful, but your sorrow shall be turned into joy. Ye now have sorrow: but I will see you again, and your heart shall rejoice, and your joy no man takes from you" (John 16:20,22), "The kingdom of heaven is like unto treasure hid in a field; the which when a man hath found, he hideth, and for joy thereof goeth and selleth all that he hath, and buys that field" (Matt 13:44); "His Lord said unto him, Well done, good and faithful servant: enter thou into the joy of thy Lord" (Matt 25:21).

The Joy Jesus Had

There is the joy that Jesus had, and gave to Christians: "These things have I spoken unto you, that my joy might remain in you, and that your joy might be full" (John 15:11). There is the joy that marks the Christian life: "And the disciples were filled with joy, and with the Holy Spirit" (Acts 13:52). In this Acts passage joy ranks with the filling of the Holy Spirit.

The Joy That Belongs To Christmas

So what is this joy that belongs to Christmas? What does that pair of 2:10s really mean? They mean that there is no everlasting joy apart from a saving relationship to God. The joy that belongs to Christmas is a product of our relationship to God. Let us try to define the biblical kind of joy; the kind of joy that you and I possess as redeemed children of God. Christian joy is a mixture of belief, peace, and hope. Leslie Weatherhead once said that the opposite of joy is not sorrow; it is unbelief. So Christian joy is not necessarily a bubbling kind of happiness which you may or may not possess as part of your psychological makeup; it is more stable and deeper in its flow.

Christian joy is a joy that has its beginning and ending in the world above; the joy that belongs to Christmas is a rope dipping down into this world and sweeping back up again into glory. To borrow an image from childhood, Christians relate to joy like little girls play jump rope. Remember how two little girls—or sometimes the girls would cajole us boys into holding the rope—would take the rope and begin to swing it in a great big rolling motion? I can still clearly hear the slapping of the rope on the pavement on its downward swing. Then some little girl would get courageous and duck into that magic circle, skipping as the rope made its turn over and under her. That's what happens to the Christian when we allow God's joy to be the rope; we can get caught up in the rhythm of it, and experience the joy, too.

Christmas Joy In The Heart Of God

For behind the Christian joy that we experience is the joy of God. The Bible speaks of angelic joy at creation—a reflection of God's anticipation of joyful fellowship with mankind. Christian joy begins in the heart of God, and is the force behind creation itself. God's joy is behind the incarnation, too. The purpose of the incarnation was to set forth a way to restore sinful humanity to our Heavenly Father. That is why the angels sang of good tidings of great joy—God has set forth on the search for fellowship with mankind again.

Christmas Joy In Jesus' Life

This Christmas joy is seen reflected in the life of Jesus. In John 15 Jesus spoke of his joy which would remain in the disciples, and in Hebrews 12:2 the writer describes Jesus this way: "Jesus the author and finisher of our faith; who for the joy that was set before him endured the cross, despising the shame, and is set down at the right hand of the throne of God." The joy of the Father's plan and hope and dream of reconciling mankind enabled God's Son to accept the incarnation and endure the death on the cross. The joy of Christmas is that the result of sin—the hostility of man to God, the gulf of guilt, the curse through the ages—can through the birth of this baby be removed. Isaac Watts said it well in that verse often deleted from the beloved Christmas carol, *Joy To The World*:

> *No more let sins and sorrows grow,*
> *Nor thorns infest the ground;*
> *He comes to make his blessings flow*
> *Far as the curse is found.*

The Purpose of Christmas Joy

The joy that belongs to Christmas begins in the heart of God. And when we read of the purpose of creation, the purpose of the incarnation, the promise of the Holy Spirit, the experience of the Christian walk and the hope laid up for us in heaven—all these are clothed with joy in the Bible. Why? It is because Christmas means a release from sin and guilt; a second chance; a future happiness that leaks into this world.

The Joy that Belongs to Christmas

There is a worldly joy and a worldly happiness of this season which cannot face the realities of life. We know that at this season of the year there are even more depressed people, more people who try to take their lives, more people who see little purpose in life or reason for living, than at any other season of the year. The worldly joy of Christmas cannot face that truth. But the joy that lives in the heart of the Christian knows there is more beyond this world. We have heard the Master say, "Be of good cheer, for I have overcome the world."

Do you have that joy in your heart? That sturdy, sustaining peace and hope and joy that walk hand in hand through the years in the knowledge of forgiveness and peace with God? That is what Christmas is all about.

Packaging Christmas

Matthew 2:1-12

Suppose for a moment that until this morning you had lived on a remote island in the South Pacific all your life. You have spent your life climbing cocoanut trees, picking up shells on the beach; doing whatever it is they do on remote islands in the South Pacific. Suddenly you find yourself plopped down in Memphis, Tennessee, in the middle of the Christmas season. Everything you see is foreign to you. You have never heard of Christ, or Christianity, or Christmas. The year of our Lord 1989 means nothing to you; in your land time is counted by big events—this is the 13th year after the big volcano blew up. You are bombarded on every hand with the crass commercialism of Christmas, the gift-giving emphasis, the street-corner Santas, the nativity scenes, the church extravaganzas, the Christmas trees. What would your reaction be! Would you have trouble figuring out what Christmas is all about? Would you wonder how it all fits together— the Santas, the manger scenes, the Christmas trees and the gift-giving? Some folks say it just doesn't fit together! Some legal opinions say

Christmas is now simply a secular holiday and ought not be given religious overtones. Most of us know better than that, but we can all agree there is a great deal of confusion about the meaning of Christmas.

Packaging a Mystery

I think I would say to our visitor from the South Sea island, and to all of us who are dismayed with the materialism of the season, that part of the confusion of Christmas is due to the fact that we stand before a mystery every Christmas; and that Christians always feel a divine compulsion to explain it, "package" it, if you will, and urge it upon an unbelieving world. Folks in public relations talk of "packaging" a celebrity or a new perfume or a new idea, and what they mean is that for our society to understand, to accept, to embrace a particular person or plan or product it must be presented in the clearest, best, most attractive and most meaningful way possible.

The message of Christmas is a mystery, as Paul often says. It is so wonderful, yet so strange and out-of-place in this world. There is mystery aplenty in the virgin birth, the wondrous guiding star, the wise men from the east. But the deeper mystery and deeper miracle is far more than the events which took place on the plane of human experience. And if we stumble over those, and many folks do, how shall we grasp the greater mystery and miracle—that the mighty God became weak, human flesh? And that He did it for our redemption?

Surely, the very idea of God Almighty coming to earth in Jesus Christ is a mystery beyond our capacity to understand. Sadly enough, those who had the best background, the best chance to hold in their hands and hearts the great mystery, did not understand or accept it. John's Gospel puts it succinctly: "He came unto his own, and his own received him not." It is not easy to package such a mystery as Christmas contains, and much of the confusion of Christmas and its celebration comes from our efforts through the centuries to explain, to "package," if you will, this unexplainable mystery of the ages.

How do you package a Mystery?

So how can we package something so unbelievable, so undeserved, so unexplainable, so unearthly and wondrous as the mystery of Christmas? Consider the facts of the mystery. First, Christmas celebrates the special moment when God burst fully into history as one of us; that moment when eternity broke through into time; the hinge of history, that special event which divides all history into two sections: before and after. Second, Christmas celebrates the fact that the creator chose to step into His creation on behalf of sinful men. He chose to become like us, and suffer and die on our behalf, so that we might someday become like Him. All preaching is an attempt to "package" this mystery. Christmas celebrates an act of God; an act of God for the salvation of sinful men, something God did for us. Something we desperately needed to happen, something God put into the prophets' hearts, something which came to pass in the fulness of time. This is the heart of the Christian celebration of Christmas, however it is "packaged." The elements of the mystery of Christmas form a half circle, described so eloquently by Paul in Philippians 2, a stooping down, an enduring of the pain and sin of humanity, a lifting of mankind to glory.

Christmas then, is all about the giving of a great gift to mankind, salvation from sin. The writer to the Hebrews puts it so beautifully in Hebrews 2:14-17. Christmas is a calling forth from darkness into light those who dwell in the land of the shadow of death. It is the announcing of a great news, the emancipation of mankind from the bondage of sin and the devil. How, then, can we "package" that message effectively for today, and what has all that to do with Santa Claus and Christmas trees and cards and gifts?

How the Gospels package Christmas

Consider first how the Gospel writers "packaged" that mystery. Each writer chose, under the guidance of the Spirit, certain aspects of the wonderful unfolding events of the first Christmas to emphasize, and spoke especially clearly to certain groups of people. Matthew emphasized the fulfillment of prophecy about Jesus, the longed-for Messiah.

In Matthew's Gospel we also read of the Wise Men and realize he is emphasizing the universal nature of the Good News of Jesus; we see Herod's anger and see behind him the opposition of the devil to God in Christmas. Luke tells us of the shepherds, of the fact that there was no room in the inn, and of God's choice of a ordinary girl as the mother of the Saviour; he is emphasizing the stooping down of God in human flesh, and the rejection of the divine gift.

Thus the very Gospel writers, through their chosen emphases, under the Holy Spirit "packaged" the Gospel, "packaged" Christmas for the people they especially had in mind. And the Gospel began its journey through the centuries and to the ends of the earth. And that kind of "packaging," that kind of emphasizing of certain facets of the story, we can understand. But where does Santa come into this "packaging?" Is he just a corruption of a Christmas message that is too great to comprehend, to understand, to realize? Or do we have in Santa efforts to package the Christmas truths in these centuries since that first Christmas?

Packaging Christmas Over the Years

There is the perennial debate over the reality of Santa Claus. May I speak a word in defense of Santa, and the Christmas tree, and the giving of gifts—as a part of "packaging" Christmas in our time. Our office manager was telling me a few days ago about their little boy Matthew seeing a Santa on a shopping parking lot. Little Matthew grew so excited at the sight of Santa, he almost had conniption fits! His parents had apparently not been looking for Santa on every corner as Matthew had, and even assured the tot that Santa was nowhere around. But at his insistence they walked around on the parking area, and sure enough, there he was! Now this particular Santa was a bit the worse for wear; both his clothes and his beard needed some work! Close up he was enough to make one doubt the reality of Santa Claus! And so it was that, after they left, Matthew's father began some heavy duty explaining about how everyone who looks like Santa really isn't Santa; some are helpers and such. The little fellow looked up at his daddy and, with shining eyes and that sincerity that only a three-year-old can muster: "I know, daddy, I know—but this one was the real Santa!" I seriously doubt that Santa is going away, or that God has anything against Santa! Rightly understood, the tradition of Santa can be a beautiful carrier of eternal truth about the divine mystery of Christmas.

In the 4th century there was a good and great bishop of the church in Asia Minor named Nicholas. There are many legends connected with this bishop, one of which tells of his parents dying when Nicholas was but a boy. He became very religious, and attended church faithfully. When the bishop of the area died, the church leaders were told in a dream to stand at the door of the church, and the first person to come in named Nicholas was to be the next bishop. And in came the young man Nicholas. Over his protests, he was made bishop. The real Nicholas died about 350 a.d. Revered for his faith, miracles are said to have accompanied him.

One famous legend is that of the 3 bags of gold. It is said that to provide a dowry for each of the three daughters of a righteous but poor man, Nicholas threw a bag of gold in the window of their humble home as each girl reached the marriage age. The 3 bags of gold have, through the centuries, been associated with Saint Nicholas in stories and paintings. He became the patron saint of bankers and moneylenders and pawnbrokers, hence the symbol of the 3 golden balls. Because he loved children and gave them gifts, his feast day, December 6, was a great occasion in many European countries, and in the 1800's it was merged with Christmas and symbolized the marvelous gift of God in sending Jesus. And the gifts of the Wise Men were symbolized in the idea of St. Nicholas bringing gifts to children, and in the giving of gifts in general at Christmas. And over a period of time Saint Nicholas' name became "Santa Claus," because it sounds like that when said fast!

The Christmas tree. It is said that Martin Luther, walking home one night at Christmas Eve through the forest, marveled at the wondrous

Packaging Christmas

sky full of stars gleaming through the evergreen trees. Later he went out and cut a fir tree and put candles on it to represent the starry night on which Jesus was born. Some legends say the tree represents the world, the large star atop the tree the Christ child, and the small lights stand for our individual lives.

How would you package Christmas?

The miracle of Christmas is that God cared enough to become one of us; to be born in a manger and to die on a cross for our sins. That's the miracle; that's the message; that's the reason for the season. And it's bigger than we can grasp, but our task as the company of the redeemed is to proclaim the Christmas mystery. Santa and the Christmas tree are part of the packaging of Christmas in years gone by. How can we best do it? Let me make some suggestions about recovering a deeper meaning of Christmas.

First, be mindful of Scripture. Know what really happened on the first Christmas. That is why we always need a strong emphasis on the nativity scene. Second, be mindful of the origins of the Christmas traditions. Many of them are really beautiful ways the Christmas mystery was "packaged" in the past. Why not pour forgotten meaning back into those traditions? Teach your children the story of the first St. Nicholas (Santa Claus), and how his bringing of gifts echoes the great gift of God's love in Jesus. Every gift we give points us to the gift of Jesus. Tell your children about Martin Luther and the Christmas tree; remind them that some lights twinkle and some are dark and some burn bright—just like people's lives. Third, experience the Christmas mystery for yourself. Ponder the Scripture and hear the angels sing; go to the stable with the shepherds in a time of meditation in your heart; with the Wise Men bring your gift to the Holy Child. Let Christ be born in your life today.

The Peace of Christmas

Luke 2:9-14; Ephesians 2:14-17

My Mother used to say, in the midst of bringing up five boys: "Oh, for a little peace and quiet around here!" Is that the kind of peace on earth the Christmas angels sang about? What is biblical peace? What kind of peace are you looking for?

Christmas Card Peace

It is clear that the peace so prominent in the run-of-the-mill Christmas cards is a peace between nations. The kind of peace efforts one is usually involved with in order to get the Nobel Peace Prize (so why did sometime terrorist Yassar Arafat receive such an honor yesterday?) Christmas card peace usually represents the kind of peace Neville Chamberlain sought at the Munich Conference with Hitler and Mussolini in September of 1938; he came back to England bubbling with victory, waving his briefcase with the signed pact as he stood in the

The Peace of Christmas

door of the airplane, proclaiming it meant "peace in our time." Before the ink was dry Britain was plunged into a war which would eventually be the worst war of all time.

There are some haunting words in the beautiful Christmas song by Henry Wadsworth Longfellow:

> *I heard the bells on Christmas day*
> *Their old familiar carols play,*
> *And wild and sweet*
> *The words repeat,*
> *Of "Peace on earth, good will to men!"*
>
> *And in despair I bowed my head;*
> *"There is no peace on earth," I said,*
> *"For hate is strong*
> *And mocks the song*
> *Of peace on earth, good will to men!"*

Those words are understandable, especially when we realize that Longfellow had just received word of the death of his son in the Civil War. According to the Guinness Book of World Records, during the past 3,500 years of human history there have only been 250 years of peace.

Your Peace Agenda

Now that record is bad enough, but there is a similar lack of peace in individual lives. The Bible speaks of the turmoil in our lives: "The wicked are like the troubled sea, when it cannot rest, whose waters cast up mire and dirt" (Isaiah 57:20). We hear the Psalmist yearning, "Oh that I had wings like a dove! For then would I fly away, and be at peace" (55:6).

All of us would agree on the importance of world peace; but I doubt that peace is on your personal "front burner." Most folks need peace in the personal realm—peace with other folks they can't get along with; peace in work relationships; peace in home relationships; peace with the things that cannot be changed; peace with ourselves in our goals and ambitions in life; peace in the midst of illness; peace with our handicaps; peace with the reality of aging and approaching death.

The Angels' Peace

Since there is clearly no change in the warlike nature of nations, and most folks yearn for an elusive peace in their personal lives, we have three options about those angels: (1) they were wrong, out of touch with the way things are on the earth; (2) they were dreamers, thinking of the millennium; or (3) they were promising a real and practical peace which we have so often misunderstood. I think that is the case. And I am convinced that we cannot interpret or understand the angels' message of peace apart from the occasion that brought them to the sky over Bethlehem.

So, what brought the angelic chorus to that shepherd's field that first Christmas eve? The chorus was responding to the announcement the Angel of the Lord had just made to the shepherds. Look at the announcement in Luke 2:10-11. He announces good news. This news will result in great joy for everybody. The good news is that a Saviour is born that night in Bethlehem; he is the Messiah and Lord. Then, the Angel of the Lord gives mundane directions on how to find the child who is the source of peace. Then the angel chorus appears and sings of peace.

Whatever peace the angels had in mind, it was a peace resulting not from the absence of anything, but from the presence of God with man. It was a peace not imposed on people, but a peace which was the result of an inner relationship to God. (Look at v. 14 in a modern translation: peace among men with whom He is pleased.) It is a peace not associated with kings and force, but rather with stables and a baby and shepherds and weakness and love. It is a peace brought by angels, not by armies. It is a peace bought with blood—the blood of the Messiah. It is a peace readily available, and available to each of us—this day, unto you.

Bethlehem: Bridging The Gap

The peace of the angels, the peace of Bethlehem, is both an inner peace and a peace with God. There can be no inner peace transcending this world apart from peace with God. If you will study the biblical uses of the word peace, you will note an interesting thing. Over 50 times in Exodus and Leviticus alone, we see references to making peace with God, making a peace offering. And these references to the need of making peace begin with the giving of the Law. Once the Israelites became aware that the true and living God is a holy God, and that He has set forth laws and commandments for our own good, they felt a realization of sin and failure; they felt a sense of alienation and lostness; they felt a need to bridge the gap between themselves and God. As long as the gap is there between imperfect people and a perfect God; between a holy God and sinful people—there will be a longing for a peace this world cannot give. And so the event at Bethlehem had to do with bridging the gap between man and God.

The Babe Is Our Peace

Turn now to Ephesians 2:12-17. Peace with God comes only through the blood of the one born in Bethlehem. Here we read that without Christ we are far off from God, people without God in this world, and people without a hope beyond this world. But through the blood of Christ we have been brought near to God, for he is our peace. What those angels knew in the sky above Bethlehem that night was that God's plan for this baby included crucifixion. For Jesus did away with the noose of the Law by his own blood and made peace between us and God (v. 15-16). The end result of Jesus being born in Bethlehem and dying on the cross is summed up by Peter as he preaches to Cornelius in the tenth chapter of Acts, verses 36-43 : To him give all the prophets witness, that through his name whosoever believeth in him shall receive forgiveness of sins. So in the babe is our peace.

When God Is Pleased

Whether we speak of global peace or our own inner peace, the source of that peace is Jesus Christ. Remember the angels' song: Peace among men with whom He is pleased. It is only through Jesus that God can be pleased with us. Paul says it in Romans 5:1: Being justified by faith, we have peace with God through our Lord Jesus Christ. And only when God is pleased with us, when our life is in harmony with God's will for us, can we have inner peace. And it is only when mankind has inner peace that the world will experience peace.

A Prescription For Peace

But, talk about it as we will, we keep coming back to the fact that so many people, even Christians, do not have an inner peace. Norman Vincent Peale tells about the typical businessman who had an appointment with a doctor and arrived in the waiting room at exactly the appointed time, three o'clock. The doctor was a little late, and the businessman fumed and paced back and forth in the waiting room. When the doctor did get to him and he was led into the examination room, the doctor said, "Sit down." "I don't have time to sit down," replied the businessman. "Well, what is your problem?" said the doctor. The man proceeded to tell how run down and tired and overworked he was. The doctor put the blood pressure cuff on the man's arm and began to pump away. Then he gave that mysterious, wise look doctors try to have, and commented, "You aren't run-down; you are all wound up!" "Then give me a prescription and let's get on with it!" Said the man. The doctor thought a moment and then began to write on a prescription pad. "Will you follow my instructions exactly?" "Of course," said the man impatiently.

He took the folded prescription to a pharmacist. The pharmacist looked at the paper, then looked oddly at the man. "We don't stock this medicine here," he said. "Well, where can I get it?" "Here," said the pharmacist, handing over the paper. On it was written, "Take three doses every day of Colossians 3:15. The businessman went home, got out a Bible, and read Colossians 3:15: "Let the peace of God rule in your hearts."

How To Experience Peace

That's the prescription most of us need. First, peace with God, and then God's peace within our hearts to enable us to deal with the chal-

The Peace of Christmas

lenges of each day. The peace the angels spoke about is personal peace with God and an inner personal peace which comes as a result.

Peace Comes Through Salvation

Exactly what must we do to experience this good news which results in great joy and peace? First, believe the message of the angels that the Messiah is born in Bethlehem, for peace comes through salvation. Accept the biblical teaching that this Jesus came to die for our sins, and by his death and resurrection has opened the possibility of forgiveness of sin and peace with God. Confess your sins and your faith to God, asking Jesus to be your Lord and Saviour. Follow the admonition of the Bible in publicly taking your stand as a believer in Jesus.

Peace Comes Through Submission

Second, understand that peace comes through submission to God's will and law and plan for your life. Listen to the Bible: "O that you had harkened to my commandments! Then your peace would have been like a river" (Isaiah 48:18). "Great peace have they who love thy law; nothing can make them stumble" (Psalm 119:165). "Thou wilt keep him in perfect peace whose mind is stayed on thee, because he trusts in thee" (Isaiah 26:3). Jesus said, "My peace I leave with you: not as the world gives . . ." (John 14:27). Only through submission to the Living Word of God, Jesus, can we have peace; only through submission to God's Laws can we have peace.

Peace Comes Through Service

Third, understand that peace comes through service to God. It is true that you can work yourself into a frenzy and a breakdown even doing God's work. But most Christians would have more inner peace if they got involved in the ministry and outreach of the church. Too many of us give our time and our abilities and our very lives to second rate causes in this world. And we wonder why we have no peace.

Compassionate Words From Hell

They sang of peace; a peace we all need and can all attain. Listen again to the words of Edmund Sears' beautiful Christmas carol:

> *All ye, beneath life's crushing load,*
> *Whose forms are bending low,*
> *Who toil along the climbing way*
> *With painful steps and slow,*
> *Look now! for glad and golden hours*
> *Come swiftly on the wing;*
> *O rest beside the weary road,*
> *And hear the angels sing!*

Which Jesus in the Manger?

Luke 2:10-16

There is a beautiful Christmas song titled *Some Children See Him*
Some children see him lily white,
With tresses soft and fair;
Some children see him bronzed and brown,
With dark and heavy hair;
Some children see him almond-eyed,
With skin of yellow hue;
The children in each diff'rent place
Will see the baby Jesus' face like theirs,
But bright with heav'nly grace.

Notice that the children in the song see Jesus as like them. But it's not just the children who do that!

The Mirror Of Scholarship

As this century opened, scholars were rocked by Albert Schweitzer's **Quest of the Historical Jesus** (1906). Schweitzer said scholar after scholar had sought to find the real Jesus behind the gospels, yet as they stared into the deep well of the Bible, came up with their own reflection. That is, the Jesus they found always sounded remarkably like the scholar doing the research! More popular studies had titles like **In His Steps** and **The Man Nobody Knows**. Thoughtful works, to be sure, yet the Jesus they present sounds a lot like the authors! And now, at the close of the century, we have Schweitzer's book being reissued in paperback, in the midst of a spate of books in recent years seeking to paint the "authentic" Jesus, with titles like **Jesus the CEO; The Jesus I Never Knew**; and **Jesus in Bluejeans**, not to mention *Jesus Christ Superstar* a generation ago.

Who Is This Child?

The problem of deciding who this child in the manger really is began at his birth. Whose Jesus is in the manger? In the Bible we read of Herod's concept of Jesus—when he heard of the birth of Jesus he assumed the child in the manger was a rival king to be assassinated. As the shepherds stood by the cradle, they saw a Messiah, a Saviour for oppressed Israel. The innkeeper no doubt saw a child who had created an inconvenience in a busy innkeeper's life. Remember the Christmas song with the line, "Do you see what I see. . ." Each of us sees something different when we come to the manger. Skeptics see Jesus as a lunatic while liberals see him as idealistic, brave and kind. Reformers see him as bold, visionary and impatient. Some Jewish scholars find Jesus to be a pretty good Pharisee, and believers see him as the virgin-born Son of God. We see him as we want him to be.

The Jesus I'd Prefer To Know

For instance, let me describe the Jesus I'd put in the manger; the Jesus I'd prefer to know. He would not have a typically Jewish look, to begin with; he'd look like southern American of English heritage.

He would be middle-class, have my traditional values, be patriotic, always agree with my theological views and never condemn me, and would do about what I would do. He wouldn't ever run afoul of the law, and he would have a college education and drive a nice car.

Your Jesus may look very much like the Jesus I have pictured, because you and I have many of the same values. And if we wear the popular WWJD (What Would Jesus Do) bracelets, it's really no strain; because basically our Jesus would do what we feel comfortable doing. No doubt this picture is overdrawn, and I am sure that most Christians are honestly seeking to follow Jesus.

The Problem With My (And Your) Jesus

The problem with a Jesus shaped in my image or your image is that he is powerless to deal with sin and evil, with death and the devil. He is as powerless as we are! A Jesus in my image may die with me; but he can never die for me and for my sins.

How can we get a true and honest picture of the real Jesus in the manger? It is impossible for us to be completely objective about Jesus, but a starting place is to confess that what I have said has a great deal of truth. Then we can try to set the real Jesus free; unchain him from our prejudices and viewpoints. To try to get closer to the real Jesus we need remember what the prophets and others said about him; we need to remember what he himself said and what he did. Then see the picture that emerges. The prophets are summed up in Isaiah's great promise: He shall be the *Wonderful Counselor, Mighty God, Everlasting Father, Prince of Peace.* For over 2500 years believers have applied these words to the babe in the manger. The angels told the shepherds that a Saviour was born this day in the city of David. At Jesus' baptism God himself spoke: This is my beloved Son in whom I am well pleased. When John the Baptist saw Jesus coming, he announced: Behold the Lamb Who takes away the sin of the world. Jesus said of himself, He who has seen me has seen the Father. He healed the sick and raised the dead.

This Child Is God's Son

This babe in the manger is God's Son. He is virgin-born and sinless. The scriptures tell us he is God wrapped in human flesh; he is the very character and essence of Almighty God who created all this universe; he is very God of God; begotten, not made. He was with God in the beginning, and through him was everything made. So this one is not like you and me; he is without our sins and prejudices. He is Almighty God.

This Child Is God's Plan For The Ages

This Jesus in the manger is the fulfillment of God's plan for the ages, as Paul puts it. This child is the green-beret force of God's attack on the domination of this world by Satan. In the very first book of the Bible it is prophesied that the seed of Eve would one day bruise the head of Satan even while Satan bruised his heel. And so, even though there was no room in the inn for this child, he is no homeless child, as Hillary Clinton recently proclaimed him. Mary and Joseph have come on a journey to Bethlehem they think, to pay taxes, but in reality the mighty plan and prophecies of God are unfolding, for the Anointed one who will bring God's grace to mankind must be born in Bethlehem. There is nothing about the birth, life, death and resurrection of this child that is happenstance. These tiny hands were foreordained to be nailed to the cross for our sins. It is God's way, the only way, of redeeming you and me from our sins.

This child in the manger has saving grace in those hands one day to be nailed up. This child will be a man for others. He will spend hours daily listening to God the Father; in what he says and does he will bring the gift of salvation to all who will believe he is God's son. In what he says and does he will hold before us the model of what a redeemed person is to be like. He calls us to live out, as he did, his words about turning the other cheek, going the other mile, forgiving each other. He comes not as one of us, just kinder and nobler and wiser, calling us to a higher level of goodness. He comes from the world beyond, to challenge the devil, to break his power over us, to set us free to become the person God intends us to be. Only then can we be the new humanity God started in the stable.

So let us not load this child in the manger down with our ideas of how he must look, or what, when he is a man, he must do and think. Let him be a stranger; let him come into our lives as one from beyond our world—one who brings the light of salvation into the darkness of our sin. Let him call us from distant places to kneel before him; let him pierce our evil hearts with his life of turning the other cheek; let him sear our consciences—our white, middle-class, comfortable consciences. Let us not mold him to our desires, but let us be molded into his image by the forgiving grace he brings as he marches to the cross.

The kings from the east brought gifts to this child. It is a time for us to bring gifts to this child. Let us bring him the only gift that really matters—our sinful life in faith and trust, to be remade by this child.

Christmas Expectations

Luke 2:8-15

Christmas is not just another day, like the third Thursday in August, or the fourth Monday in February. We have certain expectations of this day. Christmas has a cargo of meaning for us. So let me ask: What does Christmas mean to you? What do you expect from Christmas?

Our Expectations

If I ask that of a child, I will no doubt be told that Christmas means new toys and games; and many adults may expect much the same out of Christmas—grown up toys! In fact, someone said the main difference between boys and men is the price of their toys! The Christmas expectations of some folks may be quite simple: that it bring a day off from work, or a visit to relatives and loved ones. Some expect merely an endless round of parties, while still others—many others— expect Christmas to bring a time of grief and depression. The poet Tennyson, thinking of his brilliant friend, Arthur Hallam, who was engaged to Tennyson's sister but died at the age of 23, wrote:

> *The time draws nigh the birth of Christ,*
> *With trembling fingers did we weave*
> *The holly round the Christmas hearth*
> *A rainy cloud possess'd the earth,*
> *And sadly fell our Christmas-eve.*

Counselors tell us more people are depressed at holidays than at other times through the year. Many say they will be glad when Christmas is over because it only reminds them of a loved one who is gone, or of a marriage broken, or a sad memory. And so we all have our own expectations of Christmas.

Their Expectations

The people involved in the first Christmas had their expectations, too. Look at the scene described in our text, Luke 2:8-15. What kind of expectations do you think those poor shepherds had as they headed for Bethlehem? They had already been treated to an appearance by an angel, a heavenly choir, and the message that the Saviour is born—in a stable! Verse 15 rings so true: "Let's go see what all this means!" Yet when they got there, what they saw was an ordinary baby, an ordinary man and woman with him. Did it meet their expectations?

Or consider the Wise Men in the second chapter of Matthew's Gospel, journeying from the East, coming from such a distance that it apparently took them weeks or months of traveling. What did they expect of Christmas when they began to ask around, "Where is he that is to be born King of the Jews?" And when they received the word of the prophecies that the Messiah would be born in Bethlehem and hurried there, what do you suppose they were expecting? A humble house, a poor man and his very young wife, and an ordinary looking baby? Somehow that question always comes to my mind as I look at the magnificent nativity paintings of men like Brueghel and Rubens.

Or take Herod—I suppose of all those involved in the first Christmas, his expectations seem most foolish to us across the years. For the more he thought of Christmas, the more troubled he became. His expectation of Christmas was that it would threaten his rule, his throne, his way of life—and he sought to do away with the baby. Imagine anybody today seeing Christmas as a threat to their way of life! How foolish that seems to a society that has turned Christmas into the biggest money-making time of the year! Our world has not taken Christmas seriously enough to consider it a threat!

Behold now the expectations of Simeon and Anna, the aged pair who greeted Mary and Joseph and Jesus when they came to the temple to present Jesus to the Lord, as was done with all Jewish boys. Read Simeon's blessing in Luke 2:29-32; do you suppose, as he waited day after day, year after year, looking for the Anointed, that he was expecting a baby? Perhaps a warrior king; perhaps a prophet, but a baby?

It is clear that those involved in the first Christmas did not fully understand what God was up to, and had various expectations. And our expectations of Christmas as a society are even more distant from God's plan for Christmas. Maybe the main tie between the 1st century and the 20th century at Christmas is found in Luke 2:16, where we read of the shepherds coming to the manger in haste! The furious pace, the after-Thanksgiving shopping rush, the hurrying from one party to the next, the haste—that we have in common with the shepherds!

God's Expectations

It is fine to look at what the shepherds and the Wise Men and Herod expected from Christmas, and to see how we, too, have definite expectations of Christmas—but what are God's expectations for Christmas? After all, it was His idea in the first place. Think with me about two aspects of God's expectations: what God intended in the first Christmas, and what God intends Christmas to mean to you this year.

God's Expectation for the First Christmas

God's beautiful intention in the first Christmas was to come among us and bring us salvation. Look at Matthew 1:21 "thou shalt call his name Jesus: for he shall save his people from their sins." That prom-

Christmas Expectations

ise of salvation is a golden thread in the appearances in the Biblical accounts; it is the message of the angel to the shepherds: "I bring you good tidings of great joy, which shall be to all people. For unto you is born this day in the City of David a Saviour, which is Christ the Lord" (Luke 2:10-11). And Simeon's comment: "For mine eyes have seen thy salvation..." (Luke 2:30). The widow Anna "spoke of him to all them that looked for redemption in Jerusalem" (Luke 2:38).

The Evangelist Matthew also reminds us of the words of the prophet that "they shall call his name Emmanuel, God with us" (Matthew 1:23). The divine purpose in Christmas is to reverse the curse upon all of us—the curse of sin and its consequences. And that could only be done if God came down here, with us, among us, as one of us—and somehow, as He lived among us, paid the penalty of our sins. That is what Paul is talking about when he proclaims the good news that just as by one man sin came into the world, so also by one man came the possibility of salvation for every man! That's the expectation God had in the first Christmas; so beautifully put in the Medieval Latin Carol of the 14th century:

> *Good Christian men, rejoice*
> *With heart and soul and voice!*
> *Now ye hear of endless bliss:*
> *Jesus Christ was born for this.*
> *He hath opened heaven's door,*
> *And man is blest forevermore.*
>
> *Now ye need not fear the grave:*
> *Jesus Christ was born to save;*
> *Calls you one and calls you all,*
> *To gain his everlasting hall.*

God's Expectation for This Christmas

And, just as we as children and adults have our expectations for this Christmas, so does God. For those who are Christians, who have already experienced that great salvation through Jesus; that release from sin's power and guilt, that peace with God which can only come through the shed blood of Christ, that joy that runs too deep for words—what is God's expectation, His desire, for you at this Christmas? It is that you find, in the midst of all the bustle and rush, tinsel and commercialism, a recommitment to your Saviour. Christmas comes at the close of the year—a year not fully used by any of us to witness for Jesus as we should have. Every Christmas finds us closer to that day when we go to be with Christ, and in the beautiful carols and moving scriptures we ought to feel our hearts melt in confession and recommitment.

For those who have not been saved—remember the name the angel gave the Christ-child: "Call his name Jesus: for he shall save his people from their sins." For you, God has some very specific expectations for this very Christmas. First, Christmas is intended to speak to that need in your life for a Saviour. Through some song, some sermon, some word, some verse on a Christmas card, through some gentle nudge, God intends that you become aware of your sins and aware that there is a Saviour. Second, God intends that you see that somebody's approach to the meaning of life is absurd—either the world's way with its materialism even at this time of the year, or God's way in sending a baby into the world via a cattle stable to be the Saviour of mankind. And last, God's expectation is that you will be stirred in your heart to reach out for this salvation—to feel it in your heart, to think it in your head, to confess it with your lips.

Whose expectations of Christmas will come true?

The Great Reunion

Luke 16:19-31; Luke 13:28-29

Remember the old-fashioned family reunions that used to be so popular? They're coming back—I got an invitation just the other day. I can remember some of those reunions in my childhood; the fun of seeing distant cousins, the tables of fried chicken and all kinds of pies, how the grown-ups would sit on the porch and rock and talk while we kids played Cowboys and Indians. Sometimes the reunions would be held on the grounds of the old country church under the old wooden arbor. The grown-ups would catch up on all the family gossip, and then stroll around the old cemetery and quietly talk of those who had died. No doubt there was talk of a great and wonderful reunion after this world.

There's Going to be a Reunion

And it was fitting that the talk should take that turn, for one of the most certain facts in this world is the certainty of a reunion after death. The feeling that this world is not all, that there is another world in which we will see loved ones and friends, is a common element in nearly all great world religions. I see this common belief in the great reunion as further proof of the yearning of all mankind after the God whom we are privileged to know most clearly as the Father of the Lord Jesus through whom, and whom alone, we have salvation.

There's going to be a reunion because this is part of God's great design for mankind. God's intention in creating man was to enjoy fellowship with us. This wonderful intention was twisted by wilful sin on the part of Adam, and this same drama is played out in every life. But God will yet have His eternal fellowship, in a world beyond this one where there is no sin or death, with those who choose to have it so. There will be a reunion because of the sense of justice in the heart of man. Everybody does not get a fair deal in this world. Another world is demanded for the scales to be balanced. There will be a great reunion because God's Word teaches it, from Jesus' parables to his words to the thief on the cross, from Paul's letters to the magnificent passages in the book of Revelation.

Not Whether, but Which Kind

There is clearly going to be a reunion, a meeting again with friends and loved ones. The huge, looming question is not whether but what kind of reunion you are headed for. A recent Gallup poll shows that 71% of Americans, seven out of ten, believe heaven exists, while only 53% feel hell is real. Which indicates most Americans think they're going to a great reunion in heaven. But as the old song has it, "Everybody talkin' 'bout heaven ain't going there."

There really are two kinds of reunion possible after death. Each of us chooses one of these two kinds of reunions. There is the possibility of a sad reunion and there is the possibility of a glad reunion. I want us to look at both briefly because these two different reunions are equally possible.

The Sad Reunion

The most striking illustration of the sad reunion is the parable of the Rich Man and Lazarus in Luke 16. We understand that we are examin-

The Great Reunion 347

ing a parable, and that our Lord, and the rest of the New Testament, are much more interested in the future state of the saved than of the lost; nevertheless there are surely valid lessons for us as we examine this illustration.

Here we see a man in hell (v. 23). Notice his situation. *First, this scene takes place in the trash can of eternity.* For that is exactly what hell is. God is not in the business of gloating over those who go to hell. Hell is not primarily intended as a place of punishment and torment, but as a place of eternal separation from God. God does not force Himself upon anyone—here or in the next world. Hell is the place of disposal, a cosmic trash can. Indeed, According to Matthew 25:41, hell was prepared as a cosmic trash can into which God planned to dispose of Satan. For anyone to go to hell means, above all else, to be eternally separated from God; out of God's heart, God's mind, God's presence, and God's concern. Let us never forget that God has done everything He can to keep anyone from going to hell.

Second, the rich man is in torment. I do not pretend to know all about the fiery torments of hell. Hell is described in many terrible pictures in the New Testament; sometimes as burning fire and sometimes as the opposite—outer darkness. I simply remind you that if the fire of hell is not literal—and it may not be—then it is a symbol of some more horrible fate, for a symbol is never as great or terrible as the reality it portrays.

Third, the fact that this man was in hell was not a matter of predestination but of choice. Now look at verses 27-28. Here we see a couple of things that ought to open our complacent eyes! Notice that it only takes about five minutes in hell to make an unbeliever into a tremendous missionary! In the first five minutes in hell this man shows more concern and compassion for the spiritual welfare of his family than perhaps in the past sixty years!

And realize that here we are talking about a reunion that this rich man in hell doesn't want to happen! Here is the possibility of a sad reunion with his five brothers; he begs that something be done to keep them from a dreadful reunion with him in this place! And the frightful thing is that the comments of both Abraham and the Rich Man indicate that the choice is up to the brothers. Listen, brethren: we choose whether we will be part of a sad or a glad reunion. It is a thought to make each of us tremble; the poet is right when he declares that life is real, life is earnest and the grave is not its goal—we are determining in these days our eternal destiny. Jesus said so often in John's Gospel—read through chapter three—that we judge ourselves here and now; the great day of judgement will only be a time when the verdict we have passed on ourselves will be revealed for all the world to see.

The Entrance to the Sad Reunion

Now folks, mark this down: there is only one way to get a ticket to that sad reunion in hell. You cannot be a part of that terrible scene by committing some terrible sin—murder, bank robbery, adultery, etc. The only way to the sad reunion in hell is by rejecting Jesus of Nazareth as your saviour. We generally think of this sad reunion in hell as a bunch of bad people, and we assume we are not going to be there. But there will be many nice people in hell; folks who wouldn't steal your purse or your car. Let us remember that hell is, first of all, the trashcan of eternity, the disposal of those who have no place for God in their life during these years on the earth.

I plead with you—plan to miss this sad reunion in hell! Even if your friends and family choose to go there, I can assure you on the basis of this scripture that, if they love you, once they are there they would give anything to keep you from joining them there.

The Glad Reunion

Let us turn our thoughts to a happier reunion, a glad reunion in heaven. Compare the Luke passage about the Rich Man in hell with the picture of the Redeemed in Revelation 7. But first we must note that there are many pictures of heaven in the New Testament. One of my favorites is found in Luke 13:28-29 where Jesus says they shall come from the east and from the west, from the north and from the south, and shall sit down in the kingdom of God. The idea is comparing heaven to a

The Great Reunion

feast (See also Luke 14:15-24; Matthew 25:1-13; and the references in Revelation to the marriage feast of the Lamb). Some rabbis in Jesus' time thought that when the Messiah came, a new age would begin, an eternal banquet at which the Gentiles would serve the Jews, the sea monster Leviathan would be the meat, and each grape would produce 40 gallons of wine at Messiah's table. That is the background of the pictures of heaven as a feast in the Gospels. It is a wonderfully old-fashioned idea of a great reunion complete with dinner on the grounds!

Many are the ways Christians have described that time of great and glad reunion. I glanced through a couple of old hymnbooks in my library and saw these hymn titles describing heaven: *The Unclouded Day, Where the Gates Swing Outward Never, The Home of Endless Years, The Beautiful Land, Where We'll Never Grow Old, There is a Land of Pure Delight, Rest Over Jordan, Keep Tenting To'ard the Highlands, World of Wondrous Beauty, Gathering Home,* and *The Open Gate.* But ask some basic questions about this reunion in which folks will be coming from all points on the globe to the Kingdom of God (this is the same multitude we see in Revelation 7).

Who will be at this glad reunion? There is but one basis on which a person gains entry to this glad reunion of heaven: a saving relationship to Jesus. Mere church membership will mean nothing, a knowledge of the facts about Jesus won't count for a thing, good deeds and a shining reputation will get you nowhere on that Judgement Day. It matters not who you are, who you know, or what circles you travel in. The only thing that counts is a relationship of trust and commitment to Jesus of Nazareth, the Son of God. And this relationship must have begun in this world to be recognized in the next. An old hymn expresses this well, *My Jesus, I Love Thee.*

> *My Jesus, I love Thee, I know Thou art mine;*
> *For Thee, all the follies of sin I resign;*
> *I'll love Thee in life, I will love Thee in death,*
> *And Praise Thee as long as Thou lendest me breath;*
> *And say, when the death dew lies cold on my brow;*
> *If ever I loved Thee, my Jesus, 'Tis now.*

What will we do there? Will we do in heaven the same things we do at a reunion here? Well, yes and no. We won't eat the finest fried chicken and lemon pie in the world, for that existence is different from this earthly one. That we surely learn from 1 Corinthians 15. And Jesus said there would be no marrying and giving in marriage (Mark 12:25). But He surely does not mean we renounce all the depth of our relationships so dear to us on the earth. No, heaven is a different kind of existence, and we shall be equipped to fully enjoy and participate in that life.

It will be a reunion, however, and that means we will know others from our pilgrimage here on earth. And we will get to meet and enjoy saints of the past, from Abraham to David to the disciples to Paul. When I compare the thrill of walking in Jerusalem on this earth to walking in that new Jerusalem, the Holy city, and talking with Abraham and Moses and David and Peter and Paul, then I realize with Paul that it has not entered into the heart or head of man to plumb the glories God has prepared for His children in heaven.

Reunion with our families, with saints gone on before; but most of all it will be a time of fellowship with God. We shall be with God. And please don't think of some ethereal vapor, or a grandfatherly type figure—the clearest picture we have of what God is like is what we see in Jesus! And Jesus said to those raw-boned, impulsive, sinful yet committed disciples: I go to prepare a place for you . . . that where I am, you may be also. He spoke of heaven as a great mansion with many rooms, by the way.

We often sing of what won't be in heaven. It is so true that there will be no sin, no sorrow, no sickness, no death, no disappointment—for all these things vanish with this broken, weary old earth. But there is one thing to be found in heaven that we generally don't think about—our treasures! The Bible urges us to lay up treasures in heaven . . . I think it means simply to lean on God down here on the earth; to trust Him and serve Him and tell others of His love. So remember what we sing: On Jordan's stormy banks I stand and cast a wishful eye to

The Great Reunion

Canaan's fair and happy land where my possessions lie . . . The possessions that really count are in heaven.

There are hints, in parables, of rewards in heaven although the Bible is not much interested in that. At the old reunions we used to sing, Will There Be Any Stars In My Crown? I do not think it will make much difference; maybe our reward is in our capacity to enjoy heaven.

One last word: the glad reunion, like the sad reunion, is eternal. Surely it is as the hymn Amazing Grace puts it: When we've been there ten thousand years, Bright shining as the sun, we've no less days to sing God's grace than when we first begun!

One old hymn says: *One sweetly solemn tho't comes to me o'er and o'er; I'm nearer my home today, than ever I've been before.* So we are. But which final home? Which final and eternal reunion—a sad or a glad one?

Made in the USA
Columbia, SC
11 October 2022